# SCRIM

# SCRIM
## THE MAN WITH A MIKE

William Renwick

Victoria University Press

TE WHARE WĀNANGA O TE ŪPOKO O TE IKA A MĀUI
VICTORIA
UNIVERSITY OF WELLINGTON

VICTORIA UNIVERSITY PRESS
Victoria University of Wellington
PO Box 600 Wellington
victoria.ac.nz/vup



First published 2011
Reprinted 2011



National Library of New Zealand Cataloguing-in-Publication Data

Renwick, W. L. (William Leslie), 1929-
Scrim : the man with a mike / William Renwick.
ISBN 978-0-86473-695-6
1. Radio broadcasters—New Zealand—Biography.
2. Scrim, Uncle, 1903-1987. I. Scrim, Uncle, 1903-1987. II. Title.
384.54092—dc 22

This book is published with the generous assistance of a grant from the
Alexander Turnbull Library Endowment Trust

Printed by PrintStop, Wellington

To the memory of my mother and father
and my Andin grandparents,
followers of Uncle Scrim

# Contents

# Illustrations

# Introduction

It seemed that everyone in the Newton gully listened to Uncle Scrim on Sunday evenings, and those who didn't were told what he had said by neighbours or workmates. One of the first things my father did when he at last got a job again was to buy a radio on time payment so that he and my mother could listen to Uncle Scrim. My parents said I was too young to listen to him. I was sent to bed with my two younger brothers before he came on the air. I would try to stay awake until the end of the session. I was not interested in hearing the man whose voice was droning on indistinctly through the wall. I was waiting for 'The Stranger of Galilee', the song the woman sang when the man stopped talking. Eight years old, I thought it must be the most beautiful song in the world.

I read *The Scrim-Lee Papers* soon after it was published in 1976. It was clearly a partisan account. I waited for someone to write an even-handed account of the background to Lee's expulsion from the Labour Party and Scrim's dismissal from the National Commercial Broadcasting Service. But no one did.

Then, some nine years ago, Elizabeth Alley told me about the collection of materials about Scrim that the Broadcasting History Trust, of which she was a member, had gathered in the course of its work. The trust was winding up and was about to deposit its Scrimgeour material in the Alexander Turnbull Library. Would I like to look through it, she asked, and might I, perhaps, be interested in doing something with it? I read enough of the material to realise that I was indeed interested in writing an account of Scrim's notable contribution to radio broadcasting in this country.

I am most grateful to Elizabeth Alley for alerting me to the Broadcasting History Trust materials on Scrim. They are an indispensable trove for anyone with an interest in his life. Together with the large, disparate Scrimgeour Papers that had been deposited in the Alexander Turnbull Library some years earlier, they have been the main source for this account of his life.

It is a pleasure to acknowledge my debts. The Turnbull Librarian granted unrestricted access to the library's collections of Scrimgeour material. Many Turnbull Library staff smoothed my way through a great deal of manuscript, newspaper, oral, and visual material. The director and staff of New Zealand Archives facilitated my trawl through official papers relevant to Scrim's broadcasting years, first as director of station 1ZR, then of station 1ZB, and later as controller of the National Commercial Broadcasting Service. The librarian in charge of the Manuscripts Collection in the Auckland Public Library gave access to the John A. Lee Papers. Thanks are also due to The New Zealand Film Archive, the Television New Zealand Archive, Sound Archives, the personnel division of New Zealand Defence, and the Registrar of Births Deaths and Marriages.

Thanks, too, to the six scholars who have assisted me in the writing of the book. Barry Gustafson and Allan Davidson commented on working drafts of all the chapters as they were written. Patrick Day commented on working drafts of the broadcasting chapters. Malcolm McKinnon commented on working drafts of the chapters dealing with the depression years, the Savage government, and with Scrim's recalcitrant relationship with the Fraser government. Elizabeth Alley and Elizabeth Caffin commented on the entire text in its near-final form.

I am grateful to the Alexander Turnbull Library Endowment Trust for allowing funds entrusted to it by the Broadcasting History Trust to be used for the publication of this book.

It has once again been a pleasure to be associated with Fergus Barrowman and his colleagues at Victoria University Press, and editor Sue Brown, in producing another handsome book.

Above all, I thank Margery, for her unflagging support throughout a project that has taken much longer than either of us expected.

# PART 1

# Finding a Vocation

## CHAPTER 1

# One of the Local Lads

A word about names to begin with. The name on the birth certificate is Colin Graham Scrimgeour, the second son of John and Bea (Robina) Scrimgeour. He was known within the family circle as Col or Colin. His workmates nicknamed him Scrim. During his seven years as a Methodist home missioner he was addressed formally as the Reverend Scrimgeour. Lena, his first wife, called him Col within the family circle and Scrim outside it. As director of the Friendly Road and in his early years as a radio broadcaster he was Uncle Scrim. He dispensed with the Reverend during his years as the controller of the Labour government's National Commercial Broadcasting Service. When he moved to Australia in 1944, his Australian friends and associates knew him as Col, and that is what his second wife, Pam, an Australian, called him. But Scrim was lodged in the New Zealand popular memory, and it was as Scrim that he was welcomed back in 1968. In this book he is referred to generally as Scrim but as Uncle Scrim in his early years as a radio broadcaster and in his association with the Fellowship of the Friendly Road.

Scrim grew up knowing that he was descended from Highland stock on both sides of his family. Both of his grandfathers had migrated to New Zealand from Perth.[1] His father, John Scrimgeour, was born on Motuihe Island in 1860, soon after his father, Peter Scrimgeour, arrived in the country, and John's two brothers and his sister were born later. Sometime in the 1890s, John took over his father's block of land at Opowhiti, in the hinterland of Poverty Bay north of Wairoa.

Scrim's mother's parents, Thomas and Ellen Clunie, had also migrated from the vicinity of Perth and settled in the Poverty Bay back country in the 1870s.[2] They had six daughters in a family of eight. Bea their second daughter, born in 1878, married John Scrimgeour.

We cannot say how much, beyond the lives of his parents and

grandparents, Scrim came to know about his forebears when he was growing up. Perhaps, in the way of Highland families, he was brought up on stories that went well back in family history. In his early twenties he heard from someone outside the family that Scrymgeour was an honoured name in Scottish history. But it was not until he was in his seventies that, thanks to the genealogical researches of his elder sister Rita, he learnt what it was that made it distinguished.[3]

The Scrymgeours entered Scottish history at the end of the thirteenth century when the leading member of the family became standard bearer first for William Wallace and then for Robert Bruce. The royal standard bearer stood next to the king in battle. The title was hereditary and remains in the family. By the middle of the nineteenth century there were several junior lines in the Scrimgeour genealogy, and Scrim's grandfather, Peter Scrimgeour's father, was from one of them.

John and Bea Scrimgeour were living through a financial crisis at the time of Scrim's birth in January 1903. The bank had called in its mortgage loan, and the family sheep-run at Opowhiti was being sold over John's head. He, Bea, their two young children, Rita and Gordon, and their newborn baby, Colin, were forced to leave the hill country station that Peter Scrimgeour had taken up forty years earlier.[4] They resettled on a small piece of land at Kaitaratahi near the Waipaoa River on the road to Gisborne.

Bad luck and difficult times were no doubt important parts of the reason why the bank called in the mortgage, but Bea put John's failure down to his conviviality. The man she had married, she would tell Scrim on her deathbed, was a handsome, charming man, but he had too many friends who enjoyed drinking with him and betting on horses. Drink had been his downfall.[5]

John's fecklessness was illustrated in the family legend of the registration of Scrim's birth. The last day for registering the birth was also the day when John concluded the sale of Opowhiti. John and his mate Colin Campbell went off to town, signed the legal documents, and drowned John's sorrows in the time-honoured Scots way over a bottle of whisky. When, late in the day, John remembered that he must also register the birth of his second son, he was lucky enough to get to the post office just before it closed. But he was fuddled and could not remember the names he and Bea had agreed to give the boy. Campbell came to his rescue. 'My first, your second,' he said, and the birth was registered as Colin Graham Scrimgeour.

Bea was exasperated when she saw the birth certificate. The family land had gone, and John could not even get his new son's name right. Her only comfort was that, born on 30 January, Scrim was an Aquarius. The stars, Scrim wrote many years later, were all she had left to believe in. But when her third son was born in 1912, John remembered his instructions. Scrim's younger brother was given the family names that had been intended for him: Norman Hugh Newall Scrimgeour.

Using language of the 1970s, Scrim wrote in his autobiography that Bea was a solo parent. John Scrimgeour seems not to have lived regularly under the family roof after the shift to Kaitaratahi. But it also seems clear that, although living the life of an itinerant rural worker, John continued to be a presence in Bea's life. She bore three more children to him after Scrim's birth.

Bea brought up her growing family and managed the small Kaitaratahi property. She appears in Scrim's autobiography as a stoically heroic woman. Leaving Opowhiti and sheep for a few cows at Kaitaratahi was going down in the world but, as Scrim remembered her, she accepted the change without getting bitter. John was her albatross, and she feared that his sons would also grow up to be shiftless. But she kept these fears to herself. Her one comfort, and it was clearly important to her, was the support of her sisters and brothers. They were a close-knit family, and three or four of them lived not far away.

Managing her farm was a continuing struggle. Her living arrangements were Spartan. She was poor and in debt. She probably never had fewer than four children living under her roof. We know about her only through Scrim's emotionally charged recollections of her last visit to him. He remembered her as quite simply the most important person in his young life, and his love for her knew no bounds. She remained in his memory as the mother who never chastised any of her children. There were no threats and punishments: please was the operative word.[6] Quick tempered himself, Scrim had good reason to remember her advice always to breathe slowly and count to ten before responding to anyone who had made him angry. He did not always follow that advice, but there were times as an adult when he commended it to others.[7]

The family lived in a small, old cottage whose inside walls were covered with the photo pages of the *Weekly News*. There was no bathroom or washhouse. The only source of warm water was a four-gallon kerosene tin that stored rain water from the roof. Bea did the family washing in a large circular tub which was kept outside the house. On Saturday evenings the tub was brought inside for the children's weekly bath. The last one in, Scrim remembered, had a cool, soapy bath. When he grew up a bit, he slept in a tent outside.[8]

Bea's farming arrangements were equally rudimentary. There was no milking shed or cow bail, no milk buckets or milking stool. Her milk pails were kerosene tins from which she had removed the lids and attached handles made of No. 8 fencing wire. The cows were milked where they could be stopped in the paddock. They were taken daily to the nearby Waipaoa River to be watered. When Bea bought a cream separator her children thought they were 'really modern'. It stood on a tree stump behind the house. Separating the cream became one of Scrim's daily tasks, and he took pride in being able to turn the handle at the right speed for a good dairy factory test. But the separator had been bought on time payment. The butter factory took it away during Bea's final illness because she was unable to keep up the payments.[9]

Bea was a dedicated gardener. Her vegetable garden, supplemented by kumara pits dug for her by some local Maori, kept the family in vegetables. Memories of her flower garden remained with Scrim all his life. He also remembered family ventures with their horse and gig. Once a year they went twenty or thirty miles to a sheep station whose owner let them camp in the shearers' quarters while they threshed and bagged cocksfoot seed which they picked on the side of the road. Bea sold the seed to augment the family income.

Kaitaratahi was no more than a dot on the map. Its attraction was its location twelve miles from Gisborne. With a river nearby, it was a popular place for drovers to halt overnight to rest and water their stock before moving them on to the Gisborne stock markets. When motor vehicles began to take over, Kaitaratahi became a popular place for a weekend drive for a picnic. It had a hotel, whose trade was not greatly hampered by the licensing law. There was a one-teacher school.

School days could not come to an end soon enough for Scrim.

Three different teachers ran the school during his time as a pupil. None seems to have been able to bring out the best in him. One told Bea that he was a bright boy but very pig-headed.[10] Verbal skirmishes with teachers gave Scrim his first lessons in having his say and defending his corner. In later life, he gave different accounts of how long he had stayed at school. In one of his autobiographical notes he wrote that he left school 'in August 1914 when I was not quite eleven and had not completed standard four'. Elsewhere he wrote that he was accepted for military service but a truant officer 'stepped in' and insisted that he go back to school and complete standard four. Another note states that 'his real education' began on the killing floor of the freezing works in 'August 1914'.[11] To have left school without completing standard four or gaining the proficiency certificate in standard six would not have been considered in any way unusual at the time. Virtually all of the employment available to teenage boys in Poverty Bay called for strength and stamina, and employers were looking for youngsters who were reliable and ready to give a good day's work for their pay.

The monthly dances and euchre evenings at the school provided the high points in Scrim's life. It was 'ladies a plate, men a shilling'. The evenings were advertised as 'Dancing without Drink', but there was always a flask for the musicians who played the fiddle, accordion, and squeeze-bag. Local men took up their positions near the door so that they could step outside from time to time for a drink. Sharp-eyed children did not ask why money changed hands during euchre games.[12]

Scrim was tall for his age. He was five feet seven and a half inches tall when he left school and would grow to be five feet ten and a half as an adult. Like his father, he could already work hard for many hours a day. He was handsome, with thick, curly chestnut hair, a quizzical smile, and a slim build. He began wearing glasses soon after he started work, and his first pair gives a glimpse of a youngster with a sense of style. He chose rimless glasses which were just then coming into fashion. For the rest of his life he would be a trendsetter in the glasses he wore. To his first wife, Lena, this was a sign of his vanity.[13]

He threw himself into the blokish subculture of rural working men. Australian mates on the killing chain greatly increased his vocabulary of expletives and taught him how to deal from the bottom of the pack. He drank whisky neat, was easy to get along with, and his mates soon found that he could string words together. By the time he was seventeen they had elected him to be their works representative in negotiations with the bosses.[14]

His mainstay for employment was the Poverty Bay Farmers Meat Company, where he was greatly influenced by the foreman, Jack Bean. Bean took him off the chain and shepherded him through a coopering apprenticeship which he completed in the quick time of two seasons. Among other things, coopering gave him an initial point of common interest with Joe (Michael Joseph) Savage, whom he met in Auckland a decade or so later.

Jack Bean was a self-educated man who had come under the influence of Tolstoy, not the Tolstoy of the novels but of the essays of his later years. He changed Scrim's 'mental attitude to life'. Scrim wrote later that his mentor 'pounded him with "Tolstoyan philosophy"' while they cut and shaped barrels and 'belted hell out of steel hoops'. Becoming aware of Tolstoy also made him aware of Jesus Christ and of the power of stories that were also parables.

Two other men took Scrim under their wing. Tom Heeney, a New Zealand boxing champion and brother of the more famous Jack, introduced him to boxing. Lin Robinson, another leading local boxer, took him over and began to train him. Robinson instilled in him what he called the basic rules of the sport: never stand flat footed; keep walking into the fight; don't be scared of blood. He also tried to get Scrim to curb his temper and remain calm in the ring. Though keen, Scrim seems to have lost most of his fights, but claims never to have walked away during one. When, as an adult, he found himself in a tight spot, Lin Robinson's injunctions would stiffen his resolve.[15] He never seems to have lost interest in the sport. During the 1950s, when he was living in Sydney, he acted as manager for Barry Brown, a promising New Zealand boxer, during his short career as a professional boxer.[16]

By the time he was nineteen Scrim was an experienced rural worker. He could hold his own in the local sawmills. He had worked with gangs laying the Gisborne–Napier railway.[17] He and a mate had worked for a while as sharpshooters in a travelling circus. He could work dogs and muster sheep. Working a team of packhorses, he had transported the first supplies into the Moki Ranges for what turned out to be the abandoned Rakaroa hydro scheme. The saddle of his horse, he said, was the most comfortable seat he knew.

Scrim was showing himself to be a young man who could accept responsibility and use his initiative. An uncle who owned the Hawkes Bay Motor Company employed him to manage the company's staging post at Wairoa. He worked for the Poverty Bay Farmers Meat Company when it was challenging the foreign-owned meat companies, and seems to have represented the company in some consultations at the port of Wanganui.[18] Managing a four-table billiard saloon when he was seventeen was probably his most demanding challenge. From his later account it can be inferred that the local police did not enforce the finer points of the law in their supervision of the saloon any more rigorously than they did over social gatherings at the Kaitaratahi school. The nearest police station, he wrote, was seven miles away and this might have explained why no checks were made on the saloon's closing hours or the age of its proprietor.[19]

Whether from rural isolation or parental indifference, religion does not seem to have had any overt influence on Scrim's upbringing. It was through the deaths first of his father and then of his mother that he had his first experiences of church services. Both parents had been stricken with cancer and had painful, lingering deaths. His father's cancer flared up while he was serving in the army in Samoa during the war, and he was invalided home. He shunned the company of anyone who knew him, but Scrim seems to have been aware of his movements. He was close to death when Scrim came across him in a bush hut where he was living with a workmate. Scrim had him shifted to Gisborne hospital, where he died in March 1920. Scrim represented the family at the funeral. He was seventeen.[20]

By this time, Bea was also coming to the end of her own desperate fight with cancer. Three bouts of surgery had left her weak and dispirited and she could no longer manage her farm. Her sisters took her into their care and made arrangements for her children. Scrim's elder brother Gordon was brought home to run the farm. The younger children were sent to stay with Clunie aunts. Scrim, then aged nineteen, stayed with his Uncle Gairoch (Garry) on his farm at Paraparaumu.

★

Garry was Scrim's favourite uncle and, more than that, a hero figure who had served in the camel corps during the war. It was through writing to Garry while he was overseas, Scrim later wrote, that he first learnt how to express his thoughts on paper. Garry was breaking in a block of land under the servicemen's settlement scheme. Scrim was glad of the opportunity to work with him in what was both a formidable physical challenge and a financially risky venture.

Garry and his wife Dorrie welcomed him warmly. He enjoyed the good food Dorrie put on the table and, above all, the affectionate company of a family. Garry was milking for town supply. Scrim's working day started well before dawn, when he brought the cows in, and he would put in a seven-hour day of scrub cutting on land that Garry was bringing in to production.

Scrim's daily routine was interrupted when his mother unexpectedly arrived at the farm. She was at death's door. While he was living at Paraparaumu, she had been moved from one sister to another and then, as her condition worsened, to the Gisborne public hospital. Half a century later, Scrim's second son Gary, no doubt drawing on family oral memory, wrote a note implying that she had also become addicted to alcohol.[21] Bea yearned for Scrim. Some time in 1922 she succeeded in getting herself transferred to Porirua Mental Hospital as a voluntary patient. There it was that Scrim visited her for what was to be their last conversation.

Scrim's account of that conversation was probably not written until half a century later, but it is not difficult to read Bea's anxieties between the lines. What stayed in his mind was her statement that she had wanted to see him because he was so 'like your father when I first met him'. Mother and son would have known what was being left unsaid. John Scrimgeour had been undone by drink, gambling, and his blokey mates. Scrim had also been leading a larrikin life. Among stories about him, the most disturbing told of him being found asleep, blind drunk on the track of the as-yet-unfinished Wairoa to Gisborne railway line, at risk of being killed by any passing train. What he did remember was her hopes for him. 'I want you to make something of your life. What it is will be so much better but you will have to find it yourself and do it in your own way.' She took off her wedding ring, found her small Bible under her pillow, and gave them to him. 'It's a very poor inheritance,' she said, 'but it goes with much love.' He wiped tears from her eyes and left. He was heartbroken.[22]

Scrim wanted to get his mother out of hospital as soon as possible and take her home to die. A nurse arranged for him to meet the hospital superintendent. He was 'kindly' but he did not agree that Bea had a heart problem. Because, however, she was a voluntary patient, she could be removed. But the superintendent thought that such a request should come from one of the more senior members of her family. Scrim returned to his uncle's farm. The next day the local postmaster delivered a message. His mother had died.[23]

Scrim remembered his meeting with the hospital superintendent for what he referred to as an 'astounding revelation' he had made in the course of their conversation. The conversation had taken place soon after his mother had urged him to make something of his life. Scrim was in a highly emotional state. The superintendent asked him what he might do in life, and Scrim replied cockily that he was 'going to be a surgeon' and he would stake his reputation against the superintendent's.[24]

The superintendent seems to have let him down gently. Waging for high stakes was a regular feature of the blokes' world Scrim moved in, but his response was nevertheless, as he later wrote, astounding. There would be other moments in his life when, under stress, he would say or do things that others would consider to be disproportionate to the circumstances. Three years later a medical doctor found that he was prone to hypertension, a condition which could affect his responses in times of stress.

In Scrim's later recollection, his mother's funeral was 'a ghastly affair'. He was highly emotional. His family did not belong to the minister's congregation. He experienced the service as a 'cold ritual of Mumbo Jumbo' which bore no relationship to 'the very gracious lady who had been such a wonderful mother'. He gave voice to his sense of outrage, so he later wrote, when he said to his uncle Garry: 'To hell with the bloody church. Let them bury the bloody doctors and I'll toss the grave diggers a quid to work faster.'[25]

# CHAPTER 2

# Accidental Methodist

By the time Scrim started jotting down ideas for his autobiography he was convinced that he had never been converted to Christianity. There had been 'no sudden flash of revelation, no divine call', he wrote. His decision to become a Methodist home missioner he attributed to the influence of Jack Bean, to his reading of some of Tolstoy's essays, and to the story about Jesus driving money lenders from the Temple.[1] This selective recollection drew a veil over what he did in the months after his mother's death in response to her appeal to make something of his life.

All we know about Scrim's last conversation with his mother is what he recorded about it half a century later. What she said to him, however, made an immediate impact. In the privacy of his bedroom he started to read the Bible. Without any previous knowledge of it, he made the mistake of trying to read it from beginning to end, starting with verse one, chapter one of Genesis. But the lists of genealogies soon bored him and he gave up. Then Winifred Monk, a visiting relative, put him on the right track. She placed markers in sections of the New Testament and encouraged him to read them. He learnt for the first time, he wrote later, 'about a pretty tough character called Jesus Christ, a carpenter', and discovered where Leo Tolstoy got his inspiration from. Scrim began to think that the Jesus he was reading about might be the answer to his mother's wish for him.

He looked for a church he could attend. With his Scottish descent he looked for a Presbyterian church but found that the nearest one was thirty miles away. By chance he was directed to the Reverend Watson, the Methodist minister at Paraparaumu, who took a kindly interest in him. Before long, Scrim attended a meeting conducted by the Rev T.G. Brooke, the secretary of the Home and Maori Missions of the Methodist Church. Brooke was on the point of retirement, and his address was an appeal to young men to take up the missionary torch. Scrim was the only young man in the audience. He felt quite certain that the appeal was being addressed to him. That was how he became an 'accidental Methodist', he recalled in the biography which his friend Harry Bell published on his behalf in 1934.[2]

The Rev Watson set him to work to write a sermon, something that Scrim simply found bewildering. Then Watson invited him to accompany him to his next Sunday service at Paekakariki and read the lesson. On the way to the church, Rev Watson asked him if it would be the first time he had taken part in conducting a service, and Scrim thought it discreet not to tell him it was the first time he had been to a church service. He was very conscious of some verbal stumbles he made in his reading of the lesson, but Rev Watson thought well enough of him to suggest that he train to become a lay preacher.[3]

That required as a first step that Scrim be interviewed by a panel of Methodist ministers and church dignitaries who would assess his suitability. These he faced with a mixture of apprehension and self-confidence. The apprehension stemmed from his acute awareness of his educational deficiencies. His first interview was with Rev Keal in Otaki, and he had to steel himself to front up to it when he saw the letters BA after Keal's name on the church notice board. He was even more abashed when he found that the next minister he met, Rev Edwin Cox, was an MA.

More than that, Scrim had some explaining to do when he arrived in Gisborne for that interview. On the boat trip from Wellington he had been cleaned out at cards by a pair of card sharps and, because he arrived without any money, this became the first subject of conversation with Cox.

Scrim's story was that, though he had given up gambling, he could not stand aside while innocent players were being robbed by a 'couple of crooks'. Two card sharps, working together, he explained, could always beat any other player, and he had lost all his money. He confessed that he should have known better and had learnt his lesson. He would only bet on a certainty in future. Edwin Cox asked him how he would do that, and he replied, 'Well, I'll take a much bigger gamble and bet on the Carpenter of Nazareth.' Cox was struck by Scrim's conviction.

This is the one indication we have of Scrim's sense of vocation at this stage of his life. Twelve years later, when he had become a champion of religious tolerance, he gently reproved himself for the inflexibility of the views he held when he was starting out to be an evangelist. Significantly, his remarks on that later occasion were embedded in a salute to his mother. Had she still been alive when he started out on his ministry, he wrote, he would have been unwise enough to try to convert her through a 'fiery, not properly understood evangelism'.[4] At that time he was riveted by the image of Jesus scourging the temple and had no time for any 'Gentle Jesus stuff'.

Under Cox's guidance, Scrim prepared to become a Methodist lay preacher. Cox encouraged him to follow his mother's advice and do things his own way. Scrim wanted to be a preacher, so he must go out and preach. Jesus had started at Galilee: he must start at Kaitaratahi. Get the school's agreement to hold a religious service the next Sunday evening, Cox said, and put notices in the school, the local pub, and the freezing works telling people in the neighbourhood to bet on a certainty. Cox also urged him to tell them about his mother, and not to forget to take up a collection.

The schoolroom was nearly full for the service. Scrim recollected that 'he bluffed his way through it'. Jack Bean brought twenty timber workers. There were no hymns, 'just talk and a collection'. Scrim said that he simply told the 'truth', and it had 'a strange power'. A hat was passed round for a collection which, when counted, added up to £3. Its size impressed Cox when Scrim handed it to him. It was more, Cox said, than he took in his church.[5]

Sometime in the early part of 1923, Scrim went to Napier and preached a trial sermon before the Rev T.R. Richards and a small congregation of what he referred to as elderly men. He found it an ordeal but he passed the test. He was comforted to overhear a member of his congregation say afterwards that he thought the 'young fellow had something and meant well'. His future, Edwin Cox told him, would now be in the hands 'of a very nice fellow, the Rev Seamer', the superintendent of the Methodist Home and Maori Mission.

The Rev Seamer had already made a notable contribution to the church's missionary efforts in the course of more than twenty years, and would continue to do so for as long again. He would become a major influence during the next ten years of Scrim's life. Cox also remained an influence in Scrim's life long after he left Gisborne. He was one of a number of advocates of monetary reform with whom

Scrim kept in touch in the coming years. Scrim met him again in Dunedin in 1937 when he was launching station 4ZB. Cox was mayor of Dunedin.

There were things about Scrim that his new-found Methodist acquaintances found attractive. Keall thought he was a very promising candidate, though he had some doubts about his educational background. Cox thought he was 'a natural'. For his part, Scrim was clearly keen to prepare himself to become a preacher. One thing, however, he did not do. He did not act on Cox's advice to undertake correspondence courses in English and mathematics. He wrote to the Auckland Correspondence School and got their brochure but decided not to enroll. At one level his decision was not altogether surprising. Even secondary pupils with an experienced teacher to guide them could find Nesfield's Grammar, the text for the English course, difficult. Teaching by correspondence was in its early, rudimentary stage. But Scrim had a very personal reason as well. He was very conscious of the deficiencies of his written English and was not willing to run the risk of having them confirmed yet again by failing to pass the correspondence course.[6]

To give him some familiarity with the life of a Methodist home missioner, he was sent to Masterton and spent a week with Rev Frank Handy, a young home missioner. Handy would be admitted to the Methodist Theological College in 1924. Scrim found him warm and outgoing. Handy stressed how important it was to get to know people and try to understand them. To prepare Scrim for opposition to some of his ideas, he made a point of emphasising that 'the church is very conservative'.

Certainly Scrim gave Handy glimpses of his argumentative nature in discussions that filled the days they spent together and went long into each night. Scrim insisted that the Jesus who claimed his admiration was a tough-minded man, and he could not accept what he called 'the mystical nonsense' of God the Father and God the Holy Spirit. Also unacceptable to him was what seemed to be God's main attribute of 'handing out punishment', of which he took the crucifixion to be the worst example. Frank Handy countered by advising Scrim to put less emphasis on 'the Man from Galilee' and 'give more credit to God'. Scrim found his debates with Handy stimulating, and it seems that Handy did too. He recalled Handy's comment that it was 'good to meet a real heathen'. Scrim's summing-up was that he did not win any of the arguments but neither did Frank Handy, so they called it a draw. Handy suggested to him that even when he went to theological college he might not find the answers to issues he had raised. He also advised him to be patient. There was more to the church than doctrines.[7]

Scrim emerges from his account of his discussions with Handy as opinionated and argumentative, strongly committed to his beliefs and staunchly opposed to interpretations of the Christian story he found unbelievable. The outlines of his later secularised Christianity are not difficult to detect but there is no hint of any broad church tolerance. Interesting, too, is the no-doubt self-serving suggestion in his account that he had not been aggressive during his discussions with Handy. How much that would have been due to Handy's tolerance and how much to a growing self-discipline on Scrim's part is impossible to say, but it suggests a young man who, though firm – even rigid – in his beliefs, was learning how to contend with someone who disagreed with him.

In May 1923 Scrim wrote to the Rev T.G. Brooke offering himself for home mission work in the Methodist church. He 'felt', he wrote, 'a very strong call to take up the work of God' and had been preparing himself 'heart and soul' to do so. He had been converted for two years, and he told Brooke that it was from his own lips twelve months ago that he had 'received a call to the Methodist Church'. He was about to take his 'preacher's examination' in a fortnight's time. If his application was acceptable he would be available immediately for service as a home missioner. He enclosed a letter of recommendation from Rev E.T. Cox, MA.

In answer to a question that Rev Brooke put to him in his reply Scrim gave his birthday as 28 February 1902.[8] This was untrue. At later times in his life Scrim would be careless about significant dates in his career. He had no doubt advanced the date of his birth by nearly a year to give himself a date of birth that would make him immediately eligible for training as a Methodist home missioner. For Scrim it was probably a case of the means being justified by the end he had in view. Nor could it have been two years since he had been 'converted'. The executive committee of the Methodist Home Mission Board accepted Scrim's application. Brooke appointed him to a circuit with Putaruru as its centre, and he took up his appointment toward the end of June. He expected that, if his candidacy was accepted by the

Methodist Conference, he would enter the Methodist Theological College in 1925.[9]

Scrim knew that, with his limited academic attainments, he should undertake some further study to prepare himself for theological college. He took some theological lecture notes with him to Putaruru but they remained unread. He was reading widely, but Dr Laws' notes on the Higher Criticism and Dr Ranston's on the Old Testament were no match for Upton Sinclair and Aldous Huxley.[10]

Putaruru was the centre of the farming district that stretched west and south to the Waikato and east and north in the direction of Rotorua. The leading families had been farming in the district for a couple of generations. A cloud of uncertainty hung over the future of the district south of Tokoroa. Men who had taken up land under farm settlement schemes for ex-servicemen were being forced off their land because of mineral deficiencies in the pumice soil. The Methodists had closed their preaching place in Tokoroa, but developments were afoot that offered new hope for the district. One was an experiment in the nurturing of pine trees on pumice lands. Another was the exploratory work associated with the project to build a hydro electric power station at Arapuni.

Handy had impressed on Scrim that getting to know his community was as important to a preacher as preaching. Scrim knew that he would quickly run out of sermons. Any success he had would depend largely on creating good personal relationships with people. He welcomed the prospect of doing short stints in cow sheds and on farm operations.

Scrim lived at first in a boarding house where workers from the local sawmill also lived. His earlier associations with Jack and Tom Heeney and Lin Robinson made him 'one of them'. He launched his mission with them. He did not take up their offer to try his hand on the breaking down bench at the mill, but he agreed to play poker with them on their day off on Sunday. To keep nominally within the law, his new mates followed the usual practice of poker players, using matches as currency and converting their tallies to money after the games were over. Scrim joined them, intending to play only a few hands and then leave. But the others were not particularly good players, he had not lost his touch, and he cleaned them out. Then he allowed himself a little prideful boasting. Playing penny poker, he told them, was child's play. The lowest game he had ever played, he said, was for 3d a chip, and serious players wouldn't waste their time for less than a shilling a point. As evidence of his prowess he showed them how to palm cards, stack a deck, and deal from the bottom of the pack. Not even the great Franquin, he later wrote, could have had a better audience.[11]

His new mates decided that he was 'a good bloke', and he 'did not sound like a preacher either'. Not sounding like a preacher was clearly to his advantage in his attempt to influence the lives of these men. He was letting them know that he knew the world of poker players as a player himself. Then the fledgling evangelist took over. He declined the offer of a beer but invited his new acquaintances to his evening service. He would preach on the subject 'Put your trust in the man who never cheated'. He would expect them, he said, to give generously when the collection was taken up. The sawmillers in the district were not notable churchgoers but they all came that evening. The church steward was 'amazed' at the amount of money they put in the plate.[12]

Scrim felt much less at ease with the men and women who set the tone of the parish. He found them old, if not very old, and set in their ways. He was very aware of how young he appeared in their eyes. He had a strong, intensely felt sense of mission. But he knew little about the customs and conventions of the Methodist church, and was quick to challenge opinions he did not agree with.

Scrim did not stay long at the boarding house. Andrew and Mrs Begbie took him in as a boarder, and he lived with them for the remainder of his time in the district. The Begbies were Scots which, for him, was a good sign, and he found them generous and wise.

Also boarding with the Begbies was a young scientist, Basil Goudy, and Scrim struck up a friendship with him. Goudy was trying to find out if radiata pine could be grown successfully in the bush-sick land of the Central Plateau. The State Forest Service had established the species in some other parts of the country but did not yet know if it could survive in chemically deficient pumice soils. Goudy had a four-acre test bed close to the Begbie home. Scrim welcomed the opportunity to assist him.

Working with Goudy, Scrim planted out tens of thousands of pinus radiata seedlings. He regularly worked for a couple of hours before breakfast, and sometimes put in a ten-hour day. For Goudy it was a risk-venture. His backers were soon sufficiently confident to float a company that would establish and maintain a pine plantation for twenty years until the trees reached maturity and could be milled. Scrim had no means of knowing at the time that Goudy's experiment would be the foundation for New Zealand Forest Products, the country's largest and most profitable company in the latter part of the century.

Another prominent Methodist family in the district, the Alcorns, was also associated with Goudy's venture. Alcorn had become associated with the financier J.W.S. McArthur in setting up the Executive Trust of New Zealand Ltd, a holding company through which investors spread their risk over a number of firms and shared the profits. This venture was designed to attract small investors. A £50 investment bought a bond entitling its holder to an acre in a pine plantation and the prospect of an 8% return. The scheme was a type of commercial venture that was new to New Zealand and was very controversial. Entrenched financiers strongly opposed it. In 1934 Parliament passed legislation to quash the investment trust. McArthur was vilified at the time as a fraudster but Scrim was convinced that he was an honourable man and kept in touch with him.

Scrim also struck up a friendship with Bill Hudson, the Scottish engineer who was carrying out the site survey for what would become the Arapuni hydro dam on the Waikato River not far upstream from Cambridge. Hudson was working for the British firm that had won the contract to build the dam. Scrim spent quite a lot of time giving a hand to the team that was putting survey bores into the banks of the river. The project was experiencing the first of the problems that would plague it. Ministry of Works engineers were questioning whether the site chosen for the dam would be able to support the foundations that were to be built for it. These questions merely heightened Scrim's interest in what Hudson was doing. Was the Arapuni scheme, he asked himself, to be a replay of the abandoned Rakaroa scheme he had been involved in ten years earlier?[13]

In the course of his eight months in the district, Scrim met and became engaged to Lena Hardie. She was teaching at Hinuera some twenty miles up the road towards Cambridge.[14] They would marry two years later. On their marriage certificate she is recorded to as Caroline Lenna Hardie, but Scrim always referred to her as Lena.

A rash act brought Scrim's Putaruru mission to an abrupt end. He had, as a matter of course, followed Rev Edwin Cox's advice to advertise his Sunday sermons by placing posters in places where his parishioners could be expected to see them. The local sweet and ice cream shop in Putaruru was one of these. It was a popular gathering place for people after the Saturday night cinema show, and was particularly effective in getting his weekly message out.

On the Saturday evening that was to be harbinger of trouble for him, Scrim looked into the shop and noted that his poster was being displayed. But he was surprised when the shopkeeper told him that a 'pompous and pious person' had come to the shop and demanded that the 'indecent poster' be 'removed immediately'. The offending poster announced the subject of the text of Scrim's forthcoming sermon: 'TWINS: Man's needs and GOD's provisions to meet them.' The shopkeeper told Scrim that he had replied to the complainant that everyone knew about his 'dirty mind'. 'A bloody hypocrite' like him, the shopkeeper told him, had no right to insinuate that Mr Scrimgeour could outdo him in 'evil suggestions'. The shopkeeper had insisted that the poster remain on display until Mr Scrimgeour took it down. The complainant was the circuit steward, one of the senior office-bearers in Scrim's congregation.

It is clear from his actions at church the next morning that Scrim was angered by the circuit steward's intervention. He had a big congregation, and many of the people in it were new to him. He took the poster with him into the pulpit. He thought – 'without boasting' – that he did justice to his subject 'and to the Lord'. Before announcing the final hymn, he displayed the poster for all to see. He called on the circuit steward by name and, according to his later account of the incident, swore for the first and only time from the pulpit, calling the man a 'bloody hypocrite'. He challenged the circuit steward to come forward and take the poster, but he did not take up the challenge.[15]

After the service Scrim mingled with members of his flock in front of the church, then took the poster into the vestry. He was soon aware that the circuit steward was standing outside the vestry, so he called out to him to come in. He was, Scrim wrote, 'big, not very old, and blazing with rage'. Remembering his code as a boxer, Scrim knew that he must not strike an 'adversary out of the ring before warning him that he was a trained fighter'. When the circuit steward opened the door, however, Scrim could see that there would be no need for violence, not even a slap on the face with his open hand. The man backed away. Naming him by his full name, Scrim told him that he 'was not only a bloody hypocrite but a bloody coward as well. Get out before I throw you out.'[16]

Scrim had caused a sensation. As a probationer home missioner, he could be suspended from his duties and dismissed if judged to have brought the ministry into disrepute. He was arraigned before a committee of what he remembered as 'old and very dour looking parsons' in 'something of a cross between a lynching party and a kangaroo court'.

On the evening before the 'trial', Scrim ate with the Alcorn family as their guest. Robert Alcorn asked Scrim to let him conduct his defence. This was clearly intended to be helpful but, however kindly meant, Scrim saw it as an affront to his pride. He was 'young, fit and aggressive'. He had never walked away from a fight. This would be the first time he had ever called on anyone to fight for him. He was torn between his natural instincts and an offer intended to help him. He accepted Alcorn's advice.

The charge was of conduct unbecoming of a minister. Alcorn put his hand on Scrim's arm and delivered a speech which, Scrim said, 'would have done justice to the great advocate Clarence Darrow'. Alcorn based Scrim's defence on his convictions as a 'follower of our Lord and Master' and on the example of Jesus. Scrim was 'obeying the call of his heart to follow the Man of God who like him had spoken the truth as he saw it without fear or consequence'. He called to mind Christ's taking a whip into the temple and angrily driving out the money changers. It was Christ, too, who had called the Pharisees who 'exploited people a band of vipers and whited sepulchres. And who was it who stood by a woman who, without trial or justification, was about to be stoned to death as an adulteress? He was a humble carpenter who confronted the great and powerful for the defence of the common people who, we are told, hung upon his lips and followed him'. These, Alcorn said, were the actions of 'a very angry man who was prepared to face death rather than turn his back on sinners'.

Mr Scrimgeour, he concluded, was wrong only because the incident that many would think a trifle was to him 'a matter of principle'. He happened to know, he added, that Mr Scrimgeour was a cooper by trade, 'an occupation closely related to carpentry'. Alcorn did not think the incident called for an apology. He thought that all present should recall the warning, 'Judge not lest you be judged.' The men sitting in judgement agreed.[17]

It was a narrow escape. In the heat of the moment, Scrim had given rein to his aggressive emotions and had acted in a way that was out of proportion to the alleged offence. There would be other such incidents in the years to come, all signs of a man lashing out under stress. Fortunately for Scrim, there were people such as Alcorn who were impressed with what he had to offer and were willing to help him tame his tigers.

The Rev Seamer was one of them. He soon sent what Scrim called 'a very friendly note'. It offered him a transfer to an 'industrial area' in the South Island, where he would be able to make better use of his own industrial background. It was not until he recounted the incident in one of his autobiographical jottings – written perhaps fifty years later – that Scrim let it be known why he had left Putaruru.[18]

Kaitangata, Scrim's next mission station, was a small Otago coal-mining town on the Matua branch of the Clutha, four miles from its mouth. It had not had a Methodist missioner for several years, and church attendances had fallen away. Miners and, more to the point, miners' wives and children were the mainstays of the congregation.

Scrim arrived in Kaitangata in the autumn of 1924. The ladies guild of the church welcomed him with an afternoon tea. Men from the mine offered to take him down one of the mines. This invitation gave him an opportunity. He would be happy to go down the mine with them if they would promise a good turnout for his first service. He added that he was not a 'denominational bloke' and everyone would be welcome, especially if they could sing. The men agreed.

From beginning to end he found the mine visit menacing. The climax was a clambering inspection of a part of the mine that had been sealed off after an explosion many years before and was still on fire. A mile below ground level, he recalled, he was confronted by 'the sight of all time, thousands of tons of glowing fire'. What was it, he asked himself, that he had been looking at? Was it Dante's Inferno, Orpheus in Hades, 'or an image of the good old-time religious threat' of eternal fire and brimstone for sinners?[19]

The tour of the mine did exactly what Scrim could have hoped for. The men were open and companionable, and he was at his ease with them. They disabused him of any preconceptions he might have had. He learnt at first hand that coal mining deep underground was very hard graft in dirty, difficult and potentially dangerous conditions for low rates of pay. He discovered, too, that the men he met were as good as their word. He had a full church for his first service.

With his talent for building relationships with new acquaintances, Scrim got to know everyone in the town within a couple of weeks. He extended his knowledge of present and former residents by studying headstones in the town's cemeteries. He was pleased to find that his non-denominational approach was endorsed by the people he met. He did not think the town was divided by sectarian loyalties or by barriers based on race.[20]

The number of men in his congregation increased. Scrim had no confidence in his ability to pitch notes for hymns, so he made a point of getting a man who was a good singer to lead the singing in church. He took it as a vindication of his approach to evangelising that tough, hard-working miners did not constrain their language in his company. If, he said, swear words gave the right emphasis to what they had to say, they used 'bad language'. But giving moral values to words was in his opinion 'balderdash'. He had worked with freezing workers, watersiders, bushmen and navvies, and his own colloquial speech, he confessed, was more fluent and had greater variety than the speech of Kaitangata miners.[21] He raised this matter in one of his sermons. He often asked himself, he said, what it was that Christ said when he drove the money changers from the temple. He felt sure that the Authorised Version left out things he would have said.

Scrim wrote that he faced the first of his ethical dilemmas while he was serving in Kaitangata. We need to remind ourselves that Scrim's account of his years as a Methodist home missioner were written half a century after the events he was narrating. What he wrote about the old Kaitangata Salvationist might have been a mixture of fact and imagination. The ninety-year-old was living with the family with whom Scrim was also living. He was declining fast, but was determined to hold on to life until 'the Lord called him'. Scrim took over the duty of sitting with him at night. When the crisis came at 3am one morning, Scrim went for the doctor. Their discussion quickly turned to the doctor's ethical duty to a patient at the point of death. Not yet being aware of the Hippocratic Oath or the prohibitions of the law, Scrim pressed the doctor to prescribe something that would ease the old man's passage to the next world.

The doctor was a devout Catholic for whom such a breach of medical ethics would also imperil his own immortal soul. But Scrim wrote that he persuaded the doctor to let him have some tablets that he could dispense to the old man. The doctor gave him three tablets, the first to be given to the old man immediately, the second after half an hour if he was not already sleeping. One tablet was enough to send the old man to his rest.[22]

Scrim was soon troubled by ill health. His mention of this illness in his later autobiographical jottings suggests a strong similarity with crises in his health in the years ahead. A local doctor diagnosed a thyroid condition. This was confirmed by a Dunedin specialist, but he was more concerned about Scrim's heart. There were, he said, a heart murmur and some congestion of his lungs. Harry Bell would refer to the illness as a nervous breakdown in the biography of Scrim he published in 1934.

Scrim's congregation organised a 'welcome-back' service for him when he returned from Dunedin. He remembered the 'cheerful singing by the large male choir' and was deeply touched by the many kindnesses he received. He was on light duties for the rest of his time in the town.[23]

Before Scrim left Kaitangata the town was plunged into crisis. A massive cave-in in the No. 2 mine trapped all the men on the night shift behind hundreds of tons of rock and coal. All the men of the town turned to and, fortunately, all the miners were rescued. Scrim was a bystander to these events.

A consequence of his illness was that Scrim was unable to present himself as a candidate for admission to the theological college in 1925. His specialist doctor had recommended that he move to a warmer climate. Seamer decided to relocate him in the Bay of Islands. Scrim shifted in July.

On the way north Scrim stayed a few days in Auckland with Rev Seamer, who briefed him on the circuit he was now going to. He need not worry about getting exercise, Seamer told him. The Bay of Islands circuit was more extensive than any other. It was also the circuit with the most history and the greatest range of people. Seamer knew that, through his mother, Scrim had some familiarity with Maori. He assured him that the two Maori ministers in the circuit would give him helpful advice. Scrim should also pay his respects to Maori elders and listen to them.

Seamer may have been at least a little anxious that Scrim might still have an unintended ability to get off-side with members of his congregation. He suggested 'a little conservative caution' in his dealings with his new parishioners. 'Please don't try cutting down any flagpoles, will you,' he said as he farewelled him from the Auckland railway station.[24]

Russell was the oldest and largest Methodist congregation in the Bay of Islands circuit. Previous home missioners had lived there, but Scrim's first thought was that that would be a mistake. Russell was cut off from the mainland and, as in Putaruru, Scrim thought that the members of its congregation were old and set in their ways. Nor would living in Russell signify his intention to get closer to Maori in the circuit. Seamer agreed that he could move to Kawakawa. It had a doctor, a chemist, several shops, a pub, and a police station, and it was the place where the local newspaper, the *Bay of Islands Gazette* was published. It also had a Masonic lodge and an Oddfellows Lodge. Quite a few young people lived there, but best of all for Scrim, a coal miner lived there who was prepared to have him as a boarder.[25]

Scrim found the coal miner's family were a pleasure to live with, and his participation in household chores gave him a way into items of interest to women in the district. 'These close human contacts,' he later wrote, were as necessary a part of one's education 'as university graduation'. Most of the men of achievement in New Zealand 'were not academics or the favoured sons of wealthy people'. In the course of his life he considered himself fortunate to have opportunities to meet many of them. He wrote as one of them.[26]

By now, Scrim knew how to get to know people in communities in which he was a newcomer. He would begin his day with a stroll along the main street in Kawakawa, chatting to shopkeepers, the garage proprietor, and the hotel keeper. These regular contacts led to others. He was invited to become a member of both of the lodges that were established in Kawakawa. Through the Masons he met some of the men in the district he might not otherwise have had much to do with. As well as broadening the range of his social contacts, this gave opportunities for him to test some of the popular perceptions of Masons in the light of his own experience. Masons, he concluded, were 'just ordinary people'. It was 'rubbish' that Masons were a select group who arranged favours that were available only to fellow lodge members.[27]

He was soon on good terms with leading Maori in the district. He followed up an invitation that some Maori elders extended to him on his arrival in Russell and was honoured with a formal welcome and a hangi on his first visit to the Waiomio marae, a few miles inland from Kawakawa. Seamer had coached him on how he should comport himself on such visits, and Scrim, drawing inspiration from his mother, felt at home during the day's events. He was able to respond to the welcoming mihi with a short response in Maori. Then, speaking in English, he appealed to his hosts to take him in hand and teach him to speak Maori.[28]

During that first visit, the people of Waiomio worked out a suitable Maori transliteration of his name. Scrim became Karena, and Scrimgeour Kirimoa. This transliteration surprised Rev Oriwa Haddon when he heard about it. It broke all the rules, he said. Kirimoa meant the feathers of the moa and would only have been given to a chief of very high mana. Haddon was even more surprised that the elders had presented Scrim with a finely woven flax cloak trimmed with kiwi feathers. Oriwa Haddon's comments are left to stand without any further explanation in Scrim's autobiography. Scrim wore his kiwi-feathered cloak at the Waitangi centennial celebrations in 1940.

Scrim may or may not have had an inkling of the reciprocal nature of Maori gift giving, but the warmth of his welcome strengthened his resolve to get close to the Maori members of his circuit. He worked at his Maori. Each time he visited Waiomio, he 'did a little better'. He had a copy of the New Testament in Maori, and Oriwa Haddon guided him in his reading of it. Scrim's commitment to Maori people became an important part of his broadcasting mission when, a decade later, he became head of the National Commercial Broadcasting Service. One of his early decisions in that role was to appoint Oriwa Haddon to the broadcasting staff of 1ZB, and he appointed Maori broadcasters to the other ZB stations when they were established.

Scrim made regular visits to the nine preaching places listed in the circuit plan. When he found that some other places had not been listed, he added them. He built up his knowledge of the history of the Bay of Islands by visiting 'the famous Maori redoubts' and by seeking out Maori and Pakeha with stories to tell. From these visits and meetings he found that relationships between Pakeha and Maori were much more complex and varied and, for the most part, more distant than he had expected. Certainly there were friendships between leading Pakeha and Maori families, friendships which in some cases went back nearly a century. But the Methodist church, like the rest of society in the Bay of Islands, was made up of two cultural groupings who lived largely independently of each other.

Like most people living in the far north, Scrim made his visits on horseback. A visit to Towai to conduct a service in the local school was an eight-hour return journey. The service was always followed by a billy of tea and a scone, and any leftover scones were by general agreement given to his horse. Maromaku's reputation in the district owed much more to its pub than to the Methodist services conducted in the hall next door. The pub was an unofficial watering hole for passengers on the Opua line. Trains stopped long enough for them to buy a beer. The pub also did brisk after-hours trading on Sundays. It sold good beer, Scrim said, and did good trade on the evenings when he was conducting his church service. He did not drink beer at that stage of his life. He later thought that, if he had been 'on the ball' he would have passed the hat around the pub's illegal Sunday evening gatherings and done very well. The people who did not come to his services were in his opinion no worse than those who did.[29]

Scrim's visits to his various preaching places confirmed for him the importance of smoothing the differences between the various denominations. In several places the congregation remained much the same from week to week regardless of the denomination of the minister. Even Mormons, he remembered, were part of the congregation at Maromaku. He held his services at Moerewa in the local picture theatre.

He had a pleasant surprise when he paid the first of his regular monthly visits to Kawakawa. He found that the local school teacher had served with his father in the Samoa Relief Force during the war. The teacher was among those who formed a favourable impression of the young preacher. Scrim had the 'happy knack', he said, of making the members of his congregation 'feel he was one of themselves' and understood their personal problems.[30]

★

While he was in the Bay of Islands Scrim was given an unexpected opportunity to become better known to people in the district. The five-yearly census of the New Zealand population was conducted in March 1926. The postmaster and police sergeant at Kawakawa asked him to be the census enumerator for the district. Seamer agreed and he also authorised Scrim to keep the fee (£7 a week) in addition to his £6 a week stipend.[31]

He bought a new Triumph motorbike for £27 and took it on roads that were, he said, two chains wide and two feet deep. Where the roads were too daunting and mud was not a problem he took to the fields. He introduced himself as the local Methodist minister but did not wear his clerical collar while carrying out the duties of census enumerator. He was struck by the friendliness and generosity of the people he met. For his part, he was ready to offer a helpful pair of hands where they might be needed. He milked cows, mustered sheep, shod a station horse at one place and 'tinkered with a home electric outfit' at another. Some run holders gave him petrol in return for help in filling out their returns. He was thankful that he did not have to use the medical kit he carried with him and was not called on to assist with a confinement.

He did not do any preaching. Conversation was for him 'the best common denominator' and, he said, he did not have to invent any yarns to keep it going. He completed the census in three weeks. He slept in twenty different beds, two of them on marae. He ate all kinds of food, including fried eels, damper bread, and pork cooked in a hangi. He made many new friends. The chief census officer turned down his offer to accept a reduced fee. The task over, Scrim parked the Triumph in a shed at the back of the church and got on with his 'normal duties'.[32]

Scrim did well in the Bay of Islands. A child of the countryside himself, he seems to have had no difficulty in reaching out to make contact with people, sharing their interests, and listening to their concerns. But within himself Scrim did not feel one of them. He continued to think of himself as an outsider. Perhaps he misjudged his parishioners, but his image of them was of people standing in judgement on him. Some of the jottings he made for his autobiography give the flavour. Legends, he wrote, started to build up that he liked to spend more time with Maori than with the people who paid his salary; that he always had a saddlebag full of books but did not read his Bible; and that he drove his motorbike 'like a maniac'.[33]

Be that as it may, some people were starting to single him out as a man with potential. Sometime during 1926 he was approached by the ubiquitous Bert Davy and, in Scrim's words in one of his autobiographical jottings, 'offered a seat in Parliament'. That, of course, was more even than Davy could promise, and we can assume the astute political manager would have hedged his invitation with qualifications that the twenty-three-year-old either did not hear or screened out of his later recollection. Scrim declined the offer, as he continued to do when he received similar overtures a few years later. We do not know which political party Davy had in mind when he approached Scrim. Davy fell out with the Reform Party in the course of 1926 and began working with people who were seeking to rejuvenate the Liberals.[34]

During his time in the Bay of Islands Scrim took up an opportunity to meet Zane Grey, the renowned big-game fisher who was making his first visit to New Zealand and had set up his camp at Otehei Bay on Urupukapuka Island. It was not Zane Grey the fisherman but Zane Grey the acclaimed author of Westerns who interested Scrim. He had been a devoted Zane Grey reader during his early teens before moving on to Tolstoy, Shaw, and other authors who were not interested in 'sombreros, chaps, or six-shooters'.

Scrim was given a chilly reception. Grey was at first unfriendly to the point of rudeness, but he thawed a little when Scrim emphasised that he was interested in his books and mentioned the titles of 'half a dozen of his swashbuckling novels'. But Grey was still defensive. He knew that Scrim was a preacher, but was he also 'a kind of bounty hunter?' Yes, he was, Scrim rejoined, but he fished for souls, not swordfish, and this was an off-duty visit. He had simply come to say 'Hello', and he did not work for newspapers.

That was the turning point. Scrim knew that Grey 'hated critical journalists'. Once assured that he would not become newspaper copy, he relaxed and was an agreeable host. Scrim found him 'voluble and friendly' but a 'shy, cautious, and in some ways, strange man'. He enjoyed his host's 'excellent coffee'.[35]

⋆

There is a striking omission from Scrim's account of his time in the Bay of Islands. In April 1926, in Whangarei, he was married to Lena Hardie, the teacher he had met when he was stationed in Putaruru.[36] As Scrim's wife, Lena would be the mother of their three children, a co-worker, and a great support to him. But their marriage collapsed in 1953, and Scrim does not mention her in his autobiographical writings.

Lena's grandparents had arrived in New Zealand at about the same time as Scrim's paternal grandfather, and were among the first settlers in the Matakohe district near the Northern Wairoa River. Those who came to know Lena were in no doubt that she was a great asset to Scrim. She was attractive and vivacious and blessed with a warm personality. She had a natural poise and the accomplishments to be expected of an intelligent young woman born and brought up in rural New Zealand. She managed the home well and was a good mother. She was an accomplished sewer, had a sense of style, and made all her own clothes, including her coats. She played the piano, and brought one to the marriage. When, after her divorce, she looked back on her life, she believed that Scrim had sought to replace his mother when he married her. She smoothed Scrim's rough edges, teaching him table manners, civilising his language, and helping him with social graces.

She was a co-worker with Scrim in his church work and his later broadcasting activities. She served with him as a deaconess in the Methodist Social Service Centre. As 'Herself' she became one of the Friendly Road's favourite radio aunts in children's radio programmes. She was Scrim's right-hand person on his 'Man in the Street' sessions, standing in for him on occasions and serving as his host when he broadcast his sessions from Australia. She was president of the 2ZB Happiness Club when it started in 1937. She managed his 1943 election campaign for the Wellington Central seat. She took all this in her stride.[37]

What Lena had not expected was that Scrim's family would come with him. Less than a week after their marriage, one of Scrim's brothers arrived and lived with them for two years. Seldom a week went by without some other member of his family staying with them. They came, she said, because Scrim had a permanent job and they were assured of a bed and their keep.

★

Scrim's service in the Bay of Islands ended sooner than he expected. Sometime late in the year he received a telegram from Seamer informing him that he was to be appointed to a new position from the beginning of January 1927. He went to Auckland and Seamer acquainted him with his new duties. Seamer talked to him 'for hours' about his plans for a central mission in Auckland that would provide social services and be the centre for Methodist evangelistic effort.[38]

When he reflected on his time in the Bay of Islands, Scrim wondered about his ability to 'teach by preaching' but he was certain that he had learnt a lot. And he took some pride from the fact that he was not being transferred because he had cut down any flagpoles.[39]

# CHAPTER 3

# Bringing Hope to Down and Outs

Scrim would write in his autobiography that he had mixed feelings on his arrival in Auckland in January 1927. He was there to create a new Methodist mission, a social service centre, in a big city where he was virtually unknown. The Rev Seamer believed he was equal to the task, but would he measure up?

The church records of the time, however, convey a strong impression of a missioner who was meeting the challenges of the new position with great dedication and energy. There was unquestionably a great deal to do simply to get the social service mission started. The Airdale Street church on which it was to be based had not had a resident minister for several years. Its only regular activity was a Saturday evening meal and social hour for 'down and outs'. Its congregation had dispersed to other churches. The church and parsonage were dilapidated.

The inner-city church was well placed for Scrim's new responsibilities. It stood on the boundary of commercial Auckland and the city's poorest residential areas. Except for a doctor's residence on the corner of Symonds Street at the top end of Airdale Street, most of its houses were old, small wooden cottages. The lower end of the street, diagonally across Queen Street from the Town Hall, marked the effective end of commercial premises. The lower part of Greys Avenue, on the other side of the Town Hall, was the symbolic heart of the poorest part of the city. Its sly grog shops, opium dens and brothels excited public imagination and attracted police attention. The poor parts of the city stretched up Greys Avenue, down Hobson Street, into Freemans Bay, up College Hill to Ponsonby, and from the west side of Karangahape Road into the Newton gully.

The Roman Catholic Church had had a strong presence in this part of Auckland from the beginning of European settlement. The Salvation Army's social services went back to the 1880s. Anglicans and Methodists were relative newcomers. The Anglicans began their city mission at St Matthew's on the corner of Hobson Street and Wellesley Street West in 1920. Scrim was soon on good terms with Rev Jasper Calder, the Anglican city missioner who, as Uncle Jasper, would become a regular member of Scrim's team of radio aunts and uncles. He got on well, too, with Monsignor Holbrook who directed Catholic social services.

Scrim began by walking the poorer streets of the inner city, introducing himself to people as a newcomer and chatting to them. Many, he found, were shy of a stranger wearing a clerical collar, so he took it off. When people asked him what he was doing he said he was looking for a job and they usually assured him that he would find something.

Ready to work with him were some men and women whose enthusiasm matched his own, and they set out together to create a new church community. They renovated the church and parsonage. Scrim did a round of second-hand furniture shops and furnished the parsonage. The Rev Seamer set up a management board to guide the Social Service Centre and provide links with Auckland Methodists. The Pitt Street Methodist Church, the leading Methodist church in Auckland and the mission's nearest church neighbour, arranged for Sister Rita Snowden, its deaconess, to work full-time as part of the mission. Sister Rita Snowden was at the beginning of her career of distinguished service to the Methodist Church.

It had already become part of Scrim's style to be persuasively upbeat in what he had to say about his activities. His report of the Social Service Centre's first year recorded uniformly satisfactory progress. All its social services, it emphasised, served an evangelistic purpose. The two Sunday services – the morning service a time of fellowship for members of the regular congregation, the evening service an evangelistic service – provided 'continuing evidence of the power of God'. Meetings held on Monday and Saturday evenings for down and outs were regularly attended by men of a wide range of descriptions. Thirty or forty young women met on Tuesday evenings for 'a happy hour' of spirituality and gymnastics. Forty or more mothers met on Wednesdays, and a committee, formed from among them, assisted the deaconess in her work. On Wednesday evening, too, there was a Bible-reading and fellowship meeting. Films specially selected for children were screened on Thursday evenings, attended by 300 'poor children and their parents'. Band of Hope meetings were often held on Friday evenings. Clubs for young men and young women were operating under 'capable leaders'.[1]

Three years later the volume of work had greatly increased and the Social Service Centre was in good heart. Large numbers of people who had not previously been churchgoers were attending its Sunday services. Inspiring testimonies had been heard at communion services. There had been uplifting accounts of 'human derelicts' who were leading new lives 'without fear of hunger or hatred against the conventional order of things'. People seeking guidance on a wide range of concerns valued the guidance of the mission's workers in their lives. There was a never-ending demand, but no deserving case had yet been turned away.

The centre was grateful to its growing network of well-wishers for their continuing support. Churches throughout the province had been generous with gifts of cash and produce. Auckland businessmen were also giving generous support.[2] On Rev Seamer's recommendation the 1931 Methodist Annual Conference approved a change of name for the mission to the Auckland Methodist Social Service Mission.[3]

Men and women queueing for grocery chits outside the vestry of the Social Service Centre. (Photographer unknown, *Scrim: Radio Rebel in Retrospect*)

'Skypilot'. Gordon Minhinnick charcoal and chalk caricature (Alexander Turnbull Library Cartoon B-100- 027)

To keep in touch with adherents and provide a record of the social centre's activities, Scrim published 'The Call', a magazine that appeared three or four times a year. To add to its appeal He commissioned Gordon Minhinnick, a young cartoonist employed by the *Sun*, to illustrate it. When Scrim gained his pilot's licence Minhinnick drew a charcoal and crayon portrait of him as the reverend sky pilot. There was something about the eyes, however, that the cartoonist may not have intended to be flattering.[4]

Scrim's new responsibilities required him to find ways of making Aucklanders aware of what the Social Centre was doing. Jasper Calder had already demonstrated the importance of publicity in his work as Anglican city missioner. Always his own man, Scrim would have denied that he was following Calder's example or that he was competing with him. He was, as he always insisted, doing things his way. He was every bit as unconventional as Calder and, like Calder, he was criticised by church people of a conventional cast of mind who were often uncomfortable with what he was doing. But the Social Service Centre bore unmistakeable marks of his personality.

★

Scrim's flair and initiative were to be seen in all the mission's activities but nowhere more than in its regular film screenings. He was fascinated by movies. He was adept at taking machines apart and putting them together again. He felt sure that the mission should bring some joy into the lives of poor boys and girls. He arranged with one film distributor to let him show films in his church that were no longer in use on the commercial circuit. Another let him have a decommissioned film projector, and he taught himself how to operate it. An old tarpaulin strung across the organ pipes in the church served as a screen. The church organist played mood music. Scrim enjoyed the children's noisy pleasure.

His wish to show films during his Sunday evening evangelistic services was harder to bring about. By 1930 his congregation had outgrown the 200 seats in his church and he was looking for a larger place to hold it. The first talkies were being shown in Auckland. Scrim had the idea of holding Sunday evening services in a picture theatre and supplementing them with a suitable movie. This required the approval of the city council which, though not unsympathetic, was far from persuaded that film screenings – even free screenings – on Sunday evenings, could be approved under the film regulations. With the assistance of Brazillai Beckerleg, the unconventional barrister, Scrim got a licence. He had come to know Beckerleg through his interest in monetary reform and would get to know him better as a fellow broadcaster. One of the things he liked about Beckerleg was his 'streak of mischief'. He, like Scrim and others of their acquaintance, enjoyed opportunities to pull the leg of authority.[5]

The Sunday evening screenings in the Strand, with a community sing conducted by Tom Garland and a sermon by Scrim or some other speaker, were popular as evangelism. But they were discomfitting to many Methodists and other churchgoers who believed that popular films could have no place in the saving of souls. Opposition came to a head when Scrim screened *King of Kings*, the Hollywood sensation of the moment based on the life of Jesus Christ. Scrim believed the film was a far better sermon than he could ever hope to preach.[6] He screened it in ten weekly episodes. For the climactic last episode he invited Dr Ranston, the lecturer in Bible History at Wesley Theological College, to give an address that would bring the series to a close. Scrim was criticised by fellow Methodists for involving Dr Ranston in this venture. But he was compensated when the

American owners of the film did not ask for their usual very high royalty payment.[7]

Scrim's responsibilities required him to give spiritual comfort to patients in the city's hospitals and perform the functions of a prison chaplain. For his hospital visits he formalised the practice he had followed in Putaruru and Kaitangata. The needs of patients were more important to him than whether or not they were Methodists. He arranged with ward matrons to make lists of patients who were not being visited by other clergy or who were very sick or at death's door. These were the patients he visited. But if they indicated that they would prefer to be visited by a minister of some other denomination he let the relevant minister or priest know. He left his telephone number with his patients and assured them that they could ring at any time.

He recalled two cases in particular that affected him deeply. One, a middle-aged woman who was dying of cancer, reminded him of his mother. He wrote that he arranged for her to be given pills that eased her suffering and ended her life. The other was the distraught, heavily pregnant twelve-year-old girl who arrived unannounced on the doorstep of the Airdale Street parsonage. His brief account does not mention the delivery of her baby on the kitchen table but he leaves no doubt about its emotional impact on him.[8] As with the account Scrim gave of the old Salvationist at Kaitangata, his heart-rending accounts of these two cases should perhaps be taken with a grain of salt. Scrim's recollections of these events were recorded in his old age and may have been based on inaccurate memories. We will see in later chapters that some at least of the recollections of his old age were fictions.

At the mental hospital he arranged to visit the most difficult cases, which meant patients restrained in straitjackets. The superintendent agreed that the patients visited were to be freed from their straitjackets while he was with them. That, Scrim believed, would give them enough freedom of movement to be able to feel that they could trust the person who had come to visit them. He greeted them with some simple, quietly spoken words: 'You are going to get well but you must believe in yourself first. Whenever you feel distressed or even angry, repeat what I say. Now breathe deeply five times, then relax. You can learn to do this even if the ties [of your straitjacket] are not loosened.' Scrim would wait until he got some sign of a response. Then he would say: 'In quietness and confidence you will find peace and happiness.' He and the patient said this sentence together and repeated it two or three or perhaps several times. These words, he told his patients, must be the first words they spoke whenever they woke up. If the words didn't come easily, they were to breathe deeply five times and they would remember them.

The nurses and medical staff became aware that Scrim had a calming effect on the patients he visited, and the hospital superintendent found an opportunity to ask him the secret of his success. No, he had not, as the superintendent surmised, been studying psychology. He owed his approach to his mother, who had coached her children to count to ten before saying anything when they were provoked. It was all a matter of building trust, he told the superintendent. Parsons were like doctors, 'they could only treat people who had faith in them'. Mental patients were first and foremost sick people, but it was clearly difficult to gain their trust in an institution that forcibly restrained them.[9]

Satisfying as he found hospital visiting, the role of prison chaplain was even more fulfilling. It gave him opportunities to do something to redeem the lives of men whom society had shunned. As a minister of religion he had the status of a friend of the court, which meant that he could represent men brought before the court who did not have the benefit of legal counsel. He soon built up a good working relationship with the police and the magistrates, and there was a steady demand for his services. Typically, he would plead for the accused to be granted bail. He was careful, he later wrote, to wear his clerical collar when acting as a prisoner's friend in court.

Some of the men he assisted were incorrigible offenders, at least a couple of whom he got to know well during his seven years as Methodist city missioner. One of these, Bastings, was an expert safe-blower. He had been declared a habitual criminal and was liable to arrest at any time without charge. Scrim got to know him well enough to use him as a babysitter, and considered him the best babysitter he had. Bastings stayed with the Scrimgeours on occasions when he was out of prison, something that the police knew about. But when Bastings came under police suspicion for a couple of safe-blowings that showed signs of his handiwork Scrim persuaded him to 'do a bunk' to Australia.

Arthur J. Cocker was another man whom Scrim assisted. Cocker was a banker by profession who always identified himself in court as a gentleman. He was an alcoholic. He was also an accomplished organist who filled in for church services when he was in prison. The prison chaplains knew that the music for their services would be in good hands when Cocker was in prison.[10]

Acting as a friend of the court Scrim had to make quick assessments of the men he assisted, and he was liable to make mistakes. The only story he told against himself in his autobiography was about one of these. A man was before the court on a charge of stealing a typewriter valued at £10. Scrim offered to put up bail of £10. This surprised the magistrate, who adjourned the case and asked Scrim to see him in chambers. It was the magistrate's typewriter that had been stolen. Scrim was reprimanded.

But there was usually a silver lining to Scrim's stories. The news of his reprimand quickly got around. He was welcomed with loud clapping on his next appearance in the prison pulpit. He was learning what it felt like to be applauded. The magistrate and Scrim were the only parties to the private conversation in the magistrate's chambers, and it seems most unlikely that the magistrate would have had any interest in breaching its confidential nature.

Scrim made an effort to gain some understanding of the prisoners' culture. He was fascinated by their currency of plugs of tobacco through which prisoners transacted business among themselves. Cat's whisker crystal sets, hacksaw blades and other attractive trade goods had their price. The results of two-up and other games of chance were tallied in tobacco plugs. The currency had built-in protections. Laying bets with a bookmaker 'outside' might land a bookmaker in prison but there was no risk for those who made their transactions 'inside'. Nor was there any danger that a 'welsher' would disappear. The punishment of a few days on bread and water was not considered to be much worse than the usual prison rations. Prisoners' tallies of plugs were converted into pounds, shillings and pence when they were discharged.[11]

Scrim arranged for students from the Methodist theological college to assist in the conduct of his prison church services. He also invited prominent people to share the pulpit. The prison authorities were impressed when Peter Dawson, the renowned Australian baritone, turned one service into a vocal concert. They were less impressed when Scrim invited Rosie and Nina Scott, two 'beautiful' young women and 'accomplished artists' to sing popular melodies instead of dull hymns. The Scott sisters had a large following among music and drama followers in Auckland. [12]

The question was where to draw the line. Scrim knew that the point about popular songs was that they were indeed popular. If the churches were to reach out to men and women who felt that they were marginalised or, as with prisoners, rejected by society, they must accept them as they were. That meant sharing with them the songs they themselves enjoyed singing. That came naturally to Scrim. He was untutored in matters of musical taste and opinion. There were few traces of music of any kind in the life of his family nor, apart from hymns, in the rural church congregations he had been associated with. Like everyone else, Scrim knew what he liked, and what he liked was shaped by the music he listened to. He liked to be entertained and took it for granted that others did too.

Scrim was relieved to find that there were no Methodists among the prisoners. He wondered light-heartedly if that was because Methodist criminals were too clever to get caught. More seriously, he knew that that saved him from a conflict of conscience. He opposed capital punishment and rued the possibility that he might be called on to stand with some criminal at the moment of his execution. During his years as a prison chaplain he did not have to face that dilemma.

The issue he did have to face was no less challenging and it was much more complex in its implications. From the time of his arrival in Auckland he was deeply involved in doing what he could to bring relief to people who were sick, poor, derelict or without proper housing. The men and women who queued outside his vestry each afternoon were one sign of their numbers. The men who attended the social occasions for down and outs were another. Scrim decided that he must make it his business to meet these men in their own haunts, in the back streets of the city and on the wharves where they slept at night.

Scrim's illness while he was serving in Kaitangata had meant that Seamer must abandon his plan for Scrim to enter Wesley Theological College in 1925. In 1927, with Scrim now living in Auckland, Seamer arranged with Dr Laws for him to attend two lecture courses as a part-time student. Scrim was enrolled in Dr Laws' lectures in the Higher Criticism and Dr Ranston's course on the Old Testament. It is clear from what Scrim later wrote in his autobiographical jottings that being a student – even a part-time one – chafed, and the arrangement does not seem to have lasted very long. Scrim was no more accepting of pupil status at twenty-four than he had been at any earlier age.

The decision to have him take courses at the college brought into play Scrim's attitudes to authority. Serving as home missioner in three circuits, he had been his own master, deciding what should be done, when it could be done, and then doing it. Attending lectures at the theological college made it clear to all, however, that he was a student subject to the authority of its two lecturers. So Scrim set about making arrangements that showed that he was also in control. With a nod to Dr Ranston, he arranged for some theological students to gain practical experience of what he called the 'lower criticism'. Having students assist him with his prison services was one example. Having senior students to assist him in his work with unemployed men in downtown Auckland was another. Les Horward, one of the senior students, accompanied him on his first foray.

Scrim had developed good working relations with local newspaper reporters when he was working in Kaitangata and in the Bay of Islands. He arranged for a reporter and a photographer from the *Sun,* a refreshingly new but short-lived Auckland newspaper, to accompany them. Dressed in the cast-off clothing of unemployed men, Scrim and Horward spent three days and two nights among men sleeping rough on the wharves and in nearby streets. The *Sun* responded with a photograph on its front page and a sympathetic story.[13]

Scrim's visit confirmed what he already knew: clothing made a huge difference. Men wearing dirty clothes were convinced that well-dressed people looked down on them. They felt uneasy and out of their element on Queen Street. Many of them thought that well-dressed people feared that they would attack them. Some of these men, Scrim felt, were unemployable but most wanted work and were keen to get it. The little talk there was of Bolshevism was from men who were probably unemployable. It seemed, too, that the genuinely unemployed men disdained men who did not want to work.

The men he met spoke with gratitude of individual acts of goodwill from 'members of the cloth'. But they were dismissive, sometimes

Living 'rough' on the wharves. (*Sun*, 27 August 1927)

in strong terms, of the church and other charitable organisations, and got in touch with them only as a last resort. His overwhelming impression was that these men were alienated from society and they knew it. Most of them did not want temporary relief. They wanted a steady job and with it the recognition of being an accepted member of society.[14]

Working with unemployed men made Scrim realise the inadequacy of what he was doing. No church mission or charitable organisation was able to provide steady work for able-bodied men, not even for the comparatively small numbers who were unemployed in the late 1920s. The great increase in unemployment during the early thirties made that only too obvious.

Most of the down-and-out men Scrim dealt with in his work had wives and children for whom they were not providing. The wives and children were bearing the real burden of destitution. His mission reached out to them all. His working principle at that time was that, to be effective, social services for families in genuine need would require a great deal of cooperative effort from people who might or might not be Methodists but were ready to play their part.

Helping people in hardship had its pitfalls, however. Men who could tell a plausible story were a continuing challenge. Scrim and Jasper Calder quickly earned the reputation of men who were not to be taken in by fabricated accounts of hardship. But many well-disposed businessmen in the city were less successful at distinguishing deserving from undeserving appeals. The knowledge that some of their members were being hoodwinked was unsettling, and it gave Scrim his first opportunity to devise a cooperative approach to a shared social concern.

Working with some of the city's leading businessmen, he created the Auckland Businessmen's Relief Service. This service separated the giving of money for charity from the process of making decisions on the people who were to benefit from such gifts. All members of the association had a supply of printed cards which they gave to anyone seeking assistance. Applicants filled out a card and sent it to the Auckland Businessmen's Relief Service. Scrim, acting as its executive officer, vetted applications. He then informed the relevant member of the association of the applications he deemed worthy of support, and the member took the necessary action. The scheme worked. Scrim estimated that about half the tickets distributed were returned to him, which he took as evidence of an inbuilt winnowing process.[15]

To see that something should be done was for Scrim to do something about it. The Businessmen's Relief Service showed his ability to think up a creative solution to a common problem, to win the confidence of the people whose cooperation was necessary to make it happen, and then to do what was necessary to make it work effectively. The time and effort he was putting into this responsibility was in addition to his already heavy workload as a central city missioner. He was not sparing himself. He believed that no minister of religion was working harder or for longer hours.

But his gift for making friends was serving him well. Two men in particular – Hal Pettit and Harold Jones – had come to know him well during these years and knew how hard he was working. In their different ways they succeeded in getting him to take up interests that would give him times when he could relax away from the mission. Dr Pettit was twelve or thirteen years older. He had been an Auckland Hospital Board doctor since the early 1920s. Among his wide interests he was a keen deep-sea fisherman and the honorary doctor for the Auckland Wrestling Association. He was Scrim's doctor, knew of his hypertension, and made a bargain with him. He would attend any patient Scrim sent him so long as Scrim took a fortnight off from time to time and went deep-sea fishing with him. Pettit paid the costs of these trips. Scrim was not a fisherman but was more than happy to have these opportunities to enjoy Pettit's company. Pettit was no doubt glad to be able to keep his finger on the pulse of his friend's health. The two men went on several fishing trips together during the thirties.

Scrim also attended wrestling bouts in the Town Hall as Pettit's guest, sitting in one of the two ringside seats Pettit had as the honorary doctor. Professional wrestling was a popular Monday evening entertainment in Auckland from the late 1920s until the 1950s. A great deal of interest centred on Lofty Blomfield, the local wrestler who regularly tried conclusions with visiting American matmen. Scrim was struck by the differences between boxing as he had known it and the professional wrestling bouts he attended. He was convinced that professional wrestling was a fake but was impressed with the wrestlers' abilities as actors and entertainers. On one occasion, when wrestling fans were invited to make donations for the Methodist mission, £500 was taken up. Everyone, Scrim wrote, had their money's worth and 'he was able to be a little more generous with handouts of grocery orders'.[16]

Scrim received a second offer of assistance at about the same time as the one from Pettit. It is likely that, unknown to him, Hal Pettit and Harold Jones were working in tandem. Jones was the managing director of an Auckland biscuit factory. He had come to know Scrim through the Auckland Businessmen's Association. Like Pettit he knew how hard Scrim was working and he seems also to have become concerned that the demands and pressures might be too much for him. He thought that Scrim needed the safety valve of a recreation, and suggested golf. He would be happy to buy him a set of golf clubs and pay his annual subscription to one of Auckland's best golf clubs. Scrim thanked Jones for the offer but boldly suggested that he consider making a different offer. Learning to fly was his latest enthusiasm. It was something he had wanted to do since 1929 when, with thousands of others, he had paid his ten shillings and been taken on a joyride in Francis Chichester's monoplane.[17] Would Jones be prepared to fund the cost of the course of training to become a pilot? Harold Jones readily agreed to pay the £27 for the course of instruction.

Between January and July 1930 Scrim made regular visits to Mangere aerodrome where the recently established Auckland Aero Club had its flying headquarters. The leading members of the club were veterans who had flown in the Royal Flying Corps during the war. His flying tutor, Flight Lieutenant Allan, and Squadron Leader Isitt, who examined him for his licence, were members of the air force reserve as well as members of the aero club. Scrim and Isitt would cross paths again in 1943 when Scrim was conscripted into the armed services and Isitt was chief of air staff. Scrim was proud to be one of the first hundred New Zealanders to hold a pilot's licence, and was careful to note that most of that first hundred had got their licences during the war. He also liked being mentioned as 'the world's first *real* sky pilot'. [18]

Scrim made several short flights during the rest of 1930. But flying was an expensive hobby, and there were fewer entries in his logbook for 1931. He made his longest flights in February 1931 in the aftermath of the Napier earthquake. Telephone and telegraph communication with Napier was cut off and, at the urgent request

Scrim as a pilot. (Photographer unknown, *Scrim: Radio Rebel in Retrospect*)

of the mayor of Auckland, he flew to Hawkes Bay to talk to civic leaders, assess the situation, and find out what Aucklanders could do to assist.[19] He found that the local authorities in Napier, Hastings, and elsewhere in the province had swung into action and that their emergency operations were already under way. As it happened, it was through radio broadcasts that people throughout the country received the news of what had happened during the earthquake and how the people of Hawkes Bay were coping with their tragedy. Scrim returned to Auckland three days later and reported to the mayor's office. Then he crossed the road to his mission where fifty or more people – the usual daily muster – were waiting to find out what the Methodist Social Centre could do to help them.

Scrim's standing both as a pilot and a parson made it possible for him to indulge in a stanza of self-promotion. During its early years the New Zealand air force reserve's military services called on army

Scrim invents himself as an air force chaplain. (Photographer unknown, *New Zealand Observer*, 22 April 1937, Alexander Turnbull Library NP 1621 6B)

chaplains when it needed their services. Scrim devised his own answer. Jack Seabrook, the well known car dealer, was one of Scrim's acquaintances in the Auckland Aero Club and in the Businessmen's Association. He was also a squadron leader in the air force reserve. Scrim borrowed Seabrook's uniform and declared himself to be the air force chaplain.[20]

By 1931 the issues Scrim was wrestling with were very different from the ones he had faced when he began his mission four years earlier. It was no longer a matter of whether the people seeking help were deserving or undeserving or whether they were employable or unemployable. The number of unemployed had greatly increased and the vast majority of the men he was seeing were able-bodied and wanted to earn a living. The stark fact of the matter was that the economy had collapsed. Scrim was coming to see that this new situation called for new initiatives. During 1931 and the early months of 1932 he took the lead in initiating two new relief services based on a cashless exchange of goods and services.

The first of these schemes became possible through his association with leading members of the Auckland Farmers Union. He had been interested in monetary reform since the beginning of his friendship with Rev Edwin Cox ten years earlier. Cox had gone on to be one of a group of Methodists who continued to advocate monetary reform, and Scrim kept in touch with them through his own church contacts. Scrim had come to know other monetary reformers, among them Colonel Closey and some other members of the executive of the Auckland Farmers Union. Closey had achieved fame as a brave young fighting officer during the World War and was a prominent public figure. He was also a leading monetary reformer.

Closey backed Scrim's ambitious idea of providing free supplies of meat for Auckland's poor. The Auckland Farmers Union recommended the proposal to its farmer members, many of whom were willing to donate animals. Meat works agreed to kill the animals, trim the carcases, return the offal to farmers, and despatch the trimmed carcases to distribution points in Auckland, all free of charge. Members of the Auckland Businessmen's Association would set up a network of distributors in the city who would store the meat and distribute it free to people on relief.

But the scheme also needed the cooperation of New Zealand

Railways. The various voluntary organisations involved in the scheme approached Hon Adam Hamilton seeking his agreement to have New Zealand Railways transport the meat free of charge from the various meat works to Auckland. Scrim represented the Auckland Social Workers Association in a large deputation that waited on the minister in Wellington in March 1932. He felt sure that Hamilton, the Minister of Railways who was also the minister for unemployment, would look kindly on a proposal that signified so much goodwill from so many sections of the community. But he was exasperated by what Hamilton told the deputation.

As Scrim recalled the meeting forty years later, Hamilton could not see how New Zealand Railways, with its obligation to its 'bond holders', could carry produce on any basis other than the usual freight charges. Scrim found himself in one of the situations where he did not count to ten before replying. How many votes, he asked angrily, would the minister's bond holders cast at the next election? He walked out of the meeting, feeling confident that the other members of the delegation would follow him, but they did not. They remained to listen to what Scrim characterised as a pious lecture.

Scrim did not concede that his own remarks had been a tactical blunder, but they were. Hamilton had brushed the deputation aside. Lobbying of a different sort would now be needed to revive its proposal. One of Scrim's friends in the Auckland Businessmen's Association got in touch with Gordon Coates, who intervened as Minister of Finance and arranged for New Zealand Railways to carry the produce at half rates. Members of the Auckland Businessmen's Association paid the other half and organised the distribution of the meat. Hundreds of tons of meat were distributed.[21]

Scrim's second scheme was a boot exchange for unemployed workers. A serviceable pair of work boots was an essential item of clothing for men working out of doors. But unemployed men did not have the money to buy boots or have them repaired, and bootmakers who could make them were chipping weeds on relief work. Getting the boot exchange under way demonstrated Scrim's determination to have things done his way. He took his proposal to the executive committee of his fellow social workers but failed to get them to back it. Most of them took the view that a boot exchange would lessen the demand for the services of bootmakers who were still earning a living and increase the risk that they, too, would become unemployed.[22]

Undeterred, Scrim took his proposal to the Auckland Businessmen's Association and gained its support. Some tanners donated 'seconds' and reject hides, some shop owners gave free use of their premises, and some unemployed bootmakers brought their lasts and provided a free boot repair service The scheme was well publicised, and one of the Auckland newspapers published a photograph of the bootmakers at work. But it had only a short life.[23]

Scrim may have lost interest in it. His direct involvement came to an end. No one seems to have made arrangements to ensure that it would carry on. Perhaps it folded from a lack of support from within. But it would soon become apparent that Scrim was looking for new fields to conquer.

Disaffection among the unemployed and anxiety among law-abiding Aucklanders rose steadily during the early months of 1932. There seemed no end to the numbers of workers losing their jobs. The city's relief work schemes had reached their limits. New schemes introduced by the government to direct men to rural districts had so far had little effect. In March the government introduced deflationary measures that further increased the hardship of the unemployed.[24]

There were signs of growing discontent. Auckland's Labour MPs and local leaders of the Communist Party were vying for the support of the city's workers and the unemployed. In the Domain on Sunday afternoons Jack (John A.) Lee appealed to mass gatherings to trust a Labour government to right the country's wrongs. Jim Edwards organised street demonstrations and urged members of the Unemployed Workers Association to take direct action. Despite his uncompromising rhetoric, however, Edwards had a restraining influence on demonstrations in the city during March and early April.[25]

Scrim had come to know both men. He had been an active unionist in his younger days but under Lee's influence had come to see the merits of political action in the cause of social justice.[26] But he was not a supporter of any political party. He was working with a wide range of men and women of various political sympathies. Political opinion was hardening. But the people he was cooperating with were making common cause to lessen the suffering of people in distress. Politicians were kept informed of their wishes and intentions to the extent that they might be able to be of some help. Scrim kept Savage and Lee and other Auckland MPs informed of his social service activities and was glad of their support. Others were in touch with Gordon Coates. But as late as 1932 Scrim had not registered as a voter. He would cast his first vote in the 1935 general election. It was not as a political gesture but as an act of pastoral care that Scrim was associated with Jim Edwards in the aftermath of the Queen Street riot.

The event that had led to the Thursday evening riot was a trade union demonstration that started at the foot of Queen Street and ended with a protest meeting in the Town Hall. Organised by the Post and Telegraph Workers Union and widely publicised, an estimated 15,000 people marched up Queen Street in a largely orderly, well-behaved protest, led by Lee and the president of the Post and Telegraph Workers Union. Edwards marched behind them, followed by large numbers of the Unemployed Workers Association who had joined the protest.

Only a very few of those marching could expect to get into the Town Hall. Loudspeakers had been set up to relay the proceedings of the meeting to those who would be left outside. The hall filled up, the doors were closed, the meeting got under way, and those in the hall were unaware of the drama that was being played out in the street outside.

Edwards was among those left in the street. He was once again trying to calm things down when some of the people milling around him became unruly. At the suggestion of a senior policeman monitoring the crowd, he agreed to address it, and clambered onto the plinth of the clock tower to do so. But before he could speak, a policeman felled him with his baton. A spasm of anger gripped those standing near him who saw what had happened. People surged down Queen Street, smashing shop-front windows and looting goods as they went. Some armed themselves by wrenching pickets from the fence in front of the Airdale Street church and parsonage.

Scrim was watching the crowd from the parsonage but did not see the incident that led to Edwards' felling. After the rampage down Queen Street he went out on the street and spent some time trying to persuade people not to become involved in the riot. He got back to the parsonage to find three very anxious people waiting to see him. Could he find a doctor to stitch up someone with scalp wounds? Jim Edwards was the man they were speaking about. Scrim rang Hal Pettit, who agreed to attend him. Scrim was one of the very few people who knew where Jim Edwards was during the ten weeks he was in hiding.

The Queen Street riot took everyone by surprise. The urgent question the next day was whether it was the beginning of a spate of lawlessness that would be repeated again and again in coming weeks and months. But there was no repeat of the Thursday evening mayhem. Naval ratings and members of the Waikato Mounted Volunteers patrolled Queen Street and Karangahape Road. Young men recruited from Auckland University College, St John's Theological College, Wesley Theological College, Auckland Grammar School, and Kings College were sworn in as special police. But the streets on Friday night were relatively calm. Iris Wilkinson, lady editor of the *Observer,* wrote that her only anxiety when walking along Karangahape Road was being struck by the hoof of a horse of one of the volunteer farmers patrolling the street.[27] Scrim noted the irony. Waikato farmers were donating meat to feed impoverished Aucklanders. Their sons, recruited as 'specials', were quelling potential troublemakers on the city's streets.

The city was in the grip of fear of the unknown. Letters published in the *Herald* and *Star* left no doubt that many citizens saw the riot as evidence of a communist plot. Scrim reflected the unease in the sermon he preached ten days after the riot and looting. We do not know what else he said, but in its report the *Star* picked out his remarks on the shame the riot had brought to the city. It was alarming, he was reported as saying, that people in the crowd had 'been swayed in its feelings against the forces of law and order'. Unrestrained hooligans had seized the opportunity to smash windows and open the way to a 'disastrous and costly outcome'. This had had a 'staggering effect' on the country's reputation as 'a model of rectitude in social conduct'. 'It provided for the whole world an example of mass sabotage to a reprehensible degree.'[28]

Scrim was becoming more and more convinced that the government's handling of the economic depression was shamefully inadequate. He also had serious doubts about the effectiveness of charitable assistance as the means of dealing with the plight of people living in poverty. He created an opportunity to outline his doubts to a meeting of church social workers. As an evangelist he had from the beginning had a penchant for eye-catching titles for his sermons. The title he gave himself for this talk was: Charity is twice cursed because it will never meet the need. We do not know how he developed this idea, but readers of the *Auckland Star* read about it under the headline: 'City missioner condemns charity'. A subeditor had enhanced the emotional impact of Scrim's already provocative title. Letters to the editor echoed the dismay of Methodists and other church people. He felt isolated.

Once again, Rev Seamer stood by him. Years later, Scrim wrote that Seamer accepted that what he had said was right but that he had been indiscreet in the way he expressed it.[29]

In the wake of the Queen Street riot, Scrim found a way of publicising his thoughts on what would be needed for the present reliance on charitable activity to be made unnecessary. The *New Zealand Methodist Times* published a long piece he wrote under the heading 'The Social Unrest'.[30] It was his hope, he wrote, that the *Methodist Times* might take the lead in 'a movement towards a relief of our troubles'. His piece gave a tidy summary of the 'currency reformers' critique of the current collapse of the country's economic and social structures.

No other country of the Empire, he wrote, had so much capacity for productive and profitable work. The country was crying out for development, yet 70,000 breadwinners were eking out a life of unproductive drudgery. The labour of 100,000 men was needed to bring waste land into production. Yet the government's only response to 'desperate economic retreat' had been to 'drive' town people on to farmlets to live in shanties and follow a life of 'incompetent drudgery'. For the promised 'miracle of recovery' to happen, these 'allotments' would have to be abandoned so that 'tradesmen' could escape 'peasant life' for their 'true vocation'. Distressed people asked why they should be living in want in a land of plenty. 'Many authorities' would tell them, Scrim asserted, 'that a slight adjustment of our money system would enable the wheels of exchange to revolve and the fruits of labour be made available to those who want'. People should not have to live in calamity because of the government's inability 'in the game of finance' to find a substitute 'for that rare yellow precious metal – gold'.

People were becoming aware of 'the forces that govern them'. They were also feeling 'angry and betrayed' and the privileged group, no matter 'how powerful', would not be able to withstand that anger if it were to be turned against them. Scrim feared that 'the fabric of our social life' could be 'rent to shreds'. He appealed to the Methodist Church to do what it could to prevent such a disaster. More than any other denomination, he wrote, Methodists belonged to the people and would suffer with them if disaster approached. But because they belonged to the people, Methodists could lead them. All members of the church should do what was necessary to rouse the nation to the vital importance of currency reform. Of course it was possible that, on further examination, currency reform might not do what was claimed for it. If that were to be the outcome, Methodists could 'submit to our present anguish'. But he was convinced that the present task was 'to arouse the people to demand as their human rights that this remedy be fairly examined'.

It was the first and so far as I am aware the only time that Scrim committed his views to print with the intention of reaching a national readership. It was an act of solidarity with his acquaintances in the church, with the Auckland Farmers Union, and with others who were championing currency reform. It provided the context in relation to which his dismissive remarks on charity were to be interpreted and was perhaps intended in part as a peace offering for those who had been offended by them.

The Methodist Church did not take up the challenge to become an advocate of currency reform. Members of the church who, like Scrim, believed that it deserved to be given a central place in government responses to the economic crisis would no doubt have been glad to know that they had a new ally. They would have the chance to affirm their solidarity later in the year when Major Douglas visited New Zealand. But Scrim does not seem to have played a prominent part, or perhaps any part, in that visit. He was busy arranging for evangelism to take to the air waves.

There was another sign that Scrim was becoming restless. Towards the end of 1931 he had been offered what his mission's monthly magazine called 'a valuable scholarship' to undertake a course of study in 1932 at the New York School of Social Service. To the very great relief of his fellow workers in the Social Service Centre he decided not to take up the invitation. He was then, in the words of the report, 'prevailed upon to accept the unanimous invitation of the mission officials to remain for another year'.[31]

# CHAPTER 4

# The Advent of Uncle Scrim

Scrim made his first radio broadcast sometime in 1930 in the children's session that Tom Garland conducted over 1YA. Garland was a fellow Methodist and a popular figure in the musical life of the city, and he was also becoming a familiar voice on 1YA. He asked Scrim to give his listeners an idea of the excitement of flying an aeroplane. Scrim talked about what it was like to be flying into a rainbow.

Scrim would soon become the most popular broadcaster in the country, but it was with feelings of embarrassment that he looked back on his first experience of the new medium. Speaking into a microphone, he was surprised to discover, was altogether different from conducting a church service. In church he could make eye contact with people in the back pew and was confident of his ability to hold their attention. But seated at a table in a broadcasting studio with only a microphone in front of him, he could not see his listeners and did not know how many he had and whether they were listening to him. He found, too, that the microphone was sensitive to every modulation and change of his voice. With more practice, he found that the best way of dealing with this was to speak to the microphone in sustained whispers.[1]

We don't know how much interest, if any, Scrim had taken in radio before his interview with Garland. But radio broadcasting was, with talkie films, one of the two popular marvels of the 1920s, and it is probable that, with his fascination with new inventions and his ability to take items of equipment apart and put them back again, it claimed his interest. By the time he arrived in Auckland in 1927 public enthusiasm for radio was growing rapidly and was particularly evident in Auckland itself. Of the 60,000 New Zealanders who had a radio licence in 1930, half lived in Auckland, which was home to six of the country's thirty or more radio stations.[2]

This mushroom growth had given rise to a lively community of people associated in various ways with radio broadcasting: sellers of radios and radio equipment, radio station owners and operators, musicians, storytellers and humorists, who saw new openings for their talents through radio broadcasting, and radio listeners of all ages. The people who made up this community of interest in Auckland were often referred to collectively as members of 'radio-land'. Through word of mouth, for the most part, they kept in touch with each other and with what was happening in local radio broadcasting. By the time that Scrim made his broadcasting debut, however, they were served by two weekly magazines that reported on what was happening in broadcasting. The *New Zealand Radio Record* published the programmes to be broadcast each week by all the stations throughout the country and kept readers informed of developments in Britain, the United States, and Australia. The Auckland-based *New Zealand Observer* ran a 'radio page' each week which was setting good critical standards in its comments on the radio programmes that caught the attention of its reviewer. Under its editor Gordon McLean, the *Observer* offered lively, well-informed opinions on the Auckland social and sporting scene, on local and national politics and personalities, and on musical events, stage shows, films, and radio broadcasting. It would be some years before either of the Auckland daily newspapers would publish the offerings of the local radio stations.[3]

From his first broadcasts over 1ZR's devotional sessions Scrim became a popular member of Auckland's radio-land. 1ZR was the broadcasting venture of Lewis Eady Ltd, the big Queen Street music store and, more particularly, of its managing director, Lewis Eady. In 1928 the family firm reconfirmed its importance in the musical life of the city when it moved into its palatial seven-storey building at 192 Queen Street. Its music store occupied the ground floor and the mezzanine, and there was an auditorium with seating for four hundred and suites of practice rooms on upper floors.

At the end of 1930 Lewis Eady followed the lead of three of Auckland's other music stores and opened its own radio station. He did not expect his station, 1ZR, to turn a profit but he did expect it to boost sales of radios, radio equipment, and gramophone records. Music stores had quickly become gathering places for people wanting to become acquainted with radio broadcasting and buy records and wireless sets. The main Auckland station, 1YA, went off the air at 3pm each day and, as with other radio stations, was off the air one day each week. That left ample time for Lewis Eady's customers to tune into the Auckland 'B' stations during business hours.

The other four Auckland B stations were essentially amateur operations. They might or might not employ a technician to operate and look after the studio equipment and a paid announcer for some of the time they were on air. 1ZR, however, set out to rival 1YA, the Auckland station operated by the Radio Broadcasting Company. It started off with two paid employees, Tom Garland, its studio director, and Archie Don, the studio technician. Housed on the top floor of Lewis Eady's, Garland and Don were genial hosts to the steady stream of speakers and performers who came to the studio to make their broadcasts. 1ZR was on air six days a week for between five and eight hours.[4]

Like all other stations at the time, 1ZR at first relied heavily on the playing of gramophone records. But Lewis Eady, who was a leading member of the Congregational Church, expected the station to have a religious tone. 1ZR was the first radio station in Auckland and probably in New Zealand to broadcast daily devotional services. These began early in 1931 in fifteen-minute sessions at 10am, Monday to Friday, and were conducted by a roster of clergymen from various Protestant denominations. Scrim was on this roster from the beginning. He also presented 1ZR's children's session on Tuesday afternoons.

The Airdale Street church was no more than two hundred yards from Lewis Eady's, and Scrim was always willing to stand in for other ministers who were unable to take a session. He enjoyed the challenge of such impromptu occasions. Perhaps he gilded the lily when he wrote in his autobiography that he would seek inspiration as he sprinted from his church to the studio. But his performances as a radio broadcaster tested his ability to respond quickly in unexpected situations. He was clearly a good broadcaster.

He became known to 1ZR's listeners as Uncle Scrim. Honorary uncles and aunts were an important feature of family life at the time. Close friends of a wife or husband were usually known to their children as aunts and uncles. Aunts and uncles also became a distinguishing feature of radio-land. The YA stations gave a sense of family intimacy to their children's sessions by calling their presenters aunt this and uncle that. 1ZR followed suit and went one better. All its presenters were aunts or uncles or known by some other friendly honorific.

This was all part of 1ZR's aim of fostering warm, intimate bonds with their listeners. In contrast with 1YA's announcers, who were perceived to be formal and impersonal, its presenters were open and spontaneous, just the kind of person you would like to sit down and talk to. In June 1933, when the *Observer* wrote a piece on 'Our Relatives in Radio Land', 1ZR personalities took almost all the accolades. Uncle Tom headed the list, Uncle Dudley (Dudley Wrathall), Aunt Daisy (Daisy Basham) and several other aunts and uncles received favourable mention, and Uncle Scrim received a fulsome tribute as 'probably one of the most popular individuals in the whole of New Zealand uncledom'. It was well known, the *Observer* added, that 'Uncle Scrim receives about the fattest fan mail in Auckland, and he never forgets to answer them, either'.[5]

Listeners would have been mistaken, however, if they thought that Scrim wrote personally to his many correspondents. Even if he had wanted to, he had quickly gone past the time when he could have answered his correspondents himself. There were times when a dozen typists were kept busy dealing with his correspondence. At first, Ysabel Daldy attended to his mailbag, and she also made an important contribution to Friendly Road children's sessions as Mother Macchree. She left the Friendly Road office in March 1934, perhaps after some disagreement with Scrim. In 1937, in the course of its running battle with Scrim, *Truth* published an interview with her which was highly critical of him, and included the claim that she had also drafted talks for his 'Man in the Street' sessions. Perhaps she had. But it is not easy to separate Daldy's comments from *Truth*'s journalistic embellishments.[6]

1ZR was producing much of the excitement of Auckland's radio broadcasting. But the owners of all of Auckland's five B stations knew that they were engaged in a risky venture. Unlike the A stations, the B stations were entirely self-funding local ventures, and they feared that they were being squeezed out of radio broadcasting.

The United and Coalition governments were following a path that had been set by the British government. Radio broadcasting in Britain had been run at first by a private company but had been taken over by a public corporation, the British Broadcasting Corporation, in 1927,[7] after which private radio stations were prohibited by law. The United government in New Zealand said it was following the British precedent when, in 1931, it bought out the Radio Broadcasting

Company and placed the four YA stations under the control of the New Zealand Broadcasting Board. No decision was made about the B stations, and government ministers gave equivocal answers to questions about them.[8]

Supporters of the Auckland B stations felt sure that the British policy solution would not work in New Zealand. They thought it was all very well for the British government to outlaw rivals to the BBC when British listeners could tune into dozens of other radio stations broadcasting from continental Europe. New Zealand listeners did not have that option. Only late in the evening and with good reception could they pick up some of the eastern Australian stations or KF1, the Californian station with a particularly powerful signal.[9]

Opinions in Auckland radio-land differed on the best way forward. Some B station owners were open to being bought out by the Broadcasting Board. Others wanted the government to subsidise their operations. But they were all interested in what had happened in Australia, where B stations had been given a settled place in radio broadcasting.

Australia had two parallel broadcasting systems: a national, publicly funded system run by a government-appointed corporation, and separate networks of privately owned stations that earned income from commercial advertising. This solution reflected a very close relationship between print and radio journalism. The Australian B station networks in all or nearly all states were owned by newspaper companies or by companies in which newspapers had large shareholding interests. There were no parallels to these commercial developments in New Zealand, where newspaper owners had not ventured into the ownership of radio stations and were for the most part wary of commercial broadcasting, fearing competition from radio advertising.[10]

There were few signs of the public's views on radio broadcasting. Most daily newspapers acted as if radio broadcasting did not exist. They did not write editorials on broadcasting matters, and there were no exchanges of opinion about broadcasting in their correspondence columns. There were lively debates in Parliament in 1930 and 1931 on whether to extend the licence of the Radio Broadcasting Company, and whether the state should itself administer broadcasting or create a broadcasting board, acting in the public interest, to administer it. But the vast majority of MPs were prepared to let the

New Zealand Broadcasting Board settle into its work when it took up its responsibilities in January 1932. The Rev Clyde Carr, member for Timaru, and Michael Joseph Savage, member for Grey Lynn, were the only MPs to press for further indications of government policy, but they had to be content with the postmaster general's non-committal answers to their Parliamentary Questions.

Scrim's interest in 1ZR soon extended beyond his contributions to its devotional and children's sessions. He was quite sure that the station needed a regular of income. He was equally sure that, as a defence against the inroads of the government, it must organise a support base for itself among the listening public.

IZR was quick to sign up sponsors when, in July 1931, the government allowed the B stations to undertake a limited form of commercial sponsorship. Most of its programmes had commercial sponsors when the *Observer* did a round-up of B stations in October 1932.[11] We cannot say what part Scrim played in winning these sponsorships. One sponsorship for which he was responsible, however, was the important Vacuum Oil Co sponsorship. This had grown out of his friendship with Flight Lieutenant Beaumont Sheil, who had come to Auckland in 1931 as the Vacuum Oil aviation representative.[12] Sheil had flown with the Royal Flying Corps. Scrim got to know him through the Auckland Aero Club, and both men assisted Sir Charles Kingsford Smith during his visit to New Zealand in January 1933. Scrim lured Sheil into doing what proved to be a popular series of broadcasts on flying with the Royal Flying Corps. Sheil committed himself full-time to broadcasting when, in October 1936, he joined Scrim as advertising manager for the commercial broadcasting service he was setting up.

In 1932 Scrim formed a close working relationship with Harry Bell that would also be very important to him during his broadcasting years. Bell brought with him a valuable background of experience. He had served as secretary to two cabinet ministers before moving to Auckland in the late 1920s to work for one of its local authorities. He and Scrim were made for each other. Scrim was developing a penchant for living in the public eye. Bell had a good nose for what would be newsworthy, and saw it as his task to nurture good publicity for 1ZR and for Scrim himself. Bell would become one of

Scrim's closest associates during his Friendly Road years. He was on hand when Scrim was setting up 1ZB as a commercial operation. He moved to Wellington with Scrim in 1937 to become part of his head office inner circle. Then he went to Christchurch to be the 3ZB station director. But we shall see in chapter 11 that, as time went on, Bell had his detractors among Scrim's other senior colleagues. There was thought to be good reason for investigating Bell's probity as a manager but Scrim was prevaricating.

Scrim and Bell had their first success in September 1932 when, with financial assistance from an unnamed source, the *Observer* began publishing notes supplied by 1ZR.[13] The *Observer* already published information supplied to it by 1ZM. Access to its pages gave both stations a much-valued means of communication with listeners. The *Observer* was read by people whose opinions mattered. It had taken up the cause of the B stations and would be a helpful advocate for them during the uncertainties of the years to come. 1ZR's weekly notes appeared on the page facing the *Observer*'s weekly radio review. These told readers what Uncle Tom, Uncle Scrim, Aunt Daisy and other station personalities were doing. The adulatory tone of its notes about Scrim were particularly noticeable.[14]

To build social bonds with listeners Scrim moved in March 1933 to set up the 1ZR Radio Club. His personal popularity and that of Tom Garland was confirmed when he was elected president and Tom Garland the club secretary.[15] Lapel badges identified club members and made them visible to other members. Before long, the *Observer* was reporting that the 1ZR badges – a blue microphone in bronze with a silver edging – were much in evidence on the streets.[16]

The 1ZR Radio Club organised socials, dances and other social gatherings to encourage its members to become known to each other. Its first club picnic was held on Pine Island, the small island a quarter of a mile offshore from the beach at Herne Bay, and attracted a crowd of 700 in indifferent weather. It was a sign of Scrim's wide circle of friends that Flight Lieutenant D.M. Allan treated the picnickers to twenty minutes of stunt flying.[17]

After listening to Scrim for two years, Gordon McLean decided in December 1933 that the time had come for the *Observer* to analyse the secret of his popularity with listeners. It was, he wrote, a mixture of voice and manner. Scrim's excellent phrasing and enunciation set him apart from most radio speakers. His voice had no traces of 'affectation, stiltedness, detachment and condescension'. He also had 'the gift of the human touch. His personality puts him close to every listener as one man to another.'[18] McLean's analysis dealt solely with Scrim's effectiveness as a communicator. Later in the decade he would apply his critical attention to what Scrim was saying as well as the way he presented it, and his comments would become more critical than commendatory.

People closely associated with the Auckland Social Service Centre would not have been surprised when Scrim confirmed that he would resign from the Methodist Home Mission Service at the end of 1932. In the year since he had foreshadowed that decision his enthusiasm for radio broadcasting had become increasingly evident. 1ZR announced in December that Uncle Scrim would become the station director in the New Year. It also informed listeners that its denominational devotional services would no longer be broadcast in the New Year. Listeners were left to wonder what might replace them.

Scrim resigned from the Methodist Auckland Social Service Centre from the end of 1932. With the superannuation allowance he received from the church and financial assistance from Ernest Davis he took out a mortgage on a property in Kohimarama. Sometime later, he and his family moved to a larger house that had been built for him on the heights behind St Heliers Bay close to Ernest Davis's residence. The move from Airdale Street to St Heliers signified a very large change in social associations. So, too, did the Morris Sixteen saloon that he now drove. Scrim was beginning to live in the manner of a successful Auckland businessman.

During January 1934, Scrim, Beau Sheil and John Stannage worked together on what would later be remembered as Sir Charles Kingsford Smith's last barnstorming tour of the country. Stannage had been Kingsford Smith's radio operator on his flight from California to Australia. Offering joy rides at a pound a ride in his 'old bus', Kingsford Smith was a great summer drawcard. Scrim was with him on the last of these local appearances and flew with him from Thames to Mangere. To his great surprise, Kingsford Smith invited him to fly the plane once it was airborne, and he was at the controls until

Kingsford Smith took over just before landing. The flight became one of Scrim's fondest memories. It was also his last recorded flight as a pilot.[19]

Scrim made sure that 1ZR listeners were kept informed of Kingsford Smth's tour. 1ZR interviewed him when he landed at Mangere, and made relay broadcasts of his civic reception at the Town Hall and the gala ball at the Peter Pan Cabaret at which he was the guest of honour. The *Observer* reported that 1ZR's coverage of his visit to Auckland would have done justice to a royal tour.[20]

Any guessing about 1ZR's future was put to rest in February 1934 when the station ventured into the new realm of radio evangelism. It was not, as Scrim liked to claim, the first radio church in the world.[21] Father Coughlin, broadcasting extensively throughout the American mid-West had preceded him by three years. The call sign was still 1ZR but Scrim's station was now to be known as the Fellowship of the Friendly Road. It would not be a church in the usual sense of the word. It would not be an organised body. It did not have doctrines that members were expected to subscribe to. It accepted that there would be a wide range of belief and unbelief among its listeners. It was open to members of all denominations and none. It welcomed Catholics and Jews as warmly as it welcomed Protestants. Poverty would not rule anyone out. Wealth could not buy a place. It was reaching out, too, to the much larger mass of people who, though they might have a church connection, did not go to church very often if at all.

What did not need to be mentioned was Scrim's quietly compelling voice. The message and the messenger were indistinguishable. To thousands of men and women whose lives were being blighted by the Depression and to those living through personal tragedies or misfortunes his Sunday evening broadcasts were a looked-for solace. More than anyone else in New Zealand at the time, he had the knack of communicating with people. He held his audience with his distinctive radio voice and lack of airs. He spoke simply and with great personal assurance. He spoke from the heart to the heart.

It is unlikely that Scrim ever presented anything over the air that would be recognised as a sermon with the usual sequence of text, exposition, application. Stories were his stock-in-trade. He had an uncanny ability to take everyday occurrences as his starting point and transform them into parables in the telling. He talked about things that people could readily relate to. His stories illustrated the importance of acts of kindness and sympathy, of the courage that enabled people to live through moments of adversity, and of hope for the future. His voice was unobtrusive and quietly compelling. Listeners felt that he was talking to them personally. They listened and were won over.

He also made sure that his listeners knew that he had been through hard times himself. He had, he said, known most of the 'darker sides' of life – 'lack of money, lack of health, lack of what are called "good times"'. But he still thought that life, 'take it by and large, is a lovely business . . . life is worth living, and I shall think so to the end'. In his friendly upbeat way he encouraged people to be kind to each other. 'Harshness, bitterness and unkindness never settled a dispute; and we should learn surely from our close relationships in daily life, at business and at home, that anger very seldom does any good.'[22]

One of the secrets of Scrim's success was his ability to remind listeners what they already knew they should be doing for their peace of mind. His personal style and his presentation as a radio broadcaster were novel but his weekly chats were anchored in conventional homely wisdom. Most of his listeners would have had no difficulty relating what he said to their own lives, and most would have shared his lack of interest in theological niceties.

But there *were* theological objections to his recurring message. No doubt these were sometimes discussed among clergymen and interested lay people but they were slow to appear in print. The *Church Gazette*, a publication of the Anglican diocese of Auckland, may have been alone in drawing attention to Scrim's theological transgressions, and it was not until June 1937 that it did so. It dismissed the Fellowship of the Friendly Road as yet another 'fancy religion'. It belonged, in a tradition of religious 'free booters' that had no 'commission or authority to teach, and it offered an incomplete, lopsided version of religion. It used scripture readings and redemption songs, but forfeit[ed] any Christian character.' Its leader claimed to be a Christian minister, but he persistently denied the divinity of Christ. In earlier times he and his followers would have been called heretics.[23]

⋆

Harry Bell set himself the task of producing a permanent record of the founding of the Friendly Road. In 1934 he published three small booklets under the title 'Hello Everybody', the cheerful phrase with which Scrim always began his week-day devotional sessions and his Sunday evening 'Man in the Street' sessions. The booklets sold for a shilling each.

The first highlighted the friendly exhortation that headed the Friendly Road's letter head on its stationery and publicity: 'You go to your Church. And I'll go to mine. But let us walk along together.'[24] The other two booklets gave an account of Scrim's earlier service as a Methodist home missioner. This began with Scrim's mother's dying injunction to him to make something of his life, and ended with the early successes of the Friendly Road. His six years as the founder of the Auckland Methodist Social Service Centre for the poor and oppressed were well covered. Illness, referred to as a 'mental breakdown' had caused him to leave Kaitangata and prevented him from sitting the examination for entry to the Methodist Theological College.

It was an audacious publishing project and a first for the country. No other New Zealander had ever been the subject of a biography while still actively engaged in public life. As the story of a coming man, it was a shrewd venture in public relations.

In its short life, 1ZR had already earned a reputation as an innovator. It had pioneered the broadcasting of devotional services. It was using relay broadcasts to cover notable events in and around Auckland. On Christmas Eve 1932, for example, there had been relays of carols performed by the Salvation Army Band, and midnight mass at St Patrick's Cathedral.[25] The list soon included commentaries of boxing from the Town Hall, rugby league from Carlaw Park, motor racing from Western Springs, and rowing from the West End Rowing Club.

New personalities presented programmes. Of these Daisy Basham was an immediate success and for the next thirty years the country's outstanding radio celebrity.[26] Her morning recipe sessions took listeners by storm. Everything about her made her an original – her vibrant voice, her spontaneity, her breathtakingly rapid speech, her enthusiasm for whatever she was talking about, and her unerring ability to hold her listening audience in rapt attention. Her exuberantly cheerful greeting to listeners became a legend.[27]

1ZR was soon able to upgrade its equipment and accommodation. Beginning in September it had a stronger signal which was being heard from as far as Timaru. As part of 1ZR's policy of openness, it offered a standing invitation to members of the public to visit the station at any time.[28]

Scrim remained on the list of Methodist preachers and conducted services in various city and suburban churches from time to time. But it was as a preacher in the Fellowship of the Friendly Road that he now baptised infants and officiated at marriages and funerals. He baptised infants on the first Sunday of each month during his broadcast 11 o'clock service.[29] Most of his wedding ceremonies also took place in the broadcasting studio, but he was happy to marry couples in other places if that was their wish. If we can believe what he wrote later in one of his autobiographical jottings, the services he conducted were much modified versions of the standard Christian forms of service. His published statistics for 1934 record that he baptised more than 300 children, conducted 100 funerals, and claimed that his 209 marriage ceremonies were a world record for 'individual marriage ceremonies'.[30]

There were times when he enjoyed playing the showman, and for some of these he was criticised. One was for a marriage ceremony he conducted in the roller skating rink at the top of Queen Street. The bride and groom were skating enthusiasts. Scrim had not previously skated but he agreed to officiate on skates. The ceremony roused the ire of one of Auckland's ministers of religion, who issued a two-page cyclostyled broadsheet to his parishioners criticising Scrim as a 'Flipperty Jibbert parson'. The burden of the piece was that 'the "Rev" Scrimgeour did not try to act like a minister of religion. He did everything but preach the Gospel.' He flew aeroplanes, ran picture shows, took 'show girls' into the prison, but he 'did not say much about Jesus Christ'. Now he had 'disgraced the Holy Sacrament of marriage' by using a skating rink instead of the 'House of God'.

For Scrim this was criticism easily answered on the numbers. He paid for a newspaper advertisement that invited everyone who wanted to hear the 'Flipperty Jibbert parson' to come to his service on the following Sunday evening. He claimed in one of his autobiographical notes written forty years later that he had a congregation of 700 and his critic twenty-seven, including the cleric himself.[31]

★

All operators of B stations felt that they were under government siege. The postmaster general's department could put them off the air at any time for some alleged infringement of the broadcasting regulations. They also felt it was only a matter of time before the government would shut down all the B stations that it did not need to buy to augment the YA stations.

Scrim kept in touch with B stations and their supporters in other parts of the country, and was active in the moves that led to the meeting in Wellington at which the Dominion Listeners' League was established. He was elected to the executive committee of the Dominion Listeners' League and became its chairman in May 1933. The League was said to have 25,000 members throughout the country. He ensured that the League was actively engaged during the run-up to the 1935 general election.[32]

1ZR was put off the air in June 1933 for an alleged breach of the sponsorship regulations during one of Aunt Daisy's recipe programmes. Other Auckland B stations had been shut down temporarily in earlier years: 1ZQ in 1931 for breaching the sponsorship regulations; and in August 1932 1YA's relay broadcast of a public meeting in the Town Hall was interrupted to cut out the address of a social credit speaker.[33]

1ZR's suspension triggered a wave of support from Auckland's radio-land. Ernest Boucher and C.H. Pearson, the owners respectively of stations 1ZS and 1ZM, allowed Scrim the use of their stations to ensure his Friendly Road sessions continued while 1ZR was banned from broadcasting. Representatives of the Auckland radio dealers endorsed their actions. 1ZR was flooded with more than a thousand letters, telegrams, and resolutions of support.[34] Mobilising public support, the 1ZR Radio Club held a protest meeting in the Town Hall on Thursday 22 June. That was the day of the week when the weekly edition of the *Observer* hit the news-stands, and it announced itself with a billboard highlighting 1ZR's crisis. There was heavy demand for the issue. Supporting 1ZR was good for sales.[35]

Demonstrating its public support was clearly important. But the government would have to remove its ban if 1ZR were to be reinstated. Gordon Coates was believed to be sympathetic to the B stations, and the executive of the 1ZR Radio Club made sure that he was aware of what was going on. The *Observer* reported that one of Auckland 'pillars' of the Reform Party rang Coates, warned him of the 'public outrage', and urged him to get the government to 'put 1ZR back on the air and, what is more, put it back before the public meeting comes off'.[36]

Public indignation at the ban appears to have been enough for the *Herald* to publish a report of the protest meeting but not enough for it to let its readers know how popular it had been. The *Herald* put the attendance at 1500. The *Observer*'s said that there was 'standing room only' in a hall that held 2900.[37]

Then it was back to Wellington for Scrim. Leading a three-man deputation, he presented Hamilton with the resolution that had been passed at the meeting. Coates was also present. The government removed the ban, a decision which the *Observer* described as 'a dazzling display of political acrobatics'.[38] 1ZR marked its resumption of broadcasting by playing the tune 'Today I feel so happy'. Scrim kept up the momentum by announcing that the 1ZR Radio Club would hold its annual meeting in mid-July. Lewis Eady Hall was 'packed to the doors' well before the meeting began. An 'enthusiastic' audience dealt with the formal business and were then entertained to a concert of items given by the station's uncles and aunts.[39]

Opportunity once again beckoned Scrim. Over the years he had come to know Eric Baume, the one-time Auckland journalist who had recently become editor of the *Sydney Sun* newspaper. Baume was in Auckland on a return visit in early March. While there, he recorded an enthusiastic talk about the Friendly Road which he broadcast over 2UE, the radio station owned by the *Sydney Sun*. Baume felt sure that the Friendly Road would appeal to the Australian public, and urged Scrim to 'get on the first ship to Sydney'.[40]

Scrim didn't have to be asked twice, and he does not seem to have had any difficulty detaching himself from his responsibilities at 1ZR. Using the new long-playing acetate records, he pre-recorded some sessions of the 'Man in the Street' that could be broadcast while he was out of the country. Harry Bell showed him off to his best advantage in 1ZR's weekly column in the *Observer*. Listeners were writing to Uncle Scrim in ever-increasing numbers, he wrote, and ninety percent of them wished him 'God speed, success, and a safe return'. He would be away for a fortnight, but that would 'be a gracious sacrifice' if it opened up the great Friendly Road highway overseas.[41] The *Observer* had reservations. It was a good idea to spread the message of the Friendly Road to Australia, it wrote, but was it not incongruous to be associated with 2UE, 'a profit-earning station run by a sensational newspaper'.[42]

Scrim sailed on the *Mariposa*, one of the two American luxury one-class liners operated by the Matson Line on its regular Pacific service. We don't know who paid for his visit. Perhaps he made the trip as the guest of station 2UE and the *Sydney Sun*. Perhaps some of his Auckland business well-wishers paid the bills. All we know is what Scrim wrote late in his life in one of his autobiographical pieces. His head was turned, he wrote, when the chief steward told him that he was invited to be one of the passengers who would dine at the captain's table. During the previous two years or so he had become accustomed to travelling first class with a sleeper berth on the main trunk line and staying in a first-class hotel during visits to Wellington. Was dining at the captain's table another sign of his rising social status?[43]

Eric Baume knew how to go about creating a public profile for his newspaper's celebrities. Two reporters interviewed Scrim on his arrival in Sydney for a two-page spread on the Friendly Road that appeared in the *Sunday Sun* the following Sunday. So effective was the *Sun*'s publicity machine that Scrim received 2000 letters addressed to him at 2UE before his first 'Man in the Street' session went to air. He was an instant success.[44]

Baume had also set up a luncheon meeting with the chairman of the *Sun*'s board of governors on Scrim's first day in the office, and two speaking engagements in Scrim's first week with luncheon groups regularly attended by prominent business and professional men.[45] Baume threw him in at the deep end. Scrim's subject was New Concepts of Modern Society. He later wrote that he hadn't the faintest notion what he was going to say when he stood up to speak at his first meeting. But he seems to have been equal to both occasions. He spoke from a few jotted headings, and was greatly relieved by the way the speeches were received. The reporters who were present gave him a good press.[46]

Scrim ran a morning session on week-day mornings and a one-hour 'Man in the Street' session on Sunday evenings. He introduced himself to listeners with his cheerful 'Hello Everyone'. Peter Dawson recorded a theme song for his 'Man in the Street' session.

Scrim fitted very easily into the *Sun*–2UE arrangements for broadcasting. His office was on the top floor of the modern *Sun* building. His supporting staff were located next door. The broadcasting studio was on the same floor and had a direct link to 2UE. Except that everything was much less crowded, these arrangements were much the same as in Auckland. Working arrangements with his colleagues were similarly informal, all doors were open, and there were no signs of status. He was pleased to note that 2UE 'even had aunts and uncles'. The one big difference was that 2UE and the other Australian B-list stations earned revenue from commercial sponsorships and advertising. He returned to Auckland convinced that there must be a place for commercial radio in New Zealand.

Scrim's visit had been ego-enhancing. He had been treated as a celebrity and had found that he could perform in ways expected of a celebrity. He had intended to be in Sydney for three weeks but stayed nearly eight. He was invited to return to build on the initial success of his 'Man in the Street' session. That, he could now see, was the breakthrough he needed. Acetate recordings would enable him to have a presence in both countries. He felt confident that he could earn enough money in Sydney to fund the Friendly Road in both countries. He would spend six weeks by turns in Auckland and Sydney, record his programmes, and play them in one country when he was temporarily visiting the other. He returned to Auckland with renewed enthusiasm.[47]

Harry Bell had kept readers of 1ZB's weekly page in the *Observer* well informed of the impact Scrim was making on Australian audiences. Arriving as a stranger to station 2UE, he wrote, Scrim's name was now 'on the tongue and in the minds of thousands'. Even more impressive, readers were told, had been his ability to stir enthusiasm for the Friendly Road in 'the large company of hard heads' he addressed at the Million Club. Before long, Scrim would take the message of the Friendly Road throughout the English-speaking world.[48]

But 1ZR was at a crossroad. Lewis Eady had decided to sell it to the government to be Auckland's second public broadcasting station.

He had expected 1ZR to operate at an annual loss of not more than £500 a year, but the annual deficits were proving to be much greater. Earnings from commercial sponsorships had provided some financial relief but it seemed clear (and was soon to be confirmed by Hon Adam Hamilton) that they were to be prohibited. The government bought 1ZR and announced that it would stop broadcasting at the end of December.

The sale of 1ZR left 1ZM, broadcasting from Manurewa, as the only remaining B station broadcasting in the Auckland district. The executive of the 1ZR Radio Club tried unsuccessfully to buy it. They then turned their attention to purchasing the plant of 1ZB, which had also closed down recently, and getting the government to agree to transfer its broadcasting licence to the Friendly Road. The first part of these negotiations – the purchase of the 1ZM operating plant – appears to have been completed before the news of 1ZR's sale filtered through to Auckland in early September. In one of his later autobiographical pieces Scrim wrote that he had tried unsuccessfully to persuade the Methodist Church to buy the radio station and use it for radio evangelism.[49] Scrim and Lena gave diametrically different explanations for the sale of Lena's piano to meet the cost of the purchase of broadcasting equipment. Scrim said that, short of ready cash, he had asked Lena if he could sell her piano, and she had agreed.[50] Lena told their son Gary that she did not know what Scrim had in mind, he did not ask for her agreement to sell the piano, and sold it without asking for her permission and without telling her. She never forgave him.[51]

While these negotiations were under way, Harry Welsh, the chairman of the executive of the 1ZR Radio Club, was busy enlisting the support of fellow businessmen and other leading men in the city. A petition signed by twenty of Auckland's commercial and civic leaders was sent to the Hon Adam Hamilton seeking his assurance that the Friendly Road would remain on air. Though the names of the twenty men seem to have been widely known in Auckland, they were not published until early December, by which time the government had given that assurance. The *Observer*'s publication of the list merely confirmed that the city's leading businessmen and professional men were as staunch in their support for the Friendly Road as men and women in less prominent walks of life.[52]

Buoyed up with this assurance of support, and with the purchase of 1ZR sewn up or on the way to being sewn up, Scrim once again led a delegation to Wellington for discussions with Hamilton. He assured the minister that the executive of the 1ZR Radio Club would cooperate with him to find a satisfactory resolution of the problem that had arisen. The Friendly Road would not be asking for financial assistance, but its radio station must be allowed to operate independently of any control by the Broadcasting Board. It must also be granted a licence to broadcast on an operating frequency that would allow it to be heard as extensively in the future as it had been recently. But Hamilton would promise no more than 1ZR's continuation for from three to six months. There could be no guarantees after that.[53]

Donations for the Friendly Road, some of them large and anonymous, were coming in. Scrim's way of keeping the issue before his listeners, and at the same time keeping the government under pressure, was to take time during his 'Man in the Street' sessions to thank listeners for their generosity. Calling as he regularly did on the power of positive thinking, he cheerfully encouraged listeners to hope for a successful outcome. One evening he told them what the *Observer* considered to be 'a highly entertaining parable'. On his recent train trip from Wellington to Auckland, he said, he had had a dream about an 'imaginary radio station guarded by a gate marked "PR" – Peoples Rights.' When he delivered his parable he may well have known that the Friendly Road would have its station. The *Observer,* which by now was clearly on his side, remarked that Uncle Scrim's congregation was showing that it was as generous as it was large.[54]

At the end of November the 1ZR Radio Club was within days of reaching the point of no-return. Negotiations with Hamilton over the broadcasting licence had not been completed. 1ZR would broadcast for the last time on Saturday, 2 December. The club seized the moment to demonstrate the extent of its public support. It organised a public meeting to be held in the Town Hall on Sunday evening, 3 December and, should it be necessary, a grand demonstration in Carlaw Park on the afternoon of Saturday, 24 December. Arrangements were also set in train with supporters in other North Island towns to hold public meetings.[55]

The *Observer* reported an 'overwhelming' public response. It estimated that about 7000 enthusiastic people packed the Town Hall, the Concert Chamber, and the Civic and Regent theatres, and milled about outside. People had come in cars and buses from as far away as Whangarei and Dargaville and from Hamilton and Pukemiro. Hundreds, perhaps thousands, according to the *Observer,* had been unable to get into the hall.

The *Observer* saw the meeting as a 'great tribute to Rev C.G. Scrimgeour'. It had been a 'good-humoured, peaceful demonstration', with no signs of 'rowdiness'. But there could be no mistaking its 'unity' and 'singlemindedness'. It was 'a manifestation of public opinion well-nigh irresistible in its power'. Carlaw Park would be filled, it forecast, if it was necessary to hold the planned outdoor rally.[56]

The meeting passed resolutions urging the government to grant an operating licence to the Friendly Road. Those at the meeting and other supporters of the Friendly Road were urged to let the prime minister and other politicians know their views. Within a few days the prime minister Hon George Forbes received 12,000 letters from Friendly Road supporters.[57] The *Observer* stood in awe of the part of Scrim's speech that was broadcast. He had 'sailed close to the wind', it wrote, but had explained the position of the Friendly Road 'so deftly' that the authorities found no pretext for cutting him off.[58]

The *Observer* continued to be flooded with letters of support for the Friendly Road. In one week alone, it wrote, Aunt Daisy had received 700 letters bemoaning the cessation of her broadcasts. The *Observer* also found itself riding a wave of approval. In its editions of 7 and 14 December it published letters of praise for the support it was giving to the Friendly Road and the other remaining B stations. It published a piece by Daisy Basham which was as fresh and upbeat as her recipe sessions had been. 'Keep turning the magic dial,' she informed her readers, 'you'll probably hear "Good morning Everybody" before so very long'.[59]

There was public support for the Friendly Road in other parts of the North Island. An estimated 2500 (with many others unable to get inside the hall) attended a protest meeting in New Plymouth and supported motions calling on the government to allow the Friendly Road to resume. Campaign committees set up in Dargaville, Hamilton, Palmerston North and Napier were planning to hold protest meetings.[60]

Meanwhile, Scrim and Harry Welsh had gone to Wellington for

'Kamerad'. Blo cartoon. (*New Zealand Observer*, 7 December 1933)

what turned out to be several meetings with Coates, Hamilton, and officials. An agreement was reached that allowed both sides to claim it had won the points that were important to it. The government said it had agreed to an exception for the Friendly Road that was so specific that no other privately owned station would be able to use it as a precedent. There were to be no advertisements. The Friendly Road was to be wholly responsible for the station's funding. Any appeals over the air for funds were to be properly accounted for. There could be no claim on the government if the station failed and had to close. The licence was issued for no more than twelve months. Scrim does not appear to have been unduly concerned about these conditions. He was living for the moment. Such things as the renewal of a licence to broadcast could be left for the future. The public was with him now. He was confident that it would be with him in twelve months' time. The *Observer* saw the agreement as a complete victory for Uncle Scrim.[61]

★

Aunt Daisy's listeners did not have long to wait for the answer to their wishes. Scrim had bought 1ZM's plant and equipment. Ernest and Elliot Davis gave him the use of the second floor of the Queen's Arcade at the foot of Queen Street for the station's permanent accommodation. Ernest Boucher gave him use of 1ZS's storeroom space free of charge while this permanent accommodation was reorganised for use as a radio station. The Friendly Road was back on the air on New Year's Eve.[62]

This was a triumph for Scrim and Tom Garland, who had shown what an effective team they were. Garland worked quietly behind the scenes, warmly supported for his contributions as conductor of his children's choir, the Friendly Road Choir, and regular community sings. Scrim was proving to be 1ZR's special gift to radio broadcasting. He was a radio personality in his own right. All the signs were that he was a good man to deal with. He and his fellow broadcasters at 1ZR worked well together. Though he was by far the youngest among them they were happy to look to him as their leader. He had, it seems, learned that he must keep his temper when dealing face to face with Hon Adam Hamilton. As the club's president and public face he had not put a foot wrong.

The official opening of 1ZB, the new home of the Friendly Road, was a carefully stage-managed occasion of the kind that was now coming to be associated with Uncle Scrim and Uncle Tom. It was largely Garland's work. Scrim was in Sydney for several weeks at the start of the year and went away fishing for a few days after returning to New Zealand. The coming event was well advertised. Members of the Radio Club – now known as the 1ZB Radio Club – were urged to welcome Hon Gordon Coates and Mrs Coates and Uncle Scrim on their arrival at the Auckland Railway Station on the Saturday morning. The club's weekly radio notes in the *Observer* gave additional publicity.[63]

The 1ZB Radio Club's accounts of the day emphasised its enthusiastic, gala nature. The 'packed' afternoon tea party at Milne and Choyce's 'was a real Friendly Road afternoon'. The crowd at the opening ceremony in the new studios in the evening spilled out onto the ground floor of the Queen's Arcade and listened to the proceedings though loudspeakers. Michael Joseph Savage, MP was unable to attend but sent a telegram of congratulations. The chairman of the 1ZB Radio Club, Harry Welsh, acknowledged the thousands of people who had supported the Friendly Road during the difficult months it had come through, and gave special thanks to the mayor and city council for their assistance. The Friendly Road had much to be thankful for, he said, but he reminded all who were listening that more money was needed to pay for the station, and pleaded for even more acts of generosity. The studio choir sang 'old time hymns' in response to telephone requests for favourites. Neither newspaper published reports of the meeting. 1ZB broadcast Coates's speech.

Friends and supporters of the Friendly Road looked forward to an untroubled future for station 1ZB. But dark clouds were also a possibility. The members of the New Zealand Broadcasting Board were scanning the broadcasting horizon and wondering if Scrim's ambitions for 1ZB might create problems for the YA stations for which they had an advisory responsibility for the wider New Zealand public. A few days after Coates launched 1ZB in its new station he rang Charles Head, the board's general manager, to let him know that he supported an increase in 1ZB's broadcasting hours. Scrim had almost certainly lobbied him. Coates knew that, as postmaster

Opening ceremony for the new 1ZB studio, March 1934. Rt Hon Gordon Coates stands behind the table on the left, Uncle Scrim on the right. Uncle Tom is on the far left of the front row. Aunt Daisy is two in from the right of the front row. (Photographer unknown, *Scrim: Radio Rebel in Retrospect*)

general, Hamilton opposed any increase. Head reminded Coates that the board did not control the B stations and advised him to consult Hamilton, adding that the board did not favour an increase in broadcasting hours for 1ZB. It feared that, with more time on the air, 1ZB would become 'strong opposition' for 1YA. Head reported to L.R.C. Macfarlane, one of the three board directors, adding that he had gone 'fully into the question of the likelihood of Scrimgeour becoming a political menace as Father Coughlin is in America'. Coates, however, had given no indication of what he thought about the possibility that Scrim might emulate Father Coughlin.

It is not possible to say how much, if at all, radio listeners in New Zealand were aware of the radio crusades that Father Coughlin was conducting during the thirties. Perhaps he had a place in the oral culture of local radio enthusiasts but he seems to have been the subject of only one published report. An American correspondent of the *New Zealand Radio Record*, writing after the 1938 American presidential contest, wrote that Father Coughlin and his 'extremely enthusiastic followers' in his Radio League of the Little Flowers had attracted nearly as much attention as President Roosevelt himself. Coughlin was at the height of his popularity. Broadcasting at first from Detroit, his beguiling Irish-Canadian voice quickly attracted a large following. He founded his radio church in 1930, entered into a contract with Columbia Broadcasting System, was soon heard from seventeen stations in the mid-West, had a regular audience estimated to be between 30 and 40 million listeners, and received 50,000 letters a week. His Radio League of the Little Flowers provided an organisation for his followers, and this was soon superseded by the National Union of Social Justice and its newspaper *Social Justice* which he edited. Was Scrim following the same path?

At first Coughlin inveighed against money lenders and socialists, and supported Roosevelt's New Deal. Before long, however, he became rabidly anti-Roosevelt, his anti-Communism became overtly fascist and anti-Semitic, and he became a mouthpiece for Hearst's isolationism. But he lost his radio pulpit when America entered the Second World War. 'Social Justice' was convicted under the Espionage Act. Father Coughlin's days as a demagogue were over.[64]

# CHAPTER 5

# Defending Private Radio Stations

Scrim's new quarters were more spacious than 1ZR's and more accessible to visitors. The 1ZB Club had a 'nice little room with a table and chairs', and there was an open invitation to visitors, particularly country visitors to use it. Uncle Tom was often there to greet them. Aunt Daisy ran a 'Friendly Friday' hour on Friday mornings. There was a constant stream of visitors, estimated to be about a thousand a week.[1]

Scrim had been quick to use acetate recording technology for his 'Man in the Street' sessions. He as quickly introduced the related innovation of commercially produced long-playing records. The gramophone records in use when radio broadcasting got under way in the 1920s had a playing time of three or four minutes and were played on record players that turned 78 times a minute. All radio stations depended very largely on the playing of records, and programmes were successions of short items. The new long-playing records that became available in the early thirties typically played for about fifteen minutes at a much lower speed. American and British recording companies produced transcription programmes of entire operas, symphony concerts, concerts of light and popular music, plays, comedy shows, and of an entirely new type of recorded programme – the radio serial.

Transcription programmes transformed radio broadcasting. The YA stations soon used them extensively, and so did 1ZB, whose listeners began to hear programmes of Mantovani's Orchestra and other performers of light orchestral music. On Friday evenings they could hear a grand opera selected by Tom Garland and played with his interspersed commentary. Children and their parents had favourite serials to listen to. These typically ran in fifteen-minute episodes and, among other things, ensured that fifteen-minute time slots became the standard unit of 1ZB programming. With American programmes came American slang and national debates on the language habits of New Zealand children that continued for decades.

The B stations were under an obligation to pay copyright fees for the recordings they played in their programmes. These were payable to the Australasian Performers Rights Association, which protected the commercial rights of Australian and New Zealand performers, and to recording companies whose records were played over the air. The Broadcasting Board paid annual fees for the YA stations, but the B stations were expected to pay their own fees. Scrim believed that, in principle, performing and copyright fees should be paid. The question for him and for the owners of other B stations was who should pay? 1ZB and the B stations in general simply did not have the money to pay annual fees. Should not the Broadcasting Board cover the costs for all radio stations, B as well as A? The government and the B stations remained in a stand-off.[2]

Early in 1933, the British and American recording companies cut off the supply of recordings to radio stations that were not paying for the right to use them. With their close links with local music stores, most B stations were able to borrow records for broadcasting. Listeners responded generously when Scrim appealed to them to give or lend 1ZR records produced by continental recording companies.[3]

More immediate was the threat of being put off the air for some infringement of the broadcasting regulations. Scrim felt sure that 1ZR's temporary banning in June 1933 was not to be seen as an isolated event. From time to time the Post and Telegraph Department's Auckland inspectors reported occasions when they considered that 1ZR had infringed broadcasting regulations, and recommended that action be taken against it. But the Broadcasting Board was not convinced that it should intervene. Scrim, for his part, was only too happy to make the most of the continuing sense of uncertainty and made sure that his listeners were aware of it.

Scrim returned from Sydney in September 1934 convinced that the Australian arrangements for their B radio stations were much better than New Zealand's. He was becoming exasperated by what he took to be signs of the government's hostility to the B stations. He claimed that the Coalition government had agreed that 1ZB would have an increase in the number of hours it could broadcast each week. Six months later, however, that increase had still not been authorised.

Mobilising public support for 1ZB and the other remaining B stations took up a great deal of Scrim's time and energy during the eighteen months leading up to the 1935 general election. He was elected to the executive of the organisation that was set up in 1933 to protect the interests of the B stations and became its president in 1934. 1ZB's signal could be heard in many parts of the country, and Scrim was keen to reach out to listeners in other cities and towns as well. Such visits would also help the wider cause of the B stations.

Towards the end of 1934 and during February 1935, Scrim, Tom Garland and Daisy Basham made a series of planned forays to Pukekohe, Rotorua, New Plymouth, Tauranga, Whakatane, Opotiki, Wellington and Palmerston North. Some of these meetings were one-night stands, others took place over a weekend. Scrim promoted them as gala occasions, and they attracted large, enthusiastic audiences. In Rotorua the travelling party shared the stage with a local Maori choir. The combined church choirs of New Plymouth and the city orchestra performed at their rally in Pukekura Park. Mayors presided over their meetings in Palmerston North and Wellington. Collections were taken up in each centre and donated to local organisations ministering to people in distress.

Each meeting began with a long session – in Pukekohe it lasted and hour and a half – of hymn singing interspersed with 'entertaining items' given by members of the travelling party and by local artists, leading up to the climax of Uncle Scrim's address. Itinerant evangelists had used this approach effectively in the past. Visiting pop stars would use it in future. The 1ZB Radio Club's columns in the *Observer* left readers in no doubt that Scrim's forays were personal triumphs.[4] Radio broadcasting multiplied the effect. Relay broadcasts from local B stations meant that Scrim's travelling party could be picked up in most parts of the country.

A crowded meeting in the Auckland Town Hall marked Scrim's departure for Sydney in 1935. An even greater crowd welcomed him back at the end of August. The Town Hall and Concert Chamber were both filled and there was a large overflow audience in the street outside. Word had gone around that Scrim would be making an important announcement about the future of the Friendly Road. Michael Joseph Savage was among those on stage, and he spoke fulsomely about Scrim. Both daily newspapers published reports of the meeting.[5]

When he finished the broadcast, Scrim turned the microphone off and, dramatising the occasion, told the meeting that he had an important announcement to make. Because, however, he was convinced that everything he had said over the air in recent months had been 'taken down and submitted to the authorities in Wellington', he would make his announcement off the air. Then he launched an attack on the government's broadcasting policies. The Broadcasting Board had failed to protect listeners' rights, did not include listeners' representatives, and was not qualified to speak for them. Six or seven of the B stations received subsidies but the remaining thirteen had no revenue and no rights.

He had, he said, been accused of taking political action. But the Friendly Road was being forced to take public action in self-defence. All he wanted to do was 'to serve'. He did not want to 'devote ninety percent of his energies to fighting'. But he had put up with 'just as much as even I can stand'. The lack of advertising was the breaking point. He was certain that the B stations could no longer exist without the ability to earn advertising revenue. Unless that right was conceded

Scrim talking to John A. Lee after one of Scrim's well-filled Town Hall meetings in 1935. (Photographer unknown, *Scrim: Radio Rebel in Retrospect*)

'before the election or immediately after' 1ZB would close down and he would 'leave the land of his birth and might never return'.

To applause from his audience, he declared that he would do all in his power to get the correct decision on the B stations' right to advertise, and he called on the members of his audience to do the same. If any were afraid of 'political action' he would 'let them go'. His next move, he said, would be to seek a meeting of the leaders of various parties standing for election, or their representatives. He would ask them to explain their policies, and listeners would 'be able to vote in the light of their replies'.[6]

One of the most interesting features of this fighting speech was its dramatic personal note. This was new. In the past he had occasionally expressed his feelings when making his point but had not let them get in the way of his message.[7] In his early years as a Methodist home missioner he had identified with Jesus, the scourger of the Temple. More recently the Carpenter of Nazareth had been his hero. Now perhaps he was imagining himself as a prophet without honour in his own land. And was there also a hint of paranoia in what he had said?

Savage was the only political leader to meet Scrim. In the course of two hours, Scrim wrote, he and Savage discussed ways of framing a broadcasting policy that would provide a service for listeners and give relief to the B stations. Savage favoured freedom of speech 'without restriction within the bounds of decency'. It would be 'the first plank of Labour's policy' that the B stations should not only exist but should be able to 'live up to a standard of which they are worthy'. If the B stations were unable to propose a more satisfactory means of funding, he 'emphatically favoured advertising on air'. The right to advertise, if granted, should be 'unrestricted'. To Scrim, these responses were all 'pretty promising'.[8]

Scrim was determined to get the other political parties to state their policy for the B stations so, under the aegis of the Federation of B Station Owners, he invited them to reply to a questionnaire. But the federation, at the time of the 1935 election, was virtually in abeyance. Some of the bigger stations had sold out to the government. Many of those left were operated by small groups of volunteers who found the running of their station as much as they could handle, and by no means all of them saw a commercial future for themselves.

Success for Scrim's cause would rest almost entirely on his own initiative and energy. He had good backing from his team at 1ZB, all of whom, he said, were ready 'to carry the war into the enemy's camp'. He also had an energetic ally in Ian Mackay, the secretary of the federation. Mackay was four years younger than Scrim. He had become captivated by radio as a boy at Nelson College, and was a leading member of the Nelson Radio Club which operated the local station. He was secretary of the federation, and this brought him into Scrim's orbit. He and Scrim came to work very closely together during the next eight years.

The first shot in Scrim's campaign was the publication of a fifteen-page booklet, 'The Scandal of New Zealand Broadcasting', published by the 1ZB Radio Club. It was a hard-hitting critique of the government's broadcasting policies. The 1ZB Radio Club and the country's other B stations, it argued, were threatened with destruction. They were opposed by the press which, taken as a whole, feared radio broadcasting as a threat to their monopoly of advertising revenue and the publication of news. This, he argued, threatened the liberties of New Zealanders. Radio broadcasting was the greatest scientific discovery of the twentieth century. Everyone should have access to it but it was being used as a tool of a monopoly. The present policy of censorship was the greatest threat to democracy since the days of Magna Carta.

The press and the microphone were the two main channels for the expression of opinion. But the press banned the publication of opinions they were opposed to, or dealt with them in ways intended to nullify them. The current restrictions on the use of the microphone were even more repressive. Those responsible for the broadcasting regulations were deliberately applying the muzzle. No radio station was free of unwarranted interference. Even religious broadcasts were being banned. Despite statements from the Minister of Broadcasting that these restrictions were being reviewed, the gag had been tightened even further. If, for example, 'Uncle Scrim had been persuaded to offer his services as a candidate . . . he would not have been permitted to conduct his daily devotional sessions which bring comfort to countless thousands of people'.

This was making New Zealand a laughing stock. Other countries, including Australia, had allowed absolute freedom of the air without any disastrous consequences. But the curbs that the Broadcasting Board had imposed on New Zealand broadcasters had roused such intense anger that it would not be a surprise if it decided that it must remove them. There had been some mention in the press of the possibility that some political speeches might be broadcast during the coming election. But that would be only a partial freeing up and it would be temporary. The only acceptable policy was 'absolute freedom of speech' within the bounds of decency. That was the policy in Australia and in 'practically all countries where a Mussolini or a Hitler does not dictate what people should hear or think'.

It was essential, too, that the B stations be permitted to engage in radio advertising. The abolition of sponsored programmes had deliberately robbed the B stations of their slender opportunity to raise revenue. The booklet then attacked what it called 'the fallacy of the BBC model'. British experience of broadcasting was utterly unlike New Zealand conditions. There were no B stations in Britain and no need to grant them broadcasting rights. Dozens of 'high-powered' European stations broadcast from within 200–300 miles of the BBC. The B stations in New Zealand were 'stunted and starved' by government policy, and the closest alternative to the YA stations were 1200 miles away. It was chasing shadows to reproduce the British model. Australia was the country whose conditions most resembled New Zealand's. Both countries were sparsely populated and had limited resources for radio broadcasting. The report of a recent Australian royal commission had concluded that the Australian B stations were a necessary supplement of the national system.

Radio, the booklet concluded, was one of the major issues of the election. 'Fearless and definite action' was thus 'imperative'. That was why the 1ZB Radio Club was publicly declaring its position. It would be questioning the leaders of all political parties on their broadcasting policies and would publicise their answers before election day. It would be seeking definite answers to clearly stated questions. It would make sure that the parties did not evade their responsibilities by couching their replies in general terms. Its message to all listeners, printed in upper case, was to 'VOTE ACCORDINGLY'.[9]

At least 12,000 copies of the booklet were published. It was distributed by booksellers and radio clubs up and down the country, and sold for 3d a copy. Within days of publication Scrim told Ian Mackay that it was 'going like hot cakes'.[10]

Scrim then sent a questionnaire on broadcasting to the leaders of the Coalition, the Labour Party, and the Democratic Party. It sought their policy responses, it said, to the matters that were concerning the B stations and listeners generally. Would the party, if elected to power, retain the existing B stations? Should the B stations be granted increased hours of broadcasting? Would it ensure funding support for B stations? Would it allow B stations to advertise? Was it satisfied with existing broadcasting policies? Did it consider the conditions facing broadcasting in New Zealand to be more like those in Australia or in Britain? What was its position on freedom of speech over the air?

The Coalition did not reply but Labour and the Democrats did. Scrim already knew Savage's views, and the Labour reply contained no surprises. It agreed to increases in broadcasting hours for B stations. It supported the existing B stations and would find ways of supporting them financially. It would permit B stations to advertise over the air if other sources of funding were not available to them. New Zealand conditions were in its view more closely related to Australia than to Britain 'and should be dealt with accordingly'. The present control of broadcasting was unsatisfactory, 'mainly because of government policy'. The Broadcasting Board, 'while it existed', should 'have a more equitable representation of listeners'. All subjects were controversial. 'Decency and intellectual standards should be the test of broadcasting.' The present ban on broadcasting by parliamentary candidates on subjects unrelated to their political concerns 'was not common sense and should be removed'.

The Democrats would retain the B stations, and supported an increase in their broadcasting hours. They would help them to meet their copyright obligations, but they found it impossible to say if advertising on the air was unpopular with listeners. Nor could they say whether New Zealand conditions for radio broadcasting related more closely to Australian conditions or to British. The present control of broadcasting was unsatisfactory, but they did not entirely favour New Zealand 'following the BBC'. The Broadcasting Board, if it continued, should be elected by radio licence holders. Controversial subjects should be broadcast subject only to 'decency and proper organisation'. But they did not favour parliamentary candidates broadcasting on subjects unrelated to their politics.[11]

Once he received these replies, Scrim wrote a follow-up booklet, 'More Scandal in Broadcasting', to continue his attack on the government. This was published in early November. His theme was the overriding issue of freedom of speech, and he began by repeating his criticisms of the press, taking examples from the current election campaign to illustrate biased presentation of news and opinion. Then he summarised the Labour and Democrat replies to the questionnaire and castigated the Coalition for failing to respond to it. In the final analysis, he concluded, it was obvious which party gave the best replies to the questions. He would leave it to readers of the booklet to recognise the obvious for themselves and 'vote accordingly'.[12]

As president of the Federation of Owners of B Stations, Scrim took the further step of urging fellow members to vote Labour. The circular that Ian Mackay sent to members of the federation was of course a private communication. No copy of it seems to have been published or referred to in the country's press. But it was advocacy, and members of the federation were clearly intended to use it to encourage people to vote Labour.

As election day approached, emotions were running high, particularly in Auckland. Scrim was inundated with messages of encouragement and support. He said that he received 800 letters and 800 telegrams on the day before the election.[13] He also received some anonymous threats of personal injury. Rumours were circulating in Parliament and around Auckland that in his last 'Man in the Street' broadcast before the election he would urge listeners to vote Labour. There was a great deal of public interest in what he might be going to say.

That broadcast became etched in the public imagination for a very different reason. Some minutes before Scrim was to go on air, the IZB signal was obliterated by noisy interference. Normal transmission resumed shortly after. Scrim began his programme with what the *Auckland Star* said were 'some very favourable references to Rt Hon Gordon Coates and Michael Joseph Savage, the Leader of the Opposition'. But from then on his voice was crowded out in a din of noise which persisted until he had finished speaking, when the interference also ceased.[14] The 1ZB switchboard was overloaded with calls from listeners bewildered by what was happening. Scrim's colleagues in the studio, concerned for his safety, rang the police, who arranged for him to have a police escort from the studio to his home.

The question in everyone's mind was who was responsible for the jamming. By the time Scrim got to 1ZB on Monday morning he had received messages that identified a Post and Telegraph shed in

Middleton Road near the Newmarket railway station as the source of the interference. Lee had received the same information and was waiting for Scrim when he arrived at his office. Ernest Davis, the mayor, joined them. Davis rang the police, told them that he, Lee, and Scrimgeour were going to inspect the shed in Middleton Road, and instructed them that Scrim was to be given permission to enter it. In the shed they found what turned out to be a high-powered radio oscillator covered in hessian. There were signs that it had recently been in use. They shared a joke about Scrim being covered in scrim, and Lee rang Labour Party headquarters in Wellington to report the find and arrange for all Labour candidates to be informed.[15]

Coates was in Auckland, having wound up his election campaign with meetings in the city on Saturday afternoon and evening. In the course of the day Scrim met him and accompanied him when he interviewed senior Auckland officers of the Post and Telegraph Department. Scrim was entirely unimpressed with their accounts of what had happened. There were, he told a *Herald* reporter, too many contradictions, falsehoods, and denials.[16]

Coates issued a public statement which said that the government knew nothing about the jamming, and neither did any government department. He had, he said, offered Mr Scrimgeour the use of 1YA if he found he could not broadcast from his own station. The secretary of the Post and Telegraph Department, G. McNamara, also issued a statement. The department accepted responsibility for the interference, but he said it was 'wholly accidental'.[17] Full reports of the incident and of Coates's and McNamara's statements were prominently placed in Monday's *Star* and Tuesday's *Herald*, which dubbed the jamming 'the most sensational development in New Zealand's broadcasting history'.[18]

The incident was finally put to rest on 10 July 1936 during the Second Reading debate in the House on Labour's Broadcasting Bill. Jones, the postmaster general, spoke to a report he had received from the secretary of his department. This added little to what Hamilton and McNamara had said in public statements the previous November. McNamara had thought that there was a risk that, following the publication of 'More Scandal', Scrim would tell 1ZB listeners how they should vote in the general election. Hamilton had thought that Scrim should be warned that he would lose his broadcasting licence if he were to do that. But McNamara was sure that Scrim would ignore a government direction and go ahead and advise listeners to vote Labour. Hamilton asked McNamara if that meant that 1ZB must be jammed, and McNamara told him that it did. Hamilton told McNamara that he must do what was necessary to put 1ZB off the air, and McNamara went ahead and arranged for Scrim's 'Man in the Street' session to be jammed. Responding to Jones, Hamilton confirmed that, as minister, he had accepted responsibility for what the Post Office Department had done. The Hansard record of the exchanges between Jones and Hamilton was unclear and indeterminate.[19]

The Coalition government was resoundingly defeated in the election. There was rejoicing in Auckland for Uncle Scrim as well as for the Labour victory. Scrim was quick, however, to parry any suggestions that the jamming of 1ZB had had any great influence on the result. Lee also felt sure that people had already made up their minds to turn the government out before Scrim had attempted to make his broadcast. The jamming had been important, he believed, because it had kept the government under pressure until polling day. The one thing that people had wanted to talk to him about as he moved around Auckland on the eve of the election had been the jamming and Uncle Scrim.[20]

If that were possible, the jamming incident had increased Scrim's already immense popularity among Aucklanders. On the Sunday after the election, members of the Fellowship of the Friendly Road had their opportunity to express their belief in him when they celebrated their third anniversary. Two very large meetings in the Town Hall marked the occasion. A message from Michael Joseph Savage, the incoming Prime Minister, assured all present that 'the voice of the Friendly Road will live long'.[21]

There were other signs of Scrim's standing in Auckland. 'Scrim's Election', declared one newspaper's billboards. A photographic studio displayed a photograph of him in its shopfront window with a notice informing people that copies could be had inside. In coming years, that photograph, displayed alongside one of Savage, would have pride of place in countless homes in Auckland's poorer suburbs.

The *Observer* remained a firm supporter of Uncle Scrim and of the B stations. 'Well, I'll be jammed' was its editorial comment in its first number after the election. During the next few weeks, however, it considered that the prominence that was being given to the jamming and to the B radio stations was getting things out of a proper proportion. These, it reminded its readers, were 'trifling matters' when placed alongside the 'broad humanitarian issues' of the day.[22]

Scrim was news. The *Herald* published a report of an interview with him in which he gave an account of what he had done during the election campaign to highlight the plight of the B radio stations. He was self-righteous. He had not, he insisted, engaged in party politics during the election campaign. He had turned down requests from five political parties to stand for them. That number would have been six, he felt quite sure, if he had seen his Communist friends Tom Stanley and Jim Edwards before nominations had closed. In saying this, he was reminding readers of the *Herald* that he enjoyed public support right across the political spectrum. But his only interest, he said, was in principles which were in the best interests of society. The defence of the B stations was such a principle, and he had intervened during the election campaign to alert the public to the issues that were involved. 'Surely, I was not to be blamed for that,' he was reported to have said.[23]

We can be reasonably sure that the report in the *Herald* gave an accurate account of what Scrim said. A very similar report of an interview with him also appeared at the time in *Smith's Weekly* in Sydney. He was walking a very fine line. The image he presented of himself was of a man who was above politics. He had entered a public debate on a point of principle. There were political implications in the conclusions he had reached and the advice he had given, but he insisted that he was not acting as a political partisan.

One thing more needs to be said about Scrim's public stand during 1934 and 1935. With many others who had done what they could during the economic depression to improve the lot of the poor and downtrodden, he had, as we have seen, come to see that governments and government agencies must find ways of carrying the main responsibility for the provision of welfare services. He had become persuaded, too, that the central government must play a leading role in managing the national economy, particularly in relation to the intrusive influence of overseas banks. And as the director of a B radio station he had become acutely aware of the need for governments to deal fairly with privately owned radio stations in a field in which the state was itself a monopoly provider.

These were matters that deeply affected all New Zealanders. The state had become central to the nation's well-being. Governments must act in response to public opinion. As a community leader, dedicated to making New Zealand a better place for ordinary men and women to live in, Scrim had found that he was directing his efforts more and more to what be believed governments should be doing in the name of the country's citizens.

There was one clear sign of Scrim's changed perception of himself as a citizen. He registered as a voter for the first time for the 1935 general election. It seems certain that he also voted. He had urged his fellow owners of B radio stations to vote for Labour to safeguard the future of privately owned stations, and it is hard to believe that he would not have voted Labour himself. Labour's promises on social welfare and monetary policy as well as on broadcasting reflected his own convictions. Savage and Lee, moreover, were good friends and strong supporters of the Friendly Road, and he felt quite sure that they would carry out their promises. But he preserved his independence. He had not joined the Labour Party and had no intention of joining it or any other political party.

Scrim congratulates the new prime minister on election night 1935. (Photographer unknown, *Scrim: Radio Rebel in Retrospect*)

# CHAPTER 6

# The Bargain with Savage

Soon after the 1935 general election a rumour went round Auckland that the new government would appoint Scrim to chair the New Zealand Broadcasting Board. But when the *Observer* sounded him out he said that he had no ambition to join the board. It would not have been prudent for him to have added that he expected the board to be disbanded, and he did not.[1]

Scrim faced the future full of hope. He felt quite sure that under Savage's leadership with, as he expected, Lee as Minister of Broadcasting, the country would soon be put to rights. To his surprise, however, Savage did not include Lee in his cabinet. Savage told him that Lee had missed out because it had been necessary for him to include someone from Dunedin. At the time Scrim had no reason to look beyond that explanation. But in three years' time, when relations between Savage and Lee had soured, he began to understand that Savage had reasons of a more personal nature for keeping Lee out of cabinet. For the present, however, Savage had salved Lee's disappointment by making him Parliamentary Undersecretary to himself as Prime Minister.

Lee was Savage's go-between with Scrim. The two men met regularly for a yarn when Lee spent weekends in Auckland. Sometimes, however, when Lee was in Wellington or Scrim was in Sydney, they wrote to each other. The letters that have survived give glimpses of Scrim's emotional highs and lows during 1936. A letter to Lee, written at the end of a successful visit to Sydney in July, expresses Scrim's boyish belief in Savage and the Labour government.

> I have such confidence in the government that I know that within three months they will have the best broadcasting service in the world – as well as paying pensioners & returned men the highest pensions – plus monetary reforms that will make [Major] Douglas ashamed he ever asked so little. The Minister of Finance is greater than Houdini & Joe overshadows Lenin.[2]

Scrim knew that changes in the broadcasting system, though important to Savage, could not have as high a priority as other more urgent issues the government was dealing with. He knew, too, that the broadcasting of Parliament was the Prime Minister's highest priority in radio broadcasting. This may not have been something that interested Scrim at the time, and he seems to have had no part in the arrangements that came into effect in May 1936. During one of his Australian visits he had given evidence before a federal parliamentary committee that was considering whether to recommend the broadcasting of parliament. If an autobiographical note written forty years later accurately reflects his attitude at the time, he advised the committee not to do so.[3]

Scrim expected that the national broadcasting system the government would establish would have much in common with Australia's but with some important differences. He envisaged a national broadcasting service controlled and managed by the state. The Broadcasting Board would be disbanded. The B stations would remain under private ownership and control, and he expected that they would band together in a national federation of local stations. They would be allowed to earn revenue from radio advertising, but there would be state subsidies for stations that chose not to become commercial broadcasters.[4] Scrim knew that some such arrangement would be needed to satisfy the differing views of B station owners. Savage and Lee were fully aware of his views. Savage kept him informed of the progress of the government's deliberations, and Scrim made sure that he had the Prime Minister's ear when he thought it might be necessary.[5]

Early in the year Scrim proposed to Savage that he invite an Australian he had come to know to advise the government on technical aspects of broadcasting. Savage decided, however, to seek technical advice from within New Zealand.[6] Savage called Scrim in to assist in the drafting of the government's broadcasting bill when he and his colleagues had resolved the policy issues.[7] Scrim was also conducting his own canvass of Auckland businessmen. From early in the year he had firm commitments from several of them to branch out into radio advertising as soon as it was legal to do so.[8]

Scrim was caught by surprise by the funding crisis that hit 1ZB in April. The Friendly Road and station 1ZB had begun the year on a particularly high note. Eric Baume had been holidaying in Auckland during January, and he and Scrim shared the stage of the Town Hall for another crowded meeting of Friendly Road supporters. Scrim was given a large, affectionate farewell when he left in early March for Sydney to continue his work there for the Friendly Road. He took his family with him and does not seem to have set a date for his return to Auckland. Harry Bell was running 1ZB in his absence.

But Scrim's assurances to his supporters had backfired. He had told them that they could look forward to a secure future. All they needed to do was be patient. Many Friendly Road members had taken him at his word and had discontinued their donations to the Friendly Road, whose revenue suddenly slumped. Soon after he arrived in Sydney he received an urgent message from Bell telling him that 1ZB was out of funds. Bell had had to withdraw money from Scrim's personal account to keep the station running. The future looked bleak and he urged Scrim to return to Auckland 'immediately'. Bell could not see how 1ZB could carry on unless Scrim borrowed from 'some of those wealthy friends of yours'. Scrim returned to Auckland early in April.

Scrim was disconcerted, too, when he heard that the government did not want to leave the B stations in the ownership of private operators. A discussion with Lee over Easter convinced him that he must talk to Savage. 'I'm in a fix all ways,' he wrote to the Prime Minister. Scrim had arranged to meet B station owners in Wellington on the following Thursday. More than that, he told Savage, 1ZB was in financial trouble and might not be able to keep going for more than a month or so. He asked Savage to meet him if at all possible before he met the B station owners 'so that [he] could be clear which way to influence them'. He would be in Wellington on Tuesday. Would Savage be able to see him? Would it also be possible for him to meet members of the cabinet to place a case before them?[9]

We hear no more about the B station owners, who were presumably left on a limb. Savage responded to Scrim's financial predicament by providing government funding for 1ZB's operating costs from the time that he became minister in charge of broadcasting in July. That decision, which had no legislative backing, will have become apparent only to the very small number of people who studied the small print in the National Commercial Broadcasting Service's (NCBS) first annual report, and that report would not be tabled in Parliament until late in 1937.[10]

It seems unlikely that Savage consulted Fraser or any of his other senior colleagues before deciding during the 1935 election campaign to support the introduction of commercial broadcasting. Fraser had said in 1932 that he would agree to advertising only under strict conditions. Nash was even more firmly opposed.[11] Savage, on the one hand, and Fraser and Nash, on the other, reflected differences of opinion among operators of B radio stations. Outside Auckland there seems to have been little if any interest in radio advertising.[12]

Savage had to work hard to get his cabinet colleagues to agree to include commercial broadcasting within the jurisdiction of the national broadcasting service they were now setting up. In May, there was an 'impasse' over 'southern objections'. From Sydney, Scrim sent Lee a telegram with suggestions for breaking it. Perhaps everyone's interests could be met, he wrote, by introducing an 'experimental plan' for Auckland and offering subsidies elsewhere with provision to 'change to original plan whenever objectors desire'. An 'experiment' in Auckland would demonstrate the 'soundness of the scheme'.[13]

But Savage did not have to resort to a fallback position. Cabinet decided to invent a new type of radio station – a C class station – which would undertake commercial advertising as part of the state-owned broadcasting system. That decision removed an obvious difficulty with Savage's pre-election position on radio advertising. Newspaper interests would no longer be able to buy up B stations and dominate commercial radio as well as print media. The cabinet also decided that the government would buy 1ZB under an arrangement that would ensure that its Friendly Road programmes would continue unhindered.[14]

The rest of the policy fell easily into place. The New Zealand Broadcasting Board would be disbanded. Remaining B stations would have the option of being bought out by the government or continuing to operate with some government financial subsidy.

The Broadcasting Bill was introduced in the House on 8 June and was put through all its stages in both Houses during the next three sitting days.

Opposition speakers deplored the ditching of the Broadcasting Board and made dire predictions about the country's future under a state controlled broadcasting system. Adam Hamilton, now Leader of the Opposition, claimed that the Bill was 'the most dictatorial and autocratic measure the government had introduced'. It would not be long before the government appointed a minister of publicity or a minister of propaganda who would be New Zealand's Dr Goebbels. The Bill's provision for commercial broadcasting was equally objectionable. It was, he asserted, 'real Hitlerism'.[15] Other Opposition speakers spoke in similar terms.

Tidying up for the government, Fraser rebutted these arguments. The Leader of the Opposition, he asserted, seemed to be hallucinating when he likened New Zealand under a Labour government to Germany under Hitler or Italy under Mussolini. It was 'preposterous' to imagine that a party which had been associated throughout its history with the right to free speech would destroy that precious heritage. No Labour government would do that. Alluding to the government's recent decision to broadcast the proceedings of the House of Representatives, he affirmed that members of the National Party were, and would continue to be, on the air 'equally with ourselves'.[16]

Except for Hamilton's stigma of Hitlerism, not much was said by members from either side of the House about the Bill's provision in clause 14 for commercial broadcasting. Reading between the lines of what some of the Labour speakers said, however, it seems that, not before time, they had found a solution to a potentially troublesome issue. They knew that newspaper interests dominated commercial television in Australia. They knew that some New Zealand newspaper owners were thinking of moving into radio broadcasting. They were not going to let them become a Trojan horse for overseas business interests looking to set up in New Zealand. 'If profits were to be made,' Jones, the postmaster general said in his speech introducing the Bill, 'we see no reason why the government should not "go into the business"'.[17]

Savage's cabinet colleagues formally appointed him minister in charge of broadcasting.[18] The position of director of broadcasting was advertised in Australia and Britain as well as in New Zealand.

★

Scrim was in Sydney when the Broadcasting Bill was being put through its stages. On 9 August he and Eric Baume were the focus of attention at a large farewell meeting in the Sydney Town Hall. Scrim returned to Auckland for another of his rapturous 'welcome home' meetings in Auckland on the evening of Sunday, 16 August. The Town Hall was booked out three days beforehand. An hour or more before the meeting began, a large crowd had congregated outside the Town Hall to hear the address through loudspeakers. There was a long queue outside the Civic Theatre, which was being used for the overflow audience. Neither Auckland newspaper reported the meeting and we have no account of what Scrim said. But the *Observer* quipped in its 'Town Topics' column that he had 'stolen Hollywood's thunder with the Big Broadcast of 1936'. It noted, too, that for the first time in New Zealand he used a small lapel microphone he had brought with him from Sydney. The prime minister also made broadcasting history that evening. He sent an apology for not being able to be present but addressed the meeting from Wellington by means of a radio telephone link-up. In the *Observer*'s opinion, the size of the audience would have brought tears to the eyes of any theatre manager or showman.[19]

Less than a fortnight later Aucklanders were treated to another new turn in the Friendly Road story, when Rudall Hayward's feature film *On the Friendly Road* had its premier in the Majestic Theatre. It was New Zealand's first talkie feature film. Scrim knew Hayward, and it is likely that some if not all of the members of the cast were acquaintances. The solicitor Leonard Leary, writing under the pseudonym A.L. Altier,[20] wrote the script. It portrayed Scrim providing wise guidance to a group of local residents troubled by a deeply upsetting incident in their lives. The film opens with him in close-up, speaking into his microphone in his Friendly Road studio. In a few straightforward sentences he outlines the essence of the Friendly Road philosophy: be friendly and kind to each other, look for the best in people, hold out a hand to those in need, and have hope for the future. What follows is a dramatic illustration of these precepts in action. The calm of a small rural community is unexpectedly upset by the arrival of two armed robbers. The locals are initially at odds, distrusting each other, but one of them seeks help from Uncle Scrim and, acting on his kindly advice, they put aside their differences and work together to confront and capture the robbers. We see and hear from Uncle Scrim again in the film's last scene as he walks along the country road that has been transformed into a Friendly Road.[21]

*On the Friendly Road* played to packed audiences for its short Auckland season. It was then screened in Wellington and perhaps other centres in New Zealand. The *Observer* was full of praise. All the material in the film – the bush, the speech, the humour – 'is our own', it wrote. It could have added that so, too, was the film-making expertise, for, apart from a year or two in Australia in his early twenties, Rudall Hayward had learnt his craft in New Zealand filming New Zealand subjects.[22]

Hayward's film fixed Scrim in the public mind at the very height of his popularity. Not quite ten years earlier he had arrived in Auckland as a virtually unknown Methodist home missioner. Since then he had woven himself into the life and affections not only of Aucklanders but of vast numbers of people throughout the country. Directly and indirectly, he had become part of the lives of men and women, boys and girls, and young people across the entire social and economic spectrum. People believed in him. He had made his reputation as a church-affiliated social worker, extended it through various community welfare projects during the depression years, and crowned it through the immensely popular Fellowship of the Friendly Road. His networks of friendships and acquaintances included people of all sorts and conditions: church people, businessmen, broadcasters, doctors, lawyers, accountants, social workers, church musicians and popular musicians, popular entertainers, flyers, motoring enthusiasts, politicians, trade unionists, unemployed men and their families, sick people, prisoners and ex-prisoners. One thing had led to another, and his success as a broadcasting personality had given him an unparalleled place in Aucklanders' thoughts and affections. He would soon launch himself on the national stage as the helmsman of the Labour government's venture in commercial broadcasting. He was not yet thirty-four.

Scrim and Savage were in close consultation about broadcasting between the middle of August and 2 October. Scrim wrote in an autobiographical piece some forty years later that Savage offered him the post of director of broadcasting. He wrote that he told Savage that he had no interest in the position. The newly created position was to be filled according to the standard procedure used by the public service commissioners for appointment of permanent heads of government departments. As minister in charge of broadcasting, Savage would make the appointment on the recommendation of the public service commissioners after they had advertised the position and conducted a formal selection process. There is no doubt, as Savage would state in the House sixteen months later, that he was convinced that Scrim was an 'outstanding' broadcaster.[23] But Scrim's recollection, if accurate, implies that Savage thought that he would show himself to be outstanding in any field of applicants for the position of director of broadcasting. It further implies that, as prime minister and minister in charge of broadcasting, Savage's views would prevail in any discussion he would have with the public service commissioners on the relative merits of the applicants they were yet to consider for the position. The process of appointment ran its course. Professor James Shelley, professor of education, Canterbury College, was appointed.

Savage knew that Scrim wanted to continue working in broadcasting in New Zealand. But he also knew that he was popular with Australian audiences and could expect to earn much more there than in New Zealand. Scrim had taken Lena Scrimgeour and their children to live with him in Sydney. He was letting Savage know that he had another string to his bow.

From the memoranda Savage sent to the solicitor general in September and to the public service commissioners in early October it is clear that he and Scrim had reached an understanding of the sort of solution they could both live with. 1ZB would be the base from which Scrim would set up and run what would become a national network of state-owned commercial stations. He would be answerable directly to Savage, as minister in charge of broadcasting. 1ZB would continue to be the headquarters of the Fellowship of the Friendly Road. Scrim would maintain his connection with it, and would continue to broadcast his Sunday evening 'Man in the Street' sessions and his week-day devotional sessions. He would have the right of free speech in those broadcasts.

But there could be no legislative basis for these arrangements under the Broadcasting Act that Parliament had just enacted. Savage's memoranda to the solicitor general and the public service commissioners sought their approval for arrangements under which Scrim would become the de facto head of a separate commercial broadcasting organisation which would be entirely separate from the National Broadcasting Service, outside of the control of the public service commissioners, and directly answerable to himself as minister in charge of broadcasting.

His memorandum of 5 October to the public service commissioners sought approval for him to appoint Scrim immediately to the temporary position of 'advertising manager' to make arrangements for the organisation of commercial stations. He proposed that Scrim be employed on a salary of £500 per annum plus a commission of 7½% of the annual revenue of the commercial stations.[24]

This was an entirely novel proposal to which the solicitor general and the public service commissioners, whatever they thought of it, replied with carefully measured comments. Savage did not inform them that the cost of running 1ZB had been a charge against the Broadcasting Department since the beginning of July.

The solicitor general's reply took the prime minister through the legal and administrative obstacles to the making of an appointment along the lines he proposed. A new officer such as an advertising manager could be made under the Act, but the public service commissioners would first have to be satisfied that such a position was necessary. Exercising their authority, the commissioners could make an appointment without advertising it, but the 'ideal procedure' was to give public notice of the position to be filled and invite applications. That procedure 'was especially the case' where there would be more than ordinary interest in the position to be filled. For a position in which the officer would be engaged in competition with persons outside the public service, remuneration set wholly or in part in terms of a percentage of revenue earned, would be suitable. But it would not be desirable where the public servant was not faced with such competition. An annual salary of more than £765, furthermore, would require special parliamentary appropriation and an item in the estimates. The solicitor general's clear message was that the prime minister was wanting to put the Broadcasting Act and Public Service Act under more pressure than they could bear.[25]

The public service commissioners also offered cautionary advice. Their reply of 10 October carefully avoided saying that they approved the prime minister's proposal for a temporary appointment.

They 'noted' it, and approved Rev C.G. Scrimgeour's temporary appointment under section 45 of the Public Service Act 1912. It was their understanding, they wrote, that the appointment was 'purely temporary' pending the taking up of duty by the director of broadcasting. They approved a salary at the rate of £500 per annum, 'the rate referred to in your memorandum, as being the salary intended for the position when permanently filled'. That salary rate, they said, was set on the assumption made in the prime minister's memorandum 'that the payment of a commission of 7½% of revenue in addition to salary should remain in abeyance until the position is permanently filled'.[26] They assumed that Mr Scrimgeour would take up the position as soon as possible.

But Savage had already made the appointment when he received the public service commissioners' reply. Scrim's appointment to the temporary position of manager of the commercial stations of the National Broadcasting Service was dated 2 October. His annual salary was given as £500 and 7½% of the annual advertising revenue of the commercial radio stations. On the same day 1ZB became a government owned radio station and Scrim took up his new duties. The department of broadcasting's first annual report records the expenditure of £641 3s 6d on 1ZB's 'running expenses, 1 July to 2 October 1936'. 1ZB broadcast its first commercial programmes on 29 October. The prime minister and Scrim had both got what they wanted.[27]

The government came under a barrage of criticism as soon as Scrim's appointment became public knowledge. On 29 October, Colonel Hargest, the member for Awarua put down an Urgent Question for reply by the minister of broadcasting. Had Mr Scrimgeour's appointment been made after public advertisement of the position? If not, had the appointment been made after consultation with and approval by the public service commissioners? How did the minister justify an annual salary, estimated to amount to £8000, 'which was so greatly in excess' of the salaries payable to civil servants whose financial responsibilities were far greater than could possibly accrue to the commercial broadcasting service? Savage replied that the position had not been advertised. But 'the whole matter of staffing the service, including the appointment of the controller, had been discussed with the Public Service Commission'. The salary for the position 'was more or less of an exploratory character'.[28] Parliamentary Standing Orders did not allow further questions about a minister's answer to an Urgent Question, otherwise Hargest could have been expected to seek more information on Savage's answer, which implied considerably more consultation with the public service commissioners than had been covered in Savage's exchange of memoranda with them. No doubt he would also have been expected to press Savage to say whether the public service commissioners had in fact approved Savage's proposal.

Newspapers throughout the country reported Hargest's

'The Stranger of 1ZB'. Blo cartoon. (*New Zealand Observer*, 7 December 1936, Alexander Turnbull Library Cartoon Collection N-P 1623-1)

Parliamentary Question and Savages's reply, and editorial comment was uniformly hostile. Scrim encountered 'a lot of criticism among Labour Party people' in Auckland. But he nevertheless wrote to Lee that the 'public reaction up this way [was] marvellous'. He thought that 'press hostility' was 'defeating their own purposes'.[29]

Scrim's response took up most of his 'Man in the Street' session on Sunday, 15 November. Gordon McLean wrote it up in a full-page account in the *Observer.* Mr Scrimgeour, McLean wrote, was in 'fighting mood'. He had received hostile messages, a threat of blackmail, and some angry tokens of disapproval, including white feathers, one with a yellow streak on it. But by presenting himself as victim and 'carrying the fight to the enemy', he had shown his 'mastery of mass psychology'. Scrim spoke of the 'bitter enmity' that some people apparently felt toward him. He deplored 'the campaign of silence' waged by newspapers against 1ZB. That, McLean noted, 'was nothing but the truth'. The Auckland dailies, he said, had 'not carried a line, critical or otherwise' about the introduction of commercial radio, 'one of the most important and significant events in the history of New Zealand radio'.[30]

Scrim said that this would be the last time that he would answer his critics. He was going to get on with the job. He then spoke about his early life, the events that had led him into the Methodist church, and his recent career in broadcasting. People who thought that he had made a fortune out of broadcasting should know that he was £200 in debt from his purchase of the 1ZB station. 'About this £500 a year and 7½% – I don't think I'm going to be grossly overpaid. If I earn an annual profit of £100,000 for the State where previously it did not receive a penny my hand is not going to tremble in receiving £8000 a year.' But he did not think it was going to be as good as that. 'I don't think I'm going to be grossly overpaid.' He said he was not interested in money. His friends told him that he did not value money enough. But apart from bread and butter for his family, he had no other object in life but the Friendly Road. All other things were subordinate to it. That was why, when the government offered him the job he agreed 'to see the thing going, anyway, until we could be free of debt. I'm going to work as controller of commercial broadcasting . . . only for one thing, and that is to see my life's ideal fulfilled.'

Then Scrim abruptly introduced an entirely new subject. He appealed to all who were interested in the Friendly Road ideal to support the 'erection of the Temple of Grateful Hearts' to the memory of his mother and all the other mothers who have made sacrifices for their children. He did not, he said, apologise for asking for money for this cause, nor for the fact that he would be the sole trustee of the funds. If people thought that that was wrong, he did not want their help. But he was making support for the Temple of Grateful Hearts 'a test of the personal confidence of listeners in me'. He wanted to have twice as many active Friendly Road boxes as there were at present. Without some response to this appeal a job worth £8000 a year wouldn't hold him 'past the sailing of the next boat, but the letters of little children might'.[31]

There was paranoia in all this. Regular listeners to Scrim's 'Man in the Street' session would hear further angry outbursts from him during the next three years in which, claiming to be the victim, he attacked various 'enemies'. But they would hear nothing more from him about the Temple of Grateful Hearts. *Truth,* however, monitoring Scrim's session, heard the appeal and noted it for possible further use. A year later it ran a front-page story reminding readers of the proposal, and pointedly asked what Scrim had done to bring it into being.[32]

Scrim's address, McLean concluded, left listeners with something to think about. His acceptance of the position of controller of commercial radio had 'bewildered and puzzled' many 'warm admirers and ardent champions' of the Friendly Road. How were they to reconcile Scrim's new role, as head of a business enterprise, with his former mission? 'Did their radio idol have feet of clay? Was the worship of Christian principles being replaced by the worship of the Golden Calf?'[33]

When Savage set the basis for Scrim's remuneration no one could have foretold what commercial broadcasting would earn from advertising in a financial year. In fact, 1ZB got off to a much quicker start than Scrim had thought possible. By the end of its second week on air as a commercial broadcaster it was earning more than its weekly operating costs. During the six months to the end of the 1936–37 financial year it earned £6,462 6s 8d, which gave Scrim a total remuneration of a little over £700 for 1ZB's first six months as a commercial station. With money coming in from the other three commercial stations during the following six months, his earnings for the year would have been well in excess of any other public servant.[34]

By the time that Professor Shelley took up his duties on 1 December the course of the nascent commercial broadcasting service had been determined and its first station was on the air. Shelley had had no part in this, nor would he as director of broadcasting. Scrim would never report to Shelley or through him to the minister in charge of broadcasting. We do not know what Shelley thought when he arrived at his new desk and found that the commercial operation for which he was formally accountable under the Broadcasting Act had been removed from his responsibility. His actions spoke for him. He got on with the job of administering the (non-commercial) functions of the National Broadcasting Service.

It was all very well for Scrim to be cavalier about his salary. The question for Savage and his colleagues was whether the prime minister's decisions on commercial broadcasting could withstand the criticisms that were being levelled at them. Fraser and Nash intervened when they became aware of legal and financial implications of Savage's decision. They persuaded him to amend the Broadcasting Act to provide a statutory basis for the separate, independent commercial broadcasting service that was now being created. The 1937 Broadcasting Amendment Bill set out to make Savage's decision retrospectively legal. More urgently, Fraser and Nash persuaded him to change the controller's salary arrangement. From the beginning of the new financial year, 1 April 1937, the controller of the NCBS was listed with an annual salary of £1500. Savage told the House during the debate on the Broadcasting Amendment Bill that Scrim had asked for the change in the basis of his remuneration. Scrim may very well have made that request, but it is much more likely that Fraser and Nash, trying to limit the political damage to the government, were the prime movers.

One of the interesting things about this entire episode was the dog that didn't bark. Labour's initial decision on broadcasting policy was to have a director of broadcasting who would be responsible for commercial broadcasting as well as the national service. Its amended decision authorised positions for two permanent heads, both on £1500 a year. The Opposition let that pass without comment. In fact, the final decision turned out to be even more generous to the commercial service and more of a charge to taxpayers than it appeared. Scrim had paid Sheil the same salary as his own when he was running

1ZB as a B station, and he continued paying him the same salary as himself when the NCBS was established. The Broadcasting Act 1936 provided for a director of broadcasting who would be responsible for the state broadcasting service. But the result of Savage's backstairs negotiation with Scrim was that the annual salaries for the three most highly paid broadcasting positions were paid at the rate initially set for the director of broadcasting alone.

The *Observer* commended the government for reducing the salary of the controller of commercial broadcasting. 'Though not ungenerous, £1500 a year was not, it thought, 'too much to pay for an important executive position if the appointee can deliver the goods'. But it noted that the highest salary Scrim could have aspired to had he remained in the Methodist church was an annual stipend of £300.[35]

# PART 2

# Blowing It

# CHAPTER 7

# Up and Running

Scrim had an assured base in Auckland. But he was starting from scratch in Wellington, Christchurch, and Dunedin, where he would have either to buy or build radio stations and recruit and train staff. In all four centres he would have to sign up sponsors and broadcast programmes popular with listeners.

Scrim knew what he wanted to achieve and was brimful of confidence. He was an immensely popular broadcaster. Aucklanders from all walks of life were impressed with his leadership qualities. His work in Australia had given him some first-hand experience of the realities of commercial broadcasting. He enjoyed, and it was publicly known that he enjoyed, the personal confidence of the prime minister. But he was also carrying some baggage. We cannot say how many listeners will have felt, as the *Observer* did, that his venture into commercial broadcasting was at odds with his professions as an evangelical preacher. Nor can we say how many of his supporters will have been troubled by the insistent newspaper criticism of the very large annual salary he was said to be receiving in his new position.

He showed no sign of feeling any inconsistency in combining radio evangelism with commercial broadcasting, but the inherent tension between these aims soon became apparent. Scrim would be spectacularly successful in creating the National Commercial Broadcasting Service (NCBS). But his lapses in self-discipline in some of his 'Man in the Street' sessions and his regular commendation of the Labour government made him a target of continuing criticism. It was not until the government dismissed him in 1943 that the singularly unusual terms of his appointment became public knowledge.

Savage and the two public service commissioners with whom he had exchanged memoranda on Scrim's appointment were probably the only ones who knew how unusual the appointment was. Indeed, it was more than unusual: it was unique. In making Scrim's appointment,

Savage had purported to exercise a power under the Public Service Act that he did not have.

The Public Service Act laid down the procedure for the appointment of public servants and a variant procedure for the appointment of men and women who after service in some other walk of life were deemed by the public service commissioners to be worthy of appointment to positions in the public service. Very few appointments were made using the variant procedure. As it happened, however, it was the route by which Professor Shelley would be appointed director of broadcasting at the very time when Savage was trying to find a way of appointing Scrim as controller of commercial radio services. The public service commissioners advertised the position of director of broadcasting, managed all aspects of the appointment, identified the most suitable applicant, and made their recommendation to Savage who formally made the appointment as minister in charge of broadcasting. Once appointed, Shelley was then subject to the same conditions of service and disciplinary rules as applied to all public servants. The one difference was that his appointment was for three years in the first instance with the right of renewal at three-yearly intervals.

But Scrim's appointment was not in that mould. He was Savage's personal appointment and was answerable directly to him as minister in charge of broadcasting. The public service commissioners played no part in his appointment and he was not subject to their jurisdiction. Scrim held his position 'during the pleasure' of the governor in council, which meant for as long as he enjoyed the confidence of the governor in council – in reality the government of the day. When Savage made the appointment and placed it outside the purview of the public service commissioners he presumably thought that Scrim would never lose the confidence of the government, and neither he did while Savage was alive. But under Fraser, Scrim's relationship with the government soured and he discovered what it could in extreme circumstances mean to be employed at the pleasure of the governor in council.[1]

Scrim gave the men and women who had worked with him at 1ZB the opportunity to transfer to the new 1ZB, and most did. The notable exception was Tom Garland, whose his heart was in the Friendly Road and who kept his association with it. Garland's salary continued to be a charge on the voluntary contributions of Friendly Road members, but his accommodation within the station was provided free of charge by 1ZB. Daisy Basham transferred to the new organisation at £3 a week but was soon contracted to the advertising agency Carlton Carruthers under a financial arrangement that was never made public. She was probably not one of Scrim's inner circle after he shifted his head office to Wellington. She kept on broadcasting her immensely popular morning programme until a few days before her death in July 1963, at the age of eighty-three.[2] Dudley Wrathall, Harry Bell, and Eric Grainger also joined the new organisation. Wrathall became one of 1ZB's most popular personalities. Bell, Scrim's biographer and public relations mentor, was appointed initially to be secretary of the NCBS. Grainger became director of engineering services for the commercial network.[3]

Most of Scrim's new appointments were New Zealanders. They were appointed from within the country or from Australia or Britain, and they brought with them a wide range of experience in drama, film, vocal music, and popular entertainment as well as radio. Scrim made sure that each station included a Maori announcer.[4] Their appointment kept alive his memory of his mother's associations with Carroll and other Maori from the Wairoa area, and was one of his distinctive contributions to New Zealand broadcasting. One of them, Oriwa Haddon, with whom Scrim had worked in the Bay of Islands, now joined his ZB network. Arini Poutama was already a favourite with Dunedin listeners. Kingi Tahiwi, one of the younger members of the well-known Tahiwi family, quickly made his name at 2ZB.

Several of Scrim's initial appointees were Australians, including two of his four executive director positions, Beau Sheil, and Dorothy Wood. Sheil was by then well known to advertising agents on both sides of the Tasman, and was immediately successful as Scrim's advertising manager and, in effect, his deputy.[5] Dorothy Wood was a 'find'. Though still only thirty-one, she had already made her reputation as a soloist and radio broadcaster, had managed a musical publishing house in Melbourne, and came to New Zealand after five years as programme manager at 2GB, Sydney, Australia's biggest commercial station.[6]

Only three of Scrim's senior colleagues, one of them Daisy Basham, were over forty years old. Radio broadcasting was a young person's activity. Scrim was surrounding himself with people of about his own age. The salaries he paid his executive directors and other senior positions reflected the market realities of Australian commercial broadcasting. His own salary was not listed on staff schedules.[7]

In its new commercial lease of life, 1ZB was the flagship for the Labour government's commitment to popular broadcasting. How better to demonstrate that than by treating listeners to a celebratory party to announce its arrival? The opening broadcasting party, organised by Dorothy Wood after less than three weeks in the country, struck all the right notes and was a great success. The *New Zealand Radio Record*, with sceptics of commercial broadcasting in mind, played up the evening's 'brightness, novelty, and music'. No one's ears, it reported, would have been offended by the advertising matter broadcast during the evening, and it particularly enjoyed the half hour session broadcast from on board the luxury liner *Orion* which was in the harbour at the time. Listeners heard the 'splendid ship's band playing while passengers and guests danced' and would have been 'thrilled' to be 'getting their music from one of the most famous and newest liners in the world'. The *New Zealand Radio Record* was also taken with Dorothy Wood, 'the Australian importation', who shared the commentary on board the ship and sang a song 'quite impromptu'. The message of congratulations from the Prime Minister, speaking by radio telephone from Wellington, was another highlight.

But there were widely held doubts about 1ZB's ability to become commercially viable. Sheil quickly summed up the situation and proposed a strategy that Scrim accepted. Sheil knew from his Australian experience that the key players were the big firms that advertised nationally. He also knew that Australian advertising agencies managed the advertising for most New Zealand firms, and that those agencies depended on advice from their New Zealand representatives when deciding how much to spend on advertising in New Zealand and how to allocate it. It was clear to Sheil that the NCBS must actively engage with the leading Australian advertising agencies and, to do that, must be represented on both sides of the Tasman by agents whose first priority was to serve the ZB's commercial interests.

Using his Sydney contacts, Sheil negotiated the setting up of a new company to act for the NCBS in its dealings with Australian advertising agencies.[8] He matched this with a similar arrangement with an Auckland company to manage the New Zealand end. The Australian company, Radio Features Proprietary Ltd, had immediate success in getting Australian advertising agencies to work with New Zealand firms to sponsor advertising on radio in New Zealand.

Stannage was waiting for Scrim to give him the nod to set up Stannage Radio Ltd, as the New Zealand counterpart to Radio Vision Proprietary Ltd. Stannage resigned from his position with 1ZB, and began a working arrangement with Carlton Carruthers, one of the first New Zealand advertising agencies to be alert to the possibilities of radio advertising.

Scrim was bullish in an interview he gave to the *New Zealand Radio Record*. There had been an 'excellent' response from big business firms, he said. Advertising space was being 'very rapidly taken up' and, with only one station on the air at present, there could be 'considerable difficulty' in finding times for all the firms wanting to be sponsors.[9] He was able to tell Lee that 1ZB had broken even in its second week on air as a commercial broadcaster and was turning a profit in its third.[10] Scrim and Sheil had won the first round with newspaper proprietors

These arrangements on both sides of the Tasman were fragile at first. A few months after it was established, Radio Features came under the critical notice of the New Zealand government and was forced to restructure its shareholder financing. At its establishment, its sole preferential shareholder was the McArthur Foundation, a corporate entity that had been outlawed by the New Zealand and New South Wales governments. J.W.S. McArthur had become a hate-figure with influential members of the New Zealand and Australian business communities. In 1934 the New Zealand and New South Wales parliaments, synchronising their efforts, had simultaneously outlawed his commercial organisation. In June 1937 the New Zealand government insisted that the McArthur Foundation preferential shareholding be cancelled. Scrim had known McArthur since his Putaruru days and regarded him as a friend and an honest man. In his opinion, McArthur had been punished because he was an innovator in managing shareholder risk in the companies he was associated with.

Scrim always had the ability to put the best construction on his actions and intentions. This, and his penchant for self-dramatisation, was to the fore in a piece he wrote for the *New Zealand Radio Record* early in 1937. He knew he was in a corner over the background to his appointment, but he mentioned what he called his 'fierce critics' only in passing. People who met him, he wrote, with a knowing allusion to a popular radio serial were agreeably surprised to find that he was 'a perfectly ordinary individual', not a 'Radio Gangster Number One', carrying £8000 in one pocket and 'an incendiary bomb in the other'. He bore no ill will to any of the 'misinformed people who make the fulfilment of my ideal more difficult, for sooner or later they will be my friends'. The prospects for commercial broadcasting, he was quite sure, were promising. It was 'undeniable that success must come to every worthwhile effort and I know mine to be worthwhile'.[11]

Official statements at the time of Scrim's appointment referred to him as the Rev C.G. Scrimgeour. Before long, however, mister tended to replace reverend, a change which he seems to have encouraged. 'Uncle' was also dropped except when Scrim was replying to people who wrote to him about his 'Man in the Street' sessions. It was as Scrim that he referred to himself, and that is how he encouraged friends and acquaintances to refer to him when speaking or writing to him.

On his appointment as controller of the NCBS Scrim became a public servant and the senior officer of a government department. These changes in status and responsibility do not seem to have placed any real limits on the way he worked. Though part of the public service, the NCBS was not a standard government department. It had been set up to operate in the commercial marketplace, relying entirely for funding on revenue generated by radio advertising. While he led the NCBS, Scrim succeeded in keeping it a commercial enclave in the civil service.

His most important working relationship was with his minister. Here, too, he was in a special position. He had been associated with Savage as a friend. Now he served him as a departmental head, but it was still as a friend. Other departmental heads had their discussions with their minister in the minister's office. Scrim's meetings with Savage took place in the prime minister's home, as much as, or even, perhaps, more than in his office. Scrim may have exaggerated when he wrote in his autobiographical notes that he visited Savage almost on a daily basis, but he clearly had many opportunities to talk with him in his home. Savage liked to meet Scrim late in the day, when he could treat him to fruit cake and a glass of port.[12]

From the middle of 1939 Scrim sometimes took Ian Mackay with him for his meetings with Savage, and Mackay has left an account of the way the prime minister handled these meetings. Mackay found Savage pleasant to deal with, 'an administrator's dream'. When the principles of a submission were explained to him, he usually said, 'Well, that sounds alright to me,' and his signed approval would follow. Mackay thought even more highly of Savage when he later worked under Fraser and David Wilson, who was minister in charge of broadcasting.[13]

There were no administrative links between the National Commercial Broadcasting Service and the National Broadcasting Service (NBS). Scrim and Shelley reported separately to Savage, who decided whether there should be any coordination of effort. On the rare occasions when Savage required them to work together on matters affecting both services, they seem to have done so amicably, producing results that were acceptable to them both.[14] In all other aspects of their responsibilities, Savage left them to make their own decisions.

Savage soon let it be known that both men had his full confidence. He took an early opportunity to support Shelley's ambitious proposal for the establishment of a national conservatorium. He fully supported Scrim's plans for the rehousing of 1ZB. More, he backed Scrim publicly when, before long, he came under repeated criticism for things he had said in his Sunday evening 'Man in the Street' sessions.

There was also the usual background noise of rumour to be dealt with. One had it that Savage had not wanted Shelley to be director of broadcasting.[15] There were whispering campaigns about the government's decision to establish the NCBS and Scrim's appointment as controller. There were also rumours of bad blood between Shelley and Scrim. Savage answered the rumours simply and straightforwardly when he spoke in the House on the Broadcasting Amendment Bill in November 1937. He was satisfied, he said, that Shelley and Scrim were the right men for their responsibilities, and they both had his confidence and support.[16]

Scrim was similarly direct when, early in 1937, a journalist asked him point-blank if there were hard feelings between Shelley and himself. It was 'utter rubbish', he said, that he and Shelley 'had nearly come to blows'.[17] They were on the best of terms, and the two services were working well together. He instanced help that the commercial stations had recently received from the NBS. The NBS had allowed his people to use its studios in Christchurch and Dunedin to overcome slight delays in the completion of the 3ZB and 4ZB studios. A few months later he would have been able to say as well that 3YA had again come to the rescue when 3ZB was destroyed by fire.

But working satisfactorily together did not disbar either man from the occasional disparaging remark. When 3ZB was starting up, Scrim heard that Shelley had said disdainfully, 'Now there are two Woolworths in the city.' No doubt there were times, too, when Scrim had a cut at Shelley but none seems to have been recorded. Scrim's references to Shelley in his autobiographical notes written nearly forty years later were respectful. He kept his asperities for Fraser and the Labour government for the very different way he had been treated compared with Shelley. He had been sacked. Shelley had been knighted.[18]

Scrim and Shelley are an interesting contrast in their different styles of leadership. Shelley was a civilised man. In the course of sixteen years his contributions to Canterbury's cultural life as professor, public lecturer, craftsman, and director and performer in many dramatic productions had won him many admirers and the label 'Renaissance man'.[19] To him, radio broadcasting was a fascinating way of spreading enlightenment, and he turned 2YA into what one of his young colleagues called a 'university in miniature'. He regularly spent the evening in the control room, and when the station closed down he would invite anyone who was still in the building to gather around. 'What he had to say on many subjects enthralled them.'[20]

Scrim's way of expressing his leadership was very different. He had no reserves of erudition to draw on. He did not encourage his colleagues, as master to student, to sit at his feet. His was an interactive style. He met people on their own terms and, he liked to think, as equals. His colleagues referred to him as 'the chief', but, to him, they were all in it together. He addressed them by their first name or their nickname, and encouraged them to call him Scrim. Informality was what he sought. The door of his office was usually open. Anyone who wanted to see him could come and talk to him. His friendly approach probably set him apart from all other departmental heads at the time. He had grown up in a different social culture and it showed.[21]

Questions of Scrim's authority and independence of action soon arose in his working relations with the public service commissioners. Not long after his appointment, they sought to direct him to channel his correspondence with them through the director of broadcasting. He replied politely but firmly that he would deal directly with them. The commissioners let the matter drop. An early exchange of memos on a staffing matter also gave credence to his separate administrative status. He sought the commissioners' approval for a salary for Grainger, his chief engineer, that would be £22 a year higher than the highest paid engineer in the National Broadcasting Service. Shelley drew the commissioners' attention to the difference, pointed out the additional responsibility carried by the NBS engineer, and asked that Grainger not be paid the higher salary. But the commissioners approved Scrim's recommendation. The salary differential became one of a number of differences in conditions of service that came to be resented by NBS officers and would not be resolved until, following Scrim's dismissal in 1943, the two broadcasting services were amalgamated under Shelley's control.

Other conditions of service that applied only to ZB employees became apparent before long. One which was too visible not to be noticed caught *Truth*'s probing attention and some Parliamentary Questions from Endean, the National member for Parnell. Public servants employed by the Post Office, Railways, and the NBS, whose shifts started early in the morning or finished after public transport services stopped running, were required to make their own way to and from work. Most of them walked or rode bicycles. Scrim arranged with the public service garage for his officers to be driven to and from their radio station.

Not being bound by public service rules, Scrim made his own decisions about his personal requirements. Mackay recalled that he cultivated a 'high-spending business approach' and that his accommodation in head office was 'unnecessarily luxurious'. He had the use of an office car and a driver whom he referred to as his chauffeur.[22] He would not use a train, bus, or ferry if an air service was available, and did not seek ministerial approval until after he had completed a trip. Savage seems to have accepted Scrim's breaches of public service rules. But Wilson, who became minister in charge of broadcasting after Savage died, was annoyed when he found himself having to give retrospective approvals. When he could, Scrim ignored wartime restrictions on travel by public servants.

1ZB was becoming a crowded hive. The station was now on air eighteen hours every day. Its staff had grown to fifty-seven. The station was host as well to the announcers, programme staff, copywriters, and technicians who were being trained for the positions they would take up when 2ZB, 3ZB and 4ZB began broadcasting. Scrim no longer conducted many wedding ceremonies but Tom Garland did. Sundays were as busy as ever with Uncle Tom's children's choirs, the regular Sunday morning and evening religious services with the Friendly Road choir, and Scrim's 'Man in the Street' sessions in the evenings.

Gifford Male, the *Observer* journalist who kept tabs on the station, soon noticed the changes. In the days of the old 1ZB, Scrim's office had been redolent of his Friendly Road activities: the very large family Bible, a book of Woodbine Willie's verses, the cassock Uncle Scrim wore when he conducted wedding ceremonies, the large photographs of Uncle Scrim and Uncle Tom addressing huge gatherings, and the items of furniture with large signs announcing the names of the firms and others that had donated them. These and all other signs of the station's earlier existence disappeared in the course of 1937, to be replaced by large photographs of Scrim and other ZB personalities and publicity about ZB programmes. The ZB stations were engaged in popular entertainment, and their public spaces quickly resembled cinema foyers.

The earlier 'leisurely' air had also gone. Two clerks at the reception desk had to deal with a constant stream of telephone calls, welcome a regular flow of visitors, and attend to urgent requests for information from the station's visitors. Country visitors were becoming outnumbered by 'the busy stream of people who have come up on business, business, and nothing more'. 'Big business is being done,' Male reported. A year before, it had cost about £60–70 a week to run the station. Now it was costing about £300.[23]

Scrim was developing a mutually beneficial relationship with the *New Zealand Radio Record*. The *New Zealand Radio Record* with its specialised readership was only too happy to receive a stream of announcements about work in progress on the three southern stations, items about forthcoming feature programmes, and promotional pieces about 1ZB personalities. Scrim welcomed the opportunities that his exclusive interviews with the *New Zealand Radio Record* gave him to keep the public informed on the progress he was making in creating the national network of commercial broadcasting stations.

Scrim's Sunday evening 'Man in the Street' sessions remained vastly popular with listeners. In the course of 1937, when 2ZB, 3ZB, and 4ZB came on the air, he could be heard from virtually all parts of the country. Commercial advertisements were prohibited on Sundays, which would have helped with listeners who disliked commercial broadcasting.

But there were soon signs that Scrim was not always being bound by his own precepts. Listeners to his 'Man in the Street' session on 4 April 1937 heard an outraged Scrim assailing the nation's newspapers. Addressing his listeners as 'the controller of commercial broadcasting' and 'a Christian minister', Scrim attacked the press as a villainous institution. It deliberately degraded its readers, he declared. It suppressed ideas it did not approve. It ruined the careers of public men who incurred its disapproval. It secretly ensured that Parliament did not pass laws inimical to its interests. If the press did not get you one way, he said, they would get you another. He had often been warned by friends: 'Don't let them trap you, Scrim. If they can they will sell a woman to you. They do those sorts of things, you know.'

Scrim singled out *Truth*, which he named, for 'publishing filth and muck' and read some extracts to illustrate what he meant. He wanted an end to the publication of unseemly details of divorce cases and other court cases that were 'not in the public interest'. 'Commercial radio,' he asserted, 'was engaged in a war to the death with certain newspapers, and commercial radio was going to win.' As a Christian he called on listeners to join him in his 'campaign to stop the publication of filth'.[24]

Scrim's Sunday evening chat was a sensation. Members of the Labour government were bewildered. Both Auckland daily newspapers attacked Scrim in hard-hitting editorials. Readers would judge for themselves, the *Herald* wrote, whether, 'as a professing Christian', Rev C.G. Scrimgeour was 'displaying the restraint and decency he so freely prescribes for others'. Coming as they did from a 'civil servant', it believed that the public would see his remarks as part of an organised campaign of vilification. The *Star*'s leader was along the same lines.[25]

Only once in earlier years had *Truth* taken any interest in Scrim's public statements. In October 1928 it pinged him for making what it believed on its evidence to have been exaggerated statements about dope trafficking in Auckland.[26] Now *Truth* met fire with fire. On its front page, under the headline 'Ye Cannot Serve God and Mammon' it published an 'Open Letter to Rev C.G. Scrimgeour'. It accused him of a 'lying, libellous attack'. It was 'palpably untrue, it wrote, that *Truth* published 'filth and muck'. As a newspaper, it was 'bound by statute and common law', and kept within those bounds. The law of the land and the evidence available in the columns of *Truth* 'prove you are a liar and that you have perverted the truth in a manner that is discreditable and despicable in a Minister of Religion'. The government, *Truth* asserted, must cancel its contract with Rev C.G. Scrimgeour and dismiss him from its service. The demand for *Truth*'s issue for 14 April was so great that extra copies had to be railed up from Wellington.[27]

Scrim took up the challenge with a reply which *Truth* published on the front page of its issue of 31 April, adding its own further comments. Nothing new was added on either side. Scrim and *Truth* no doubt thought that they had each routed the other. That was the end of hostilities for the moment.

The *Observer*, meanwhile, was keeping its readers informed from its position on the cross benches. In its issues for 15 and 22 April it published lengthy pieces based on interviews with Uncle Scrim. *Truth*'s attack, it wrote, was the talk of Auckland lawyers. Public opinion, it thought, was sharply divided between pro- and anti- Scrim 'factions'. Many of his supporters had expected Scrim to hit back, but there had been no more fireworks. The *Observer* thought that his chats on 11 and 18 April had been 'very lukewarm'. He had said that his remarks had not been meant to apply to the daily newspapers but to that 'yellow rag *Truth*'. Perhaps, it commented, Scrim had concluded, on reflection, that he had gone too far. But his explanation, it added, was not good enough. He had spoken in general terms of 'the press' and 'the papers'. He was unlikely to convince his critics that he was speaking only about *Truth*.

Battle of the Billboards. (Photographer unknown, *New Zealand Observer*, 27 April 1937, Alexander Turnbull Library Collection N-P 1621-6 B)

Scrim was conceding nothing. He dismissed the controversy as a storm in a teacup which had turned out to the advantage of the commercial service. His only regret was that it had not received as much coverage in the Wellington papers as it had in Auckland. That prompted the *Observer* to ask him if he had a free hand in his 'Man in the Street' sessions. In asking that question the *Observer* was probably assuming that Scrim's outburst had become the subject of some sort of government review. Scrim took the question in his stride. He was not, he replied, restricted in any way in what he could say on the air. The prime minister had given him 'a definite assurance', and he would gladly rely on it. He did not know the fine detail of any limitations on the freedom of action of civil servants. But in his view a 'man did not sell his soul when he decided to serve the state'.[28]

There were many, the *Observer* said, who thought Scrim had made a tactical error in attacking the press and had been 'unwise' in what it had said about *Truth*. It was only partly to defend their corner, it said, that the Auckland dailies had criticised his outburst. Their real objections centred on the way he had been appointed to head the commercial service, his personal links with the prime minister, and his public advocacy of the government's policies. As an admonitory caution, the *Observer* quoted Napoleon's remark: 'Four hostile newspapers are more to be feared than a thousand bayonets.'[29]

Perhaps, the *Observer* suggested, Mr Scrimgeour's Sunday evening chats would be less controversial in future. Perhaps, too, when he became controller he should have given up any activities that could involve him in controversy. He should 'propitiate' his critics instead of 'lightly offending' them. The 'danger with radio speeches', it said archly, was that you never knew if there was a reporter in the house.[30]

Lee noted in his diary that two thirds of the cabinet would have 'butchered' Scrim, and he was not completely confident of Savage. A notorious larrikin in his own early years, Lee knew one when he met one. He felt an affinity with Scrim. He accepted that Scrim had 'been a trifle tactless'. He had started a fight he could not 'sustain', but his talk was '95 per cent good', and his comrades should be prepared to stand by him. Scrim was the sort of man who would 'see you through on the big issues', and Lee trusted him.[31]

Savage was out of the country and Fraser was acting prime minister. Fraser had had no direct involvement in Scrim's activities as director of the Friendly Road radio station, but he would have been aware of rumours about him. Now questions were being asked about the contract he had entered into with the Australian firm Radiovision Proprietary Ltd at the end of 1936. Fraser ordered a thorough investigation of Scrim's office. Some of the files in Scrim's office included correspondence from Labour MPs. Some cryptic comments in Lee's diary are the only published mentions of the investigation. Lee regarded it as an 'OGPU operation', an allusion to the infamous Soviet security agency.

Lee and Scrim were working in tandem, as they would in Scrim's later crises. Scrim, on Lee's advice, protested to Fraser, declaring that he would defend himself publicly. Lee, too, sent Fraser a letter of protest. Fraser then rang Lee, and asked him to 'call Scrim off' and tell him that there was nothing against him. Lee was very unsure of his relationship with Fraser and was not disposed to take anything he said to him at face value. He also thought that Fraser did not like Scrim. He took the phone call as a sign that Fraser had become 'scared'. He thought that Fraser was quite capable of intimidating his colleagues, but he also thought he would not want civil servants to get their hands on private correspondence. In Lee's view, Scrim was rightly 'annoyed' to be 'treated as a crook' in interviews with members of his own staff.

Emotions were running high in the closed circle of government. We cannot say whether Lee's allegation of a Soviet state style investigation was a product of his febrile imagination, a consequence of Fraser's heavy-handedness, a result of the way the investigation was carried out, or some combination of all three.

On 28 April the cabinet authorised a comprehensive inquiry into the establishment, development, and management of the commercial broadcasting stations with particular reference to the Rev C.G. Scrimgeour, including his continuing relationship with the Friendly Road. The crown solicitor and a senior Treasury officer were directed to carry out the inquiry 'forthwith'.[32] Their report seems to have absolved Scrim. Early in June he was called to a meeting with Fraser, Jones, and Lee which, Lee wrote, confirmed all his powers.[33] Scrim would continue to give his Sunday evening 'Man in the Street' sessions under the conditions that had been agreed on between Savage and himself

Scrim's attack on the press dented his credibility. He was quick to reassure his Friendly Road followers that he was still the Scrim they had come to believe in, and to reassure himself that he had their continuing support. He set a date for a Sunday evening meeting in the Auckland Town Hall. Friendly Road box-holders[34] were given the opportunity to reserve seats. A circular from Uncle Tom informed them that Uncle Scrim would present the 'full facts of the story from the inside'. Regular announcements over 1ZB spread the word. The meeting would be open to the public, but it would be a private meeting and would not be broadcast.

So great was the response that the Regent, Embassy and Plaza picture theatres were booked as well as the Town Hall and Concert Chamber. Every seat was filled. Lee attended the meeting. His diary note said all that needed to be said: '15 June. Scrim 7000. Remarkable meetings. Scrim improving as public speaker.'[35]

Scrim spent a few minutes in each of the three picture theatres and the concert chamber before the meeting began. He entered the Town Hall to the singing of the Friendly Road song, prolonged applause, foot stamping, and cheers. He began by saying that he would not 'waste time answering questions'. He often got so wild with people for what they say that he 'could tear them limb from limb'. But he preferred to take the advice that John Lee had once given him: '"He that endureth to the end must prevail." Breathe deeply and act slowly.' It is altogether likely that Lee had given Scrim that advice quite recently following his attack on the press.

Scrim treated his audience to what had become the standard account of his years as a Methodist home missioner, the founding of the Friendly Road, and his struggle to keep 1ZB on air. In his negotiations with the government he had 'absolutely insisted on the Friendly Road's right to go on'. He was unhappy that 1ZB had become a government-owned radio station. That meant a loss 'overnight' of an asset, so he claimed, of at least £50,000. Fortunately, though, there had not really been a change of ownership. From being owned 'by the many people who had funded the station' it was now owned by 'all the people of New Zealand'.

He had been accused, he said, of receiving money from the government and at the same time 'feathering his nest from the Friendly Road funds and boxes'. That was untrue. The Friendly Road's balance sheet was 'always available for public inspection'. Its accounts were 'audited by the biggest and most reputable firm in Auckland and the government'. It had not sought any funds from the government and had not received any. He had personally guaranteed the Friendly Road overdraft, which was overdrawn by £667 16s 11d.

He had only one regret about the letter he had written in reply to criticism of a certain newspaper: 'he had never caught up the loss of the twenty minutes he had wasted on dictating it.' He ended by affirming that, despite the 'important duties' he now had to 'perform', he still had the time to spread the gospel of love and friendship.

When he sat down, Uncle Tom moved a motion he had brought with him to the meeting, and it was passed unanimously. The resolution empowered Uncle Scrim to act for the Friendly Road in negotiations with the government for the sale of 1ZB. It had been a smoothly managed meeting.[36]

Scrim had one thing more for his followers. Copies of Harry Bell's *Chats: Talks on the 'Friendly Road' by Uncle Scrim* were being distributed in Auckland during June. *Chats* was a book of 127 pages. It included forty-seven chats, more than half of which had been given since 1ZB started broadcasting as a commercial station the previous October. Each chat illustrated Scrim's themes in some way: be kind and helpful to others; be positive even when the going is tough; and believe that good times will come again. The costs of publishing *Chats* were probably covered by donations. No price was listed on its cover.[37]

John Joseph McNamara cartoon of Scrim. (*Radio Record*, 18 June 1937, Alexander Turnbull Library Cartoon Collection A-354-009)

There was speculation that Scrim might buy one or other of the now redundant B stations in Wellington, Christchurch or Dunedin. But none of these would give him the minimum of one kilowatt in transmission power, so he built his own stations. He struck up good working relationships with officers of the Public Works Department who, liaising with Sheil and Grainger, made what proved to be good decisions for these centres.

Sheil selected the accommodation and took charge of its redesign for the Wellington, Christchurch, and Dunedin stations. Each one called for its own solution. He was particularly pleased with the design of the Christchurch station, considering it, when built, to be the best designed radio station in Australasia. Scrim agreed with him. When, two years later, he visited radio stations in North America, he saw nothing he considered better for its size than 3ZB.[38]

Grainger's preference for American broadcasting equipment raised a question of policy. The National Broadcasting Service sourced its equipment from British suppliers, so a modification of government

Scrim discusses the model of 3ZB with Beau Sheil. (*Radio Record*, 16 July 1937)

policy would be needed. Scrim backed his colleague, and it seems that Savage did too. 2ZB's equipment, housed in one compact cabinet, was much admired when it was installed and in use.[39]

When 2ZB was about to be opened, Scrim announced the organisational structure of the NCBS. Each station would have a station director, executives in charge of advertising, programmes, engineering, and accounting, a dozen announcers and a Maori announcer, copywriters, and technical staff, giving it a total complement of about fifty. There would also be a head office staff which, to begin with would be located with 2ZB. He, Sheil, Wood, Grainger, and Bell, the secretary of the NCBS, would move to Wellington.[40]

Scrim's responsibilities as controller were to oversee the work of his head office managers and the four station directors and keep his finger on the pulse of the NCBS's relationships with sponsors and potential sponsors, influential politicians, and movers and shakers whom it was important to have on side. It was a job he was able to make up as he went along and a near-perfect fit for his restless nature. Mackay would recall that he made frequent visits to Parliament Buildings with Scrim 'to cultivate our friends'.[41]

Scrim and his family had lived very well during their last four years in Auckland. He made similar living arrangements in Wellington. The *Observer* informed its readers that he had bought a large two-storey house in an expensive part of Lower Hutt. It soon noticed him on a fine Sunday morning wearing a duck-egg blue suit and matching pork-pie hat.[42]

In other respects, too, Scrim carried on where he left off in Auckland. The freemasonry of the sleeper carriages on the Limited Express continued. Labour MPs regarded him as one of them, and he attended their informal Sunday morning gatherings in parliament. He made some new mates. Of these, the ones he felt closest to were Dick Griffin and Jim Dyer, two Communist Party members who were his friends for the rest of their lives.[43] He now drove a large American Hudson Terraplane. He seems to have seen much less of his Auckland acquaintances. But he still kept up his summer fishing trips with Hal Pettit and John Stannage, and Pettit still monitored his health.[44]

★

A few months after the move to Wellington, Lee saw what he thought were signs that Scrim was 'unbending' and 'becoming human'. He was 'drinking an odd spot, learning to dance, and dancing with the prettiest girl'. Lee hoped Scrim would 'never settle down to rich respectability', though there did not seem to be any signs of that. For the present, however, it soon became evident that it was pretty girls who were capturing Scrim's interest. Nine months later Lee wrote that he had talked to Scrim about his 'entanglements'. It is clear from the context that these were amatory entanglements, or at the very least, dalliances. Many years later, when Lee was reflecting on his long association with Scrim, he mentioned an affair Scrim had had with a 'beauty' who had 'bumped him off at a critical moment'.[45]

The ZBs advertised their wares. They bought space in the *New Zealand Radio Record* to publicise new serial programmes and other important broadcasting events. They would have advertised in the main daily newspapers if proprietors had been willing to accept their copy. A quote from a ZB advertisement in the *New Zealand Radio Record* when 2ZB was about to begin broadcasting illustrates the NCBS's sales pitch. It listed the programmes that would be heard, and, next to each one, the name of the sponsor in parenthesis, and the assertion that they were all 'new stories, new fixtures, brisk, bright programmes of a standard never before equalled in New Zealand radio history'.[46] No one would mistake the ZB stations for blushing violets.

2ZB introduced the ZB's first major serialised drama with a gala event for theatre goers. 'One Man's Family' had been a long-running hit in the United States. It was directed and produced for the ZB network by a live cast of New Zealand actors, and the first episode was performed before an audience in the Nimmo Hall in Willis Street, Wellington.[47]

'One Man's Family' was an instant success. Listeners warmed to this ordinary American family and had little or no difficulty relating to the everyday events in their lives. It was the first of the genre of domestic family dramas that became a staple of radio and, later, television entertainment. It was followed by 'Easy Aces', which appealed with its droll humour, and by a stream of new serials. From 'The Air Adventures of Jimmy Allen', and 'Tarzan of the Apes', to

'Rebecca', Beau Geste', and 'The Dark Invader', to pick out only some of the popular ones, there were serials for all members of the family to listen to.[48] Most of the earliest of these were American productions and, among other things, they caused much public discussion about their baneful influence on the speech habits of New Zealand children and young people. Some serials were given a judicious editing before they were broadcast. But these concerns were somewhat allayed when serials made in Australia came onto the market and were broadcast over YA as well as ZB stations. Among these, 'Fred and Maggie Everybody' and 'Dad and Dave' became long-running favourites.

It was not until almost the end of the 1937 parliamentary session that the government introduced its Broadcasting Amendment Bill seeking retrospective statutory sanction for the NCBS. There was never any doubt that the Bill would be passed. That did not stop Opposition MPs from mounting a determined attack on the policy it embodied and, more particularly, raising questions about the role Scrim had played in setting up Radio Features Proprietary Ltd, and making other allegations against him.

For their part, government MPs showed more interest in raking over the ashes of the jamming incident. Lee led that counter-attack with a hard-hitting speech early in the Second Reading debate. Savage and Fraser held back and were among the last to speak. Savage was not to be drawn by the Opposition's coded attack on Scrim. He affirmed what he had already said several times in public statements during the year. He had never met a man in his life, he said, in whom he had greater confidence than the controller of commercial broadcasting. He would 'back the controller one hundred percent, all the time'.[49]

Fraser outlined the different procedures the government had used in making Shelley's and Scrim's appointments. It was, he said, open to the Opposition to criticise Scrim's appointment, and it had done so. The government had no complaint about that, and took full responsibility. Members of the public would reach their own conclusions and give their verdict at the next general election.[50]

*Truth*'s parliamentary reporter thought that the debate on the Broadcasting Bill had been 'the most hotly contested for many years'. If the government thought that it had won the debate, it wrote, it was mistaken. It had trailed a 'smokescreen' over the field but, with the battle over, the weakness of its defence could clearly be seen. To clear matters up, it should set up a royal commission. The *Evening Post* agreed. To the *Observer*, the debate provided 'the first skirmishes' of the 1938 election campaign.[51] But there was no possibility that the government would open itself to the risk that a royal commission might seek to examine the official record of the advice it had received and the decisions it had made in appointing Scrim.

The Broadcasting Amendment Act came into force on 19 November. On that day, the public service commissioners formally appointed Scrim to the position of controller, National Commercial Broadcasting Service. The appointment was for three years, at the pleasure of the governor in council, and there was a right of renewal at the completion of the three-year term.[52]

Some newspaper editorials in their comments on *Truth*'s open letter had asked why Scrim had so far not charged the newspaper with libel. Scrim used his speech at the Friendly Road anniversary celebration to give his answer. He had not made a claim, he said, he had made an offer. If the charges against him could be proved he would give £500 to charity. The *Observer* could not repress the comment that it 'must be marvellous to have a clear conscience and all that money'. *Truth* kept up its attack. It was, it pointed out, the only newspaper, apart from the *Standard*, the Labour Party's official newspaper, that supported the introduction of commercial broadcasting. But Scrimgeour and the government were avoiding the allegations that had been made against him. Scrim's explanations were evasions.[53]

Savage and Scrim received messages from people who wanted them to know how thankful they were for the Labour government and how much they valued Scrim's broadcasts. Reporting to Savage, Scrim said that letters 'had poured in from all parts of the country'. Far too many for him even to suggest that he should look at them. He did, however, send Savage a copy of the supporters' letter that 176 residents of Patea had signed and sent to *Truth*. He expressed his great debt of gratitude to Savage in a covering letter.[54]

# CHAPTER 8

# Man of Principle or Propagandist?

Nineteen thirty-eight started with one of those festive events that had become Scrim hallmarks. 2ZB hosted the finals of the countrywide competition that the NCBS had promoted to find 'our very own Deanna Durbin'.[1] Deanna Durbin, a vivacious teenager, had taken the United States by storm and had quickly become a popular international idol. The ZB's search for her national counterpart attracted a thousand applicants. There was unprecedented public enthusiasm during the preliminary rounds in the four main centres. Union Airways, which sponsored the contest, flew the four finalists to Wellington where they stayed at the St George Hotel as guests of the NCBS. Scrim presided over the function.[2]

June Barson, a thirteen-year-old from Auckland, won the contest. She and the other finalists were then treated to a fortnight in Sydney and Melbourne, where they made public appearances, recorded performances for the Australian Broadcasting Commission, and did screen tests as guests of Universal Films.[3]

The contest allowed Scrim to renew his association with Rosie Scott. Her singing career had moved on since the days when she and her sister sang for Scrim's prison services. She had recently returned to Auckland from Sydney, where she had been a student at the New South Wales Conservatorium. June Barson was one of her singing pupils.

Scrim's penchant for doing the unexpected was put to the test in February when Count Felix von Luckner, the German sea dog paid his long-delayed second visit to New Zealand. As the skipper of the raider *Seeadler* he had taken a heavy toll of unarmed merchant ships during the First World War. He had been captured in the Kermadec Islands in 1916 and detained in New Zealand for the remainder of the war. Released after the war, von Luckner had said he would make a return visit to New Zealand within two years. He did not keep to his timetable, but he created much public interest in February 1938 when he arrived in Auckland in his smart ocean-going ketch. Scrim made his acquaintance and was clearly tempted by the possibility of sailing with him to Sydney.[4] Nothing came of it, however.

Scrim's continuing professional association with Rosie Scott among others is a reminder that New Zealand in the 1930s was a mosaic of local communities. People who made their reputation in one part of the country might well be largely unknown elsewhere. That was changing, however, as the two national broadcasting services made it possible for performers to build a national reputation. As controller of the NCBS, Scrim now played a key role in creating national reputations and communities of interest. But, like everyone now working in broadcasting at the national level, he carried with him friendships and associations he had made in his local community, in his case Auckland. The question was whether he would deal fairly and consistently with colleagues regardless of his previous associations with them.

Until the time of his dismissal in 1943, Scrim successfully presented the NCBS as a big happy family of go-getters. But that is not how the people who worked within the commercial network came to feel about the organisation. Scrim became the despair of his senior colleagues, but none of them broke ranks. Even after Scrim's dismissal, the public remained unaware of their criticisms and grievances.

Two incidents in 1938 would have aroused public interest had they become known outside Scrim's head office. The first was a personal campaign by a disaffected former employee who accused him among other things of playing favourites. The second arose from the inspection report for station 3ZB carried out for the public service commissioners.

Bill Harris was the disaffected former employee. He had been sacked as 2ZB's racing reporter in March 1938. He had been good at his job but his drinking habits had brought about his dismissal. He turned against the NCBS and organised some embarrassing hoaxes against it. He also wrote a letter which made various allegations against 'The Rev Uncle Scrim & his Henchmen' but which was never published. The letter had no addressee. Some years later it came to roost in the archive of a prominent Wellington left-winger. We cannot say who Harris was writing to, whether the letter was sent, or whether, perhaps, he had written it for himself in preparation for an appeal against his dismissal. The freemasonry of Wellington's inner city public bars has always facilitated the sharing of news, rumour, and gossip among journalists, trade unionists, public servants, lawyers and others. If Harris had wanted his allegations against Scrim and the NCBS to come to the notice of officers in the public service commission he would have known how to go about it.

Harris claimed that Scrim had infiltrated the NCBS with friends and relatives, and it is true that he was employing several men and women, including some of his in-laws, who had worked with him in the old days of 1ZB. John Stannage continued to have privileged access to NCBS's head office, and that raised questions in the minds of some NCBS officers. A coterie of Scrim's senior colleagues, Harris wrote, spied on other members of staff.

Harris alleged, too, that Scrim and Sheil had received irregular payments from the Weintraubs while they were under contract to the NCBS. Harris does not seem to have provided evidence to support this allegation, which may have been based on no more than hearsay. Any suggestion that Scrim had received illegal under-the-counter payments can probably be discounted. As recently as the previous year the government had investigated his financial dealings from the time of his first involvement in radio broadcasting, and had given him a clean sheet. The provision for commission in Scrim's salary had ended on 1 April 1937. Sheil's remuneration still included £1000 a year from the ZB's sales of advertising, but that will have been dealt with as a routine accounting item. As controller of the NCBS, Scrim was operating in a goldfish bowl. Some of the people who were no doubt still taking a close interest in his business dealings would not have hesitated to take legal action against him if they had evidence of any financial impropriety.

The second matter was of the sort that could crop up from time to time in a department's relationship with the public service commissioners. One of the commissioners' inspectors had written a report on his recent visit to 3ZB that included testimony of some members of the staff about alleged indiscretions of the station director. It also raised questions about NCBS policy on relationships between members of its staff and advertising agents. Scrim, accompanied by Bell, met

Scrim depicted as Harry Bell's brain. (John Joseph McNamara cartoon, *Radio Record*, 28 January 1938, Alexander Turnbull Library Cartoon Collection S-L 1077-19)

the two commissioners and the assistant secretary of the Treasury, Ashwin, on 6 May 1938.

The meeting began with some shadow-boxing between Scrim and the commissioners. He had no difficulty agreeing that there might be prima facie reasons for investigating some of the actions of the station director, but pointed out that he had formed a good impression of the man. He also said that there were more cross-currents among the 3ZB staff than the commissioners' inspector had become aware of. If there were to be an inquiry, Scrim insisted, it must start without any preconceptions of guilt or innocence and must respect everyone's right to a fair hearing.

On working relationships with advertising agencies Scrim thought that the commissioners were fishing in a pool best left to the government's other control agency, the Treasury. He had already worked through the issues with Ashwin, and was able to say that the Treasury supported what the NCBS was doing. Ashwin said little at the meeting, but what he did say agreed with Scrim's explanations. The nub of the issue was one that had fuelled some of Harris's allegations. The possibility existed that a dishonest officer could enter into a secret agreement with an advertising agent to defraud the NCBS. Everyone at the meeting understood that. To the commissioners the problem could be resolved either by the NCBS accepting full responsibility for all contracts, or by deciding that all advertising contracts should be handled by outside advertising agents and their clients. Scrim supported the second option and said that he could see signs that it was already happening. The meeting had started frostily but this final exchange of views was perhaps a sign that the sun was beginning to shine, if not particularly warmly. Perhaps, however, it might have illustrated what Ian Mackay would later refer to as Scrim's ability to 'charm a bird out of a tree'.[5]

One of the issues in the 3ZB inquiry was the station manager's behaviour in supplying liquor at the station's Christmas party. The standing public service rule was that alcohol was banned from departmental premises. Scrim turned a blind eye to that prohibition. His own breach of the rule a few years later would add a dimension to the government's reasons for dismissing him.

The records of the NCBS that were deposited with National Archives throw almost no light on Scrim's working relations with his senior colleagues. An event that seems to have passed unnoticed was Dorothy Wood's resignation from the organisation. She had planned and managed the ZB programmes with a sure touch, but she left the NZBS some time in 1938. Perhaps she left for a better deal from her new employer. Perhaps, however, she had found her working relations with her colleagues, even perhaps with Scrim himself, less than satisfying and had opted for a change of scene. One file records Scrim's brief, faltering attempt to require his four station managers to produce monthly reports of new developments. It was introduced in March 1938. Some directors reported irregularly but one or two do not seem to have reported at all. The reports that were sent in were for the most part inconsequential. The requirement was discontinued in April 1939 when Scrim was in the United States and Beau Sheil was acting controller.[6]

Scrim's stand-off with *Truth* lay dormant until April 1938 when *Truth* taunted him with some page one allegations. He replied aggressively in his next 'Man in the Street' session. Members of trade unions around the country passed motions expressing support and confidence in him. Local Labour Party committees affirmed their support, albeit with explanations that indicated some degree of discomfort. The Taradale branch of the Labour Party, for instance, defended Scrim's chat but was 'surprised' by its 'tenor'. They saw it as 'a natural reaction' of a man who had had to withstand incessant 'attacks' and 'innuendos'. Scrim had simply let himself go, they said.[7]

The current crop of rumours had it that Scrim was about to leave the NCBS. The word was that he would 'get out from under' before the election and that the government would be happy to see him go. 'Was he about to visit America and then resign?' Male asked him on behalf of the *Observer.* That was the first he had heard about it, Scrim replied. He had, he said, not received any offers from overseas broadcasting interests. Even if he had, he would not be interested until his current three-year appointment was up. 'So that was that,' Male wrote. But it was strange, he commented, how these rumours hung around.[8]

Scrim had given a canny answer. He knew more than he had said. He harboured thoughts of visiting the United States and Canada, not in response to possible job offers but as part of his responsibilities as controller, and had put a proposal to Savage. But Savage had not wanted him out of the country during election year, and directed him to defer his visit until 1939.[9]

The thought that Scrim might go to America or Australia raised the question of what would happen to commercial broadcasting if he moved on. It was generally agreed that an incoming government would scrap state-owned commercial broadcasting should Labour lose the election, remote as that might have seemed in 1938. But a story was circulating in radio circles that a group of radio people were ready to take over the commercial stations.[10]

National Party predictions that Scrim would become the Labour government's minister of propaganda gave spice to such rumours. In May, Justin Power, a leading light in the National Party, told a meeting in Greymouth that Labour people in Wellington were openly saying that Scrim would be their candidate for Stratford. But the Stratford Labour Representation Committee scotched that sort of talk. It already had a candidate, it said, and would be sticking to him.[11]

During the second half of July Scrim and Lena went on the *Maunganui*'s Pacific Islands winter cruise. Harry Kelliher had booked the berths for his wife and himself but had given them to Scrim. Scrim did not say why he unexpectedly took an extended period of leave at that time of the year. But it is very likely that Kelliher had become aware that he needed a break and was able to arrange one for him. Scrim was under pressure from his opponents. He was no doubt pushing himself hard. Was he having a repetition of the 'mental breakdown' that had laid him low in Kaitangata thirteen years earlier? All we know is that Lee found Scrim in a highly emotional state when he was about to embark on the cruise and talked about 'throwing in the towel'. Lee thought, mistakenly as it turned out, that he had persuaded Scrim against doing that.

On his return to Wellington, Scrim sent Savage a letter of resignation. He had told Lee that, if he resigned, he would go out with an attack on 'the Enemy'. He delivered that attack in his 'Man in the Street' session on Sunday, 7 August. His venom shattered the Sunday evening calm of his listeners, estimated by the *Standard* to number hundreds of thousands.[12] Scrim singled out Justin Power in a swingeing attack on the National Party. Power was an organiser for the National Party in its Wellington division. Scrim alleged that Power was 'an unmitigated and malicious liar'. According to the *Dominion*'s report, which was probably taken from a stenographer's transcript of the speech, Scrim went on to say:

> In case you did not hear it, and in case your stenographer missed it – you are an unmitigated and malicious liar, and I will challenge you and your employers to name one charge – anyone they like – a distinct act or any distinct practice ever committed by myself – either in the commercial service or out of it. You and your friends have in times past been very free with some good suggestions about libel actions. Now this is your chance. For the third time, you – and the gang who employ you to say these things – are unmitigated and malicious liars.
>
> . . . If these people [prominent members of the National Party] were put in a sewer at North Cape and worked their way through to the Bluff they would come out as clean as when they went in.

Scrim went on to allege that members of the National Party derided him for his religion. Then he took up one of his standard themes: the misery that the recent depression had brought to people who had starved in a country flush with food and worn cast-off clothing when the woolsheds were 'packed with wool'. He finished by farewelling his listeners, whom 'he had enjoyed meeting and talking to'. He had never, he said, 'descended to the depths of insinuation of some of his critics'. He 'had never been the mouthpiece of the party now in power'.

> I want you to hear this challenge and if 'they' don't take it up they ought to shut up – please don't squeal because I use the air to do it. I am sick of lies and filthy slanders. I follow the same ideal now that led me to preach the gospel of the Stranger of Galilee.
>
> Good Night.

The fruity words and music of 'The Stranger of Galilee' ended the session.[13] No one who heard Scrim's breathtaking rant could fail to have an opinion on it. Newspaper editors up and down the country deplored the unbridled attack. They challenged his right as a public servant to use a state-owned broadcasting service to make personal attacks on his critics. It was for ministers, not officials, to answer criticisms against their department. Scrim could exercise his civil rights through the courts. On the other side of the fence, trade union branches in various parts of the country held mass meetings which unanimously passed motions urging the government not to accept Scrim's resignation. Labour's newspaper, the *Standard*, was alone in standing apart from the general press condemnation, congratulating Scrim on his 'courageous answer to [his] critics'.[14]

The *Observer* had until this time balanced criticism of Scrim's 'Man in the Street' sessions with comments supporting him for his work as controller of the NCBS. But C.W. Carrick's full-page account of his 'startling outburst' could find nothing to say in its favour. Mr Scrimgeour, he wrote, had said during his 'diatribe' that he was speaking 'without political bias'. But his speech 'was inferentially a denunciation of the National Party' as well as a 'fiery denunciation of his own critics'. His 'vilification' of Justin Power did not sit at all well, coming from a 'one-time minister of religion' and 'apostle of charity in word and deed'. The speech 'was a piece of electioneering'. But 'many members of the government would have deep misgivings about that sort of electioneering'. Broadcasting matters were likely to be of general public interest in the coming election, Carrick concluded, 'but Mr Scrimgeour had made himself a more important election issue than any of them'.[15]

Scrim had put Savage on the spot. Only two or three weeks earlier

Savage had told officials in the commercial broadcasting service that the broadcasting of political propaganda 'would not be tolerated'. Scrim had not been present, and may not have been told what had been said. But he more than anyone should have been aware of the government's position, particularly in the run-up to an election. He had blatantly breached Savage's prohibition. He had also given him the poisoned chalice of his resignation. And he was in a highly emotional frame of mind. Lee, who had been away from Wellington, rang Scrim on Wednesday, 10 August and found him so out of control that he quickly ended the call and went to meet him so that they could talk face to face.[16]

Savage could most surely have done without having to make a decision on Scrim's letter of resignation. He already had enough troublesome problems to deal with. He was anxiously watching the slide in the country's sterling balance. He and his cabinet colleagues were engaged in a fractious debate in caucus over the government's social security legislation. He had committed himself to speaking engagements in various parts of the country, was in poor health, and his doctors would soon advise him that he had cancer of the colon and must undergo an urgent operation.[17]

We do not know how much Savage was aware of the extent to which his cabinet colleagues were feeling compromised by Scrim's statements in his 'Man in the Street' sessions. But some of them were making their views known to the NCBS. Mackay was regularly rung up by Nash, Semple, Wilson and other ministers complaining about things Scrim had said. But none of them was prepared to make a formal complaint while Savage was alive.[18] Nor do we know if Savage discussed Scrim's letter of resignation with his cabinet colleagues. He knew what they thought about Scrim and probably saw no need for further discussion. Scrim was becoming a political liability. He had a huge following among people who were still recovering from their misery during the depression. But his intemperate outbursts over the air were turning former sympathisers into sceptical listeners, and many of these were becoming active opponents. Scrim was becoming the symbol of what the National Party and the editors of a large number of newspapers attacked as the failure of the government's broadcasting policy.

Savage knew that Lee was firmly in Scrim's corner. Lee had emerged as the government's strongest critic on monetary and economic policies, and in the debate over social security. But he was, with Savage, perhaps Scrim's only other remaining supporter in the Labour caucus. Lee wrote Savage a long letter urging him not to let Scrim go. He was convinced of Scrim's loyalty to Savage and himself, and to the Labour Party. Between them, he wrote, he and Savage could manage Scrim. 'Scrim can be got to do anything in the world for us,' he wrote. He could also be 'disciplined', if that was necessary, but only by people who 'had faith in him and treated him as a comrade and not as a crook'. Lee could 'do anything with him', he wrote, 'and *you yourself can because you play fair* with him, but I confess to a feeling of disgust at the way he has been handled'.[19] Lee's letter was a triumph of hope over experience. Its logic was less important than its emotional appeal. Lee had written it to strengthen Savage's resolve.

On 11 August, the *Standard* published an exclusive interview with Savage in which he announced that he had decided not to accept Scrim's resignation. He had received messages from one end of the country to the other, he said. Mr Scrimgeour would remain in his position. There were no conditions. 'He would just get on with the job.' Alone again among the newspapers, the *Standard* applauded the prime minister's announcement. The people of New Zealand, it said, 'made it quite plain "that Scrim must not go"'. They also made it plain that they did not like the Opposition's tactics, and they didn't like slander. The *Standard* said that it had received hundreds of letters from a cross section of the country. 'To read them was to be reminded that the lessons of the Depression are not forgotten and that the lessons of the last three years have been well learnt.'[20]

The *Standard* then published an exclusive interview with Scrim. He was, he said, deeply grateful for the prime minister's continuing confidence in him. In everything he did he tried to apply 'Christian ideals' to the conditions of the day. In the service of 'the ultimate ideal, the brotherhood of man,' he wanted to 'bring about better conditions for all'. The social security proposals 'were not party politics'. They were 'more truly depicted as applied Christianity'.[21]

Other newspaper editors were dismayed by the prime minister's decision. The *Press* said it was 'not easy to believe that the prime minister believes what he says'. Mr Scrimgeour had deliberately defied the government. But he remained in office, 'enjoying, as a result of his defiance, a liberty allowed to no other public servant'.[22] The *Auckland Star* bristled over Scrim's uniquely privileged position and the 'violence' of his language, and spoke for 'many people who find it intolerable'. The outcome of the resignation incident had been to 'strengthen his position at the expense of the government'. Mr Scrimgeour's proper course of action would have been either to have had his minister defend him in Parliament or seek redress in the courts.[23]

Scrim and his critics were in perpetual check to each other. The central issue had long been plain to all. Scrim's contract with Savage allowed him to express his own opinions in his 'Man in the Street' sessions, answerable only to his own judgement. That right was not available to any other public servant. Scrim, furthermore, was the head of the broadcasting service over which he was making his broadcasts. He was, as his critics pointed out, uniquely privileged. He claimed for himself that he dealt with principles, and denied that his broadcasts had a political intent. He saw himself as a man of Christian love, peace, and goodwill. He also saw himself as a victim of the innuendos and slanders of hostile critics.

His critics saw him very differently. From the time of the last election they had seen him as too close to Savage and the Labour government. They saw his appointment as controller of the NCBS as an act of political patronage. They thought it was wrong in principle for him to have retained his interest in the Friendly Road. They thought it wrong in principle and a serious mistake by the government to give him free rein in his weekly 'Man in the Street' broadcasts. Their misgivings had been confirmed by the many occasions when he had used these sessions to make political comments in favour of the government and critical of the National Party. They were affronted by his attack on the press in April 1937 and by his recent attack on members of the National Party. They deplored his loss of control of himself in those broadcasts and their vituperative nature. They wanted him to go.

These opposing sets of perceptions were irreconcilable. Scrim never seems to have understood the distinction between affirming a principle and taking public stands on controversial political matters as the head of a government department. That was illustrated once again in his interview with the *Standard*. He thanked the prime minister for his support, and then, before the government's social security proposals had been made public, gave them the seal of his approval. It was entirely proper for Archbishop Averill and others to characterise the government's social security proposal as 'applied Christianity', Scrim held that view himself, as a great many people did. But it was not open to Scrim or any public servant to be a public advocate for government policy proposals.

Scrim had become the head of a government department without any previous experience of the hothouse of Parliament. He had been quite sure that he would win over his critics, who would come to acknowledge the success of the government's commercial broadcasting service. Successes there had been. But Scrim through his own actions had conjured up critics and opponents, and now he was locked in controversy with them. He was wilting under the strain.

The intensity of feeling against Scrim was illustrated in a conversation that Lee had with Coates. Lee and Coates were old soldiers who, though on different sides in Parliament, respected each other and kept in touch. Coates warned Lee to be careful in his relations with Scrim who, Coates said, was 'a dirty lying swine'. Lee said he would take the risk.[24]

Scrim's relationship with the Labour government was more complicated than his opponents realised. He had never been a member of the Labour Party and had no intention of becoming one. That is why he believed that his favourable comments on the government were not political comment. Most members of the Labour cabinet were ambivalent about his commentaries on their policies and were as angry with him as his opponents over his broadcast on 7 August. But with Savage still staunchly supporting him, they had to endure Opposition criticism in silence.

Parliament adjourned in mid-September for the general election campaign. Scrim's 'Man in the Street' sessions included political commentary during the campaign. He also held meetings in Rotorua, Matamata, Morrinsville, Putaruru, and Tirau, and addressed large Friendly Road rallies in Auckland and New Plymouth.

We can only guess why, in the course of an election in which he was being attacked as a contentious public figure, he should visit the part of the country where he had begun his work as a Methodist home missioner fourteen years earlier. The state of his health might have provided the answer, but why should he make personal visits during a hotly contested election campaign? It is unlikely that he was in the district to give support to Alex Moncur, the Labour MP for Rotorua. Whatever the reason, it is impossible to believe that his meetings in these upper Waikato towns were unrelated to the general election.

Scrim had difficulty getting the approval of the Rotorua Borough Council for a meeting in the Majestic Theatre on the evening of Sunday, 25 September. The council gave its approval only on the day of the meeting. The *Observer* drew the inference that the council had had to be persuaded that the meeting would be a religious, not a political function. The Rotorua shopkeeper who was advertising the meeting displayed life-sized photographs in his window, one of Savage, the other of Scrim, labelled: 'the greatest brains of the age'.[25]

During the next few days Scrim met groups of people in Putaruru, Morrinsville, and Matamata. He became the focus of a noisy demonstration of disapproval when he joined a meeting that Moncur was addressing in Tirau. Scrim had found himself unable to keep an appointment that had been made for him unrelated to Moncur's meeting. He joined the meeting, he said, intending to speak after Moncur's meeting had ended. Members of the National Party from Matamata, getting wind of what was afoot, organised a convoy of cars to take supporters to the Tirau meeting. Some 400 people crowded into the hall and the supper room or stood outside. Moncur spoke for two hours. 'A furious volley of cheers, applause, cat-calls, and booing' broke out when Scrim rose to speak. 'The uproar went on for fifteen minutes.' Scrim, who had not been able to speak, sat down, and was thanked.[26]

Scrim went on to Auckland where, on Sunday evening, 2 October, he was welcomed by 4000 cheering Friendly Road supporters who filled the Town Hall and the Concert Chamber. Though well short of his largest meetings in the city, the audience was still much larger than any other speaker could command, and he would have been reassured by it. He spoke for an hour to his enthusiastic audience, giving them, among other things, an account of his Tirau meeting. At the end of his address he read out two telegrams he had received. One said, 'May God bless you and preserve you.' The other said, 'Do you think that you are the only person in New Zealand.' He was cheered off the stage.[27]

The *Herald*'s editorial spoke for Scrim's critics and opponents. A great many people detested his Sunday evening propaganda sessions, it said, and would gladly see the last of them. The *Observer* was among his critics. It reported that Scrim 'had probably never spoken better'. He had presented a 'well-tuned and very effective piece of political propaganda'. But was he aware, it asked, of the 'unfair and misleading character of his half-truths and generalisations', and his impropriety and calm presumption that, at the height of an election, he could exploit a radio monopoly which money could not buy? He did not own the commercial radio stations, the people of New Zealand did. It congratulated him on being able to arrange a dominion-wide relay of that monopoly.[28]

Garland and others in the inner circle of the Friendly Road had also been thinking about what could happen after the election. A National Party victory was very unlikely. But they thought it prudent to seek Hamilton's assurance that the Friendly Road would not receive unfriendly attention from a National government. When Scrim finished his speech, Garland proposed a prearranged motion which the meeting passed. The Friendly Road wanted to be treated on the same basis as other associations that also had legitimate claims on broadcasting facilities. It wanted to be assured that all Friendly Road sessions would 'remain undisturbed' and all 'privileges would continue in their entirety'.[29]

Hamilton was unyielding. Under a National government, he replied, the Friendly Road would have access to broadcasting facilities on the same basis as 'other associations with similar objectives'. It would be treated with 'absolute justice', but it would not be given 'favourable treatment' at the expense of 'great religious bodies and other organisations'. The sort of privilege that gave one man the right to broadcast political propaganda under the guise of religious talks 'would most certainly disappear'.[30]

On Monday, 3 October, Scrim addressed an audience in New Plymouth that filled two halls, with the people in one of the halls listening to him through loudspeakers. It had been nearly three years since he had last spoken in the town. He was greeted with 'prolonged applause' and spoke without any 'antagonistic' interruption. From the report in the *Taranaki Daily News*, we can infer that Scrim gave his standard speech of self-justification, laced with barely concealed accusations of his opponents. He 'did not care two hoots' for his

£1500-a-year job. Anyone who could do a better job could have it. But no one could take him from the Friendly Road. A man who worked only for money 'was a poor man indeed'. There would be much less bitterness in the world if the 'ideals of the Friendly Road were followed more generally'. He was not himself one 'to strike the first blow'. He stood for principles held by thousands of New Zealanders. But there were those, he warned, 'who did not want the voice of the "Man in the Street" to be heard'. They wanted to dictate 'what people should do'. He was not, he said, referring to 'those fiends of Socialists' but to the other people who stood for freedom. The freedom they wanted was the freedom to starve.

He resented 'the unfairness of some of the propaganda against him'. He had never said 'Do as I think' but had 'constantly urged people to think for themselves'. Perhaps the prime minister had lent some colour to those criticisms by 'courageously coming out and saying he was my personal friend'. But he and the prime minister were not political allies. 'Principles were above politics. If they went against their principles they not only offended their principles, they offended God.' The commandment to feed the hungry did not mean charity. It meant distributing food to all who needed it. People who allowed such conditions to exist had no right to question the morality, sincerity, or religion of anybody – he did not care what party they belonged to.

He had no bitterness, he said. He did not believe in personalities. Then, strangely, in what he must have intended to be a warning shot for some unnamed person, he said that, if he wanted to, he could make known 'certain facts' that would 'damn a certain gentleman in the eyes of decent people'.[31] Here was Scrim, the man of principle, speaking in the middle of a general election campaign. Protest as he might that he was not engaging in political debate between Labour and National, he could not expect his opponents to accept that self-description.

The *Taranaki Herald*, the evening rival of the *Taranaki Daily News*, voiced the opinions of those who would by now consider themselves variously to be Scrim's critics, opponents, and enemies. Its issue for Monday, 3 October, had a stinging attack on his speech in Auckland the previous evening. 'Once again,' it wrote in its editorial, 'Mr Scrimgeour had abused his position in his attempt to influence the coming election.' It quoted from the prime minister's statement following Scrim's broadcast on 7 August. After his latest broadcast, it wrote, 'the public must conclude either that Mr Scrimgeour is able to defy the government with impunity or that Mr Savage has not been sincere in his assurance.' Mr Scrimgeour, it said, had done more than any other man to embitter New Zealand politics. He would become 'the Dr Goebbels of New Zealand in the Socialist State envisaged by Mr J.A. Lee'. Scrim replied, hotly denying any similarity to Dr Goebbels. Never before had he been so insulted.[32]

The *Observer* wrote that Scrim campaigned for an hour in his last 'Man in the Street' session before the election. During that session he quoted from letters in his mailbag, among them a chain letter attacking the Catholic church and urging voters to return a National government.[33] The Hon W. Perry, MLC, heard the broadcast and was offended by it. He immediately wrote an open letter to Rev C.G. Scrimgeour, which he sent to the *Evening Post* for publication. Perry made it clear that he was writing as a Catholic and not as a member of the National Party, which was unaware of his letter. As a Catholic, he 'appreciated' Scrim's condemnation of a 'vile effusion' which was 'thoroughly offensive to all Catholics'. Scrim's reading the letter over the air had made it known 'to thousands, including Catholics who had never seen it'. But why, he asked Scrim, had he given it 'a wider circulation than ever before'?

What was Scrim's real reason for reading the letter? It could not have been to assist the authors of the letter. But was it 'to discredit the National Party'? And if it was not to discredit the National Party, he asked, 'why did you not tell your listeners that the letter had been publicly disclaimed by Hon Adam Hamilton, the leader of that party?' Or was the omission deliberate, so that Catholic listeners who had not read the letter or the disclaimer might be left to think that the letter had been written with the knowledge and approval of the National Party? Perry sent Scrim a copy of the letter so that he would 'have the opportunity of an immediate reply'.[34]

Perry was an experienced public figure who knew how to pin an opponent. Scrim's reply shows that he knew he had been pinned. He had been unaware, he wrote, that Hamilton had published a denial, and he presumed that thousands of other people would also have been unaware of it. 'It was only to be expected,' he said 'that Hamilton should disclaim the letter. No worthy citizen would ever allow their name to be associated with such a vile thing.'[35]

It might have been expected, too, that Scrim would have checked the facts before making his broadcast. But there had been signs for at least eighteen months that the 'Man in the Street' was sealed off in his own mental world. In April 1937 he had said he had not known that the Savage had made a critical speech about the press shortly before he had launched his own attack over the air. Now during an election campaign he had failed to notice what the Leader of the Opposition had been saying. It was careless behaviour.

Labour won the election with a larger percentage of the vote and increased numbers of Labour MPs in the House. The *Observer* offered 'Mr C.G. Scrimgeour' mordant congratulations. 'His continued success,' it said, 'just shows what can be accomplished by a clean young man who works hard and takes no interest in politics.'[36]

# CHAPTER 9

# A Gathering Storm

Getting re-elected was easier for Labour's politicians than finding an agreed basis for the appointment of cabinet ministers for their second term in government. Fraser, Nash, and most if not all other cabinet ministers expected that Savage would select the members of his cabinet. But Lee and thirteen members of the caucus argued that the cabinet should be elected on the basis of a preferential vote of caucus members. Lee had written to Savage in September to let him know that he would propose a motion to that effect at the first caucus meeting after the election.

It was an article of faith with Lee that the caucus should be the key decision-making forum in a Labour government. His political aspirations hinged on a favourable caucus vote, and he felt sure that he could garner enough votes to force Savage's hand. Win or lose he would annoy Savage on the way to a caucus decision. Savage, however, had made it clear that he would not of his own volition have Lee in his cabinet. He had won his endorsement as prime minister in the general election. His decisions could be challenged only by a vote in the party's national executive or its annual conference. He told Lee that, if he proceeded with his motion, he would resign and refer the issue to the Labour Party conference for a ruling.[1]

Savage, Fraser, and Nash mistakenly thought they had the numbers to defeat Lee's motion when it was put to the caucus meeting on 3 November. But it was passed, twenty-six to twenty-three, after a long, bitter debate. Savage reacted angrily. Only a decision of the Labour Party Conference, he said, would make him accept the motion. He stormed out of the caucus room and could not be persuaded to reconvene the meeting.[2] A few days later, on Savage's recommendation, the governor general appointed the members of an unchanged cabinet. Sullivan took over the housing portfolio. Lee remained parliamentary undersecretary to the prime minister but with no stated responsibilities.

As the one person who was on terms of close friendship with Savage as well as Lee, Scrim was soon actively engaged in efforts to persuade Savage to reconvene the caucus. One after another, Nash, Fraser, and Janet Fraser called on him and asked him if he could persuade Savage to make peace with Lee. They felt quite sure, they told him, 'that the Prime Minister's hatred of Mr Lee was killing him'. We know of these overtures from Lee's accounts of them in his diary.

From Lee's diary, too, we can trace moves that Scrim, Lee, and others took during the next month to repair the rift. Scrim was sure that Savage had become a prisoner to Fraser and Nash. He let Lee know that he was on his side in the 'scrap'. This pleased Lee, and he was also pleased to note that Scrim had spoken in the same way to Nash. Lee, who was seldom generous in his remarks about others, was impressed by these 'courageous' acts.[3]

But Lee's support dwindled during the summer months, and Savage would have known that it had. He conceded nothing to Lee when the two men met on 6 February, but he agreed to convene a meeting of caucus. A six-man committee – two Savage supporters, two Lee supporters, and two members of the national executive – reported to that meeting, which accepted its recommendations after another turbulent debate. The national executive endorsed them soon after. These decisions vindicated Savage. All that Lee had salvaged from the summer's protracted negotiations was a commitment to elect the leader of the party in the third year of each parliamentary cycle and an arrangement under which a Labour prime minister's proposals for members of cabinet were to be confirmed on the basis of votes in caucus.[4]

This left Lee all the more determined to press ahead with his campaign against Savage, Fraser, and Nash. Beginning with what became known as the 'Lee Letter', his attack on Nash's financial management, and ending with his piece 'Psycho-pathology in Politics', his attack on Savage, he carried his fight to the Labour leadership. Refused permission to publish his pieces in the *Standard*, Lee published them in *Tomorrow*, the left-wing fortnightly published in Christchurch by Kennaway Henderson. *Tomorrow* had a small circulation, but Lee's pieces, re-published in daily newspapers, were widely read.

Though the party was trying to rein Lee in, it still needed to make use of his talents. He continued to make stunning speeches in the House. He bolstered the party's campaign in the by-election in Christchurch East following the death of Teddy Howard. He made important contributions to the government's efforts to get its defence forces ready for the looming war in Europe. His reputation as a 'coming man' continued to grow inside the party, as well as, but for different reasons, with Opposition MPs and newspaper editors. Savage found himself on the defensive, turning down requests, including one from the governor general, that he take Lee into his cabinet as minister of defence.

The ZB stations were by now well into their stride and were very popular with listeners. The main issue for the government was how to provide better reception conditions for listeners in central North Island districts. From the time that 4ZB came on the air, Scrim had been beset with requests for a fifth station to be added to the network. We do not know the background to the decision, but on 10 October, in the course of his election campaign, Savage opened a new commercial station at Palmerston North. He was aware, he said, that various towns had an interest in being the permanent home for the station.[5]

Scrim found a novel way of testing the claims of these towns while at the same time providing good publicity for the NCBS. He negotiated an arrangement with the Railways Department for a first-class carriage to be converted into a broadcasting station. At relatively little cost, it became a fully self-contained broadcasting studio, control room and associated office and store rooms, with living and sleeping quarters for the two staff who lived aboard it. Painted ivory white with, on each side, a wide crimson flash in the centre of which the logo 5ZB stood out in striking blue, it evoked great public interest. The Railways Department moved the carriage from centre to centre and parked it at night in local railway yards.[6]

Scrim put Ian Mackay in charge of the operation. This was Mackay's first step up the ZB managerial ladder. He had moved quickly through the ranks as an announcer. He would soon rank with Sheil as one of Scrim's two most valued associates. He and two colleagues spent thirteen very strenuous weeks showing the flag. As the sole announcer, he was on duty eighteen hours a day, seven days a week. He and his colleagues, he wrote later, travelled like lords and worked like slaves.[7]

The mobile station's progress through the North Island was well advertised over 1ZB and 2ZB. Starting in Rotorua on 2 June, it visited Hamilton, Whangarei, Te Kuiti, Taumaranui, New Plymouth, Hawera, Wanganui, Palmerston North, Dannevirke, Napier, Hastings, ending its tour in Masterton on 21 June. Mackay wrote that about 18,000 people went through the carriage during the first few weeks. Most provincial newspapers gave it a mixed reception. One exception was the *Hawkes Bay Daily Mail* in Hastings. By arrangement with the editor, Mackay visited the newspaper offices one evening while staff were at work and, using hook-ups, made a broadcast for people in the back blocks of Hawkes Bay. The editor wrote an editorial deploring the widespread newspaper hostility to commercial broadcasting, arguing that both media stood to gain from cooperation. This would have been music to Scrim's ears.[8]

Scrim was out of the country while the mobile station was touring the North Island. In February 1939 cabinet approved the prime minister's recommendation that Scrim visit the United States and Canada to study developments in public broadcasting. Scrim had not given up his dream of an academic qualification, and he carried with him an open letter from Savage commending him to any American university that would consider him as a candidate for a doctorate in philosophy. The letter gave a warmly appreciative account of his work as a missioner, broadcaster, and head of the national commercial broadcasting service, and the very high regard in which the government held him. There are no signs that Scrim made any use of the letter. It seems most unlikely that any recognised American university at the time would have accepted anyone as a PhD candidate – not even one with Scrim's experience of broadcasting – who had had no previous record of successful university study.

The visit was expected to take four months. Sheil ran the NCBS while Scrim was away. With his nose for public relations he arranged for the *Standard* to publish extracts from Scrim's letters to himself and to Lena Scrimgeour. Two of these were published in the *Standard* on 25 May and 15 June.

Scrim concentrated his visits on Los Angeles, Chicago, and New York. He visited broadcasting studios, recording units, film studios, and television studios. The scale of American operations overwhelmed him. He saw some 'marvellous' radio programmes.

Some had as many as seven or eight popular movie stars on a half-hour programme that cost $20,000 to produce. He was disappointed to find that few of these shows were recorded and were therefore not available on transcription services.

Scrim warmed to the friendly people he met, but he still liked 'our general tone much better', and 'he saw no studio he liked better for its size than our 3ZB'. He was impressed by the fact that people 3000 miles from Los Angeles, Chicago, or New York could hear programmes 'perfectly clearly'. He was impressed, too, with the way the broadcasting corporations dealt with news. Events of national and international importance were 'hot' news within minutes. Stations that gave time to controversial speakers gave people and organisations with differing opinions the opportunity of buying time to make their views known. Many shades of opinion found expression through broadcasting. Not surprisingly, he was impressed with Roosevelt's extensive use of radio hook-ups, noting its effectiveness in countering the views of a press that was 'violently against' his administration.[9]

The two highlights of Scrim's tour were being present for the opening of the New York World's Fair and being a guest of honour for Commencement at the University of California at Los Angeles (UCLA). The New York World's Fair announced to the world that the depression was over and that American technological innovation was ushering in the future. Scrim with everyone else was mesmerised by the first public television screenings that the Radio Corporation of America, RCA, broadcast from its studios in the Rockefeller Center. He did not mention this in either of the two letters he wrote home, but he dwelt on it in considerable detail in one of his autobiographical recollections written thirty-five years or more after the event. There are good reasons for doubting the accuracy of the recollections he recorded during his later years. One of these is a detailed account of a reception hosted by David Sarnov, the legendary president of RCA, at which Scrim was, so he wrote, an honoured guest. Perhaps in preliminary conversation Scrim might have said some self-aggrandising things about himself. Inviting Scrim to speak, Sarnov is said to have warned his guests mock seriously not to play cards with him. Scrim, he said, was a minister of religion and a card sharp who knew how to stack a pack. What stayed in Scrim's mind over the years was the shapely beauty of the troupe of Rockettes who, he wrote, also graced the occasion.[10]

★

Scrim claimed that he was the first foreigner to be interviewed on American television. He had been a believer in the possibilities of television since 1927, when he struck up a friendship with a university student who was doing some practical experimentation on cathode rays in the physics laboratory of Auckland University College.[11] He had kept up with experimental developments through his working association with Grainger and others, and from reports which the *New Zealand Radio Record* published from time to time. No doubt he had also discussed them with Savage, another broadcasting enthusiast. Scott Ramsay's report for the government in 1936 had discussed international developments in television. A television studio was planned for the broadcasting house which the government planned to build.[12]

Scrim's autobiographical piece shows him entering fully into discussions on technical aspects of the medium with his hosts. RCA had decided to transmit television on 450 lines. He credits himself as saying that a higher definition would be needed to compete with film. He knew, he has himself saying, that the BBC was going for 650 lines and he believed that the Americans should go for that, too. When British and other European countries began television on 650 lines or with higher levels of definition, American television images were seen to be inferior.[13]

Scrim's visit to Los Angeles was also ego enhancing. He was present at the UCLA Commencement when degrees were conferred on 3800 graduands. That is all that he recorded in the letter he wrote at the time. His autobiographical piece was, however, fulsome and, among other things, increased the number of graduands to 5000. It recalled that the president of the university had referred publicly to favourable comments about him that had recently been published in the *Christian Science Monitor.* A report in the newspaper had linked him with Father Coughlin and Dr Goebbels as one of the three greatest broadcasters of the age. In Scrim's recollection The *Christian Science Monitor* had presented him as a white knight in contrast to the fascist Goebbels and the neo-fascist Coughlin. But a search of the file of the *Christian Science Monitor* from the beginning of March until the end of June 1939 has failed to turn up the report that the president of UCLA was said to have been referring to. Perhaps the president had mistakenly attributed it to the wrong newspaper. Perhaps Scrim's recollection was of a report that had never been published.[14]

Scrim decided to shorten his trip by a month. He returned to Auckland early in June and held a welcome home rally which his colleagues organised in the Town Hall. The *Observer* reported that 2000 people were present for the week-day meeting, about as many, it said as would fill the hall for a wrestling match.[15] Savage or Lee, the two politicians with the ability to fill the Town Hall, would have been well pleased with so large an audience. But for Scrim, who in the past had drawn crowds of up to 7000 and who the previous October had attracted 4000, it might have been something of a let-down.

Hitler and Mussolini's aggressive actions in Europe were matters of growing concern to informed New Zealanders. Franco's rebellion in Spain became a burning issue from July 1936. Attitudes towards the Soviet Union were sharply divided. Most people who kept up with foreign events did so through their daily newspaper. Some read *Zealandia* or the *Tablet*, the Catholic weeklies. A very few read the largely left-wing *Tomorrow*. The communist *Workers' Weekly* had its following. Some were also listening to BBC news bulletins and commentaries from the YA stations, and both national services were taking their first steps to broadcasts commentaries by New Zealand speakers. Occasionally these commentaries sparked a critical public reaction.

At the end of 1937 the National Broadcasting Service had to justify two talks that had been broadcast from 2YA. In one, Walter Scott, a lecturer at Wellington Teachers College, had given a talk on international events in which he spoke about Italian bombing raids on Abyssinian tribal people. He deplored these attacks but also reminded listeners that other imperial nations were still using their military power to subdue native populations, instancing recent British bombing raids in India. There were calls for Scott's suspension as a radio commentator. Opposition MPs raised the matter in the House, but Fraser, speaking for the government, upheld Scott's right to free speech.

The other incident concerned remarks made during a Sunday evening religious broadcast by a Redemptorist Monk of St Gerard's Monastery, Wellington. The monk's scorching attack on Soviet communism prompted a range of responses from listeners. Shelley issued a statement which said that the monk had departed from the agreed purposes of religious broadcasts, which were that such broadcasts were to deal with matters of religion. We cannot say whether Shelley acted on his own initiative or had been nudged by Savage as minister in charge of broadcasting. Savage was thought to be attentive to the views of Archbishop O'Shea on the Soviet Union and on the pope's role in European affairs. But the monk seems not to have been suspended from making religious broadcasts. His right to free speech seems to have been upheld.[16]

Scrim had little to say on international affairs during the years before the outbreak of the war in Europe. His one reported reference to the deepening European crisis was at the time of Chamberlain's meeting with Hitler in Munich in September 1938. Scrim's anti-war sentiments were uppermost in his mind at the time. The audience cheered when he began an otherwise controversial speech in the Auckland Town Hall by paying what the *Auckland Star* reported as a 'warm tribute' to Chamberlain's 'efforts on behalf of peace'. This was not what the communist *Workers' Weekly* wanted to hear. 'Uncle Scrim,' it wrote, 'had fallen a victim to Tory ballyhoo'.[17]

It was 1ZB's 'History behind the Headlines' programme run by Kenneth Melvin that caused trouble for Scrim. This commercially sponsored programme became very popular from the time of the Munich crisis and was soon producing three sessions a week. A nervous government suspended it. There was 'always the danger of harm coming from statements made over the air on international affairs', Savage said. Liberal and left-wing listeners would have been surprised by the decision, but the only public criticism seems to have come from the *Workers' Weekly*, which deplored the decision as 'a victory for Hitler'. In a clear reference to its local ideological enemies, it claimed that nothing in the programmes would have offended the German consul, the editor of *Zealandia*, or friends of Chamberlain.[18]

These incidents highlighted the privileged status of Scrim's 'Man in the Street' session. The *Auckland Star* wrote in an editorial that the government was acting like its predecessor, indecisively and inconsistently. It did not interfere with programmes favourable to its policies, 'the glaring example' being broadcasts by the director of commercial broadcasting. But when the government was pressured by 'sectoral groups', broadcasts were 'modified or terminated'. The remedy, the *Star* said, was to allow all points of view to be presented with equal ability and frequency. It acknowledged that there would always be practical difficulties, but the BBC was showing that they could be dealt with effectively.[19] Mention of the BBC was a reminder to the *Star*'s readers that the government had rejected control by a broadcasting corporation when it set up the state-controlled broadcasting services. But it took some comfort from the fact that listeners to the YA stations were able to hear transcriptions of BBC foreign affairs programmes.

Scrim's 'Man in the Street' sessions remained an irritation to his opponents. The National Party and various newspaper editors were monitoring his 'Man in the Street' sessions week by week. Not until November 1939, however, did he create a public sensation in any way comparable to his broadcasts in April 1937 and August 1938. Large meetings of farming organisations were held in Wellington during the last week in November. Scrim's comments on the following Sunday evening gave offence.

A report in the *Dominion* claimed that Scrim 'had blasted the Farmers' Union and had had the audacity to say that they or it were Public Enemy No.3'. Scrim denied that he had made the remark. Mr J.J. Maher, a farmer from Mangaroa who would be the National MP for Otaki in later years, challenged Scrim to repeat what he had said before a supreme court judge of his choice, but Scrim did not respond to the challenge. The Farmers' Union lobbied other organisations to support its criticisms of Scrim. The Dunedin branch of the Watersiders' Union passed a unanimous motion of support for him at a stop work meeting.[20]

For as long as he had been controller of commercial broadcasting Scrim had been trying to resolve 1ZB's accommodation problems. On his return from the United States he presented Savage with what he at last thought was the answer. It was a departure from his solutions for station accommodation in Wellington, Christchurch, and Dunedin, all of which he had found by altering and refurbishing existing buildings. He had at first thought that 1ZB's requirements could be met in the same way. With officers from the public works department he had considered various properties but found nothing that would match his brief. Meanwhile the station's main site in Queen's Arcade had become seriously overcrowded and various other temporary sites had been added to it. Only purpose-built accommodation would do. A small vacant site in Durham Lane just off Queen Street gave hope. The Public Works Department bought it.[21] Savage sent Scrim's submission to cabinet for decision in June 1939.

Scrim was unlucky in his timing. Expenditure on the government's various capital works programmes was building up and, in July, cabinet ministers were disturbed to find that they did not have any overall control of the spending decisions of individual ministers. Savage was ill at home and Fraser was running the government when this record of spending decisions came to light. Fraser ruled that the 1ZB proposal should not proceed. Building new facilities in Waiouru for the army must take precedence.

Savage was furious when Scrim told him of the decision, and directed him to bring Paddy Webb to see him the next morning. Paddy, Savage said, was the only man he could rely on in the whole cabinet. Savage told Webb to get the decision reversed, and he told Scrim to talk to cabinet ministers who could be expected to support a lifting of Fraser's ban.

A complication in Webb's love life created an unexpected difficulty for Scrim. Parliament's Lothario was at that moment being pursued by a woman claiming that he had breached his promise to marry her. The Hon Mark Fagan, leader of the Legislative Council, visited Scrim at his home and put a proposition to him which, in the circumstances, he could not refuse. Would Scrim get Paddy off the hook by finding a job for the woman?[22]

The cabinet reconsidered the 1ZB project and approved it.[23] The *NZ Listener* for 14 November 1939 published an architectural sketch of the new station on its front cover.[24] It was the only government building to be built in Auckland during the war years. The decision brought continuing criticism from Opposition MPs and groups of Aucklanders who were convinced that other projects had a greater claim to government approval. But Savage had reminded his colleagues of who was in charge. Scrim had saved Webb's bacon by adding a female member to the staff of 1ZB. The one left empty-handed was Professor Shelley, who did not have a private line to the prime minister or to other influential cabinet ministers. There were 'wry smiles', Mackay recalled, when Wilson announced that the building of Wellington's Broadcasting House would not proceed.[25] The foundations for the building had been completed on a site behind

The new premises to be erected for 1ZB. (*New Zealand Listener*, 14 November 1939, Alexander Turnbull Library New Zealand & Pacific Collection S-L 1088-1)

parliament. Often flooded after storms and known to Wellingtonians as the fish pond, the foundations remained until the project was abandoned after the end of the war.

While Scrim was in America the government had set about preparing the country for the war in Europe that now seemed to be inevitable. Both broadcasting services were classified as essential national services, and were drawn into the deliberations of the government's Organisation for National Security.

With war in the offing Scrim had to come to terms with his pacifist inclinations. We cannot say how much soul searching, if any, this caused him. Nowhere in his later autobiographical jottings does he discuss his pacifism. The peace movement had strong roots in the Methodist church and other churches during his formative years as a home missioner. When Scrim shifted to Wellington in 1937, there was considerable public support in Wellington for the anti-war movement, but there are no signs that Scrim had any association with it. His views on peace and living in peace did not determine his stance as a public figure when the crunch came in 1939.

Scrim had arranged to hold a routine meeting of his senior executives and station directors on Saturday 2 September but the German invasion of Poland overnight gave it an altogether more urgent purpose. The task was to put the National Commercial Broadcasting Service on a war footing. The verbatim record of the meeting shows Scrim clearly in control of proceedings. He introduced most topics, ensured that his colleagues expressed their views, and steered discussion to the conclusions he wanted.

His opening remarks were a mixture of factual background and generalised comments that listeners to his 'Man in the Street' sessions would have easily recognised. As the head of a popular broadcasting service he was facing the prospect of being part of the government's propaganda apparatus during hostilities that he deplored. He told his colleagues that he would not 'resile' from his 'pacifism' but neither would he let his personal views 'colour his official duties'.[26]

His use of inclusive pronouns was clearly intended to persuade his colleagues to agree with what he was saying. He emphasised the irrelevance, in the context of a war in Europe, of anything that might be said and done in New Zealand. The time had passed, he said, when anything they could have done 'might have prevented a war or lessened its impact'. They knew, he said, that the outbreak of war 'won't be altered one iota' by what happens in New Zealand. It was 'practically impossible' to prophesy the outcome, and we should all be 'exceedingly thankful' that we are 'so far removed from the centre of the conflagration and could not feel its full effects'. These sobering remarks set a context for him to refer again to his pacifism. But no one's personal opinions, he insisted, not his any more than any of his colleagues, must be allowed to get in the way of their official duties.

With the high colouring that came naturally to him, he emphasised the imperative nature of the emergency regulations that the government was at that moment bringing into force. They were to be 'read, understood, and rigidly adhered to'. No one should mistake their overriding importance. Though published in a cyclostyled document, 'they are just as important as if written in the Prime Minister's handwriting and delivered to you personally by him'. They applied to everyone, and all officers of the commercial broadcasting services must stick to them. There were to be no 'free lances'.

In the vastly different circumstances in which they would now be working, all officers must be 'business-like and efficient' in the way they carried out their duties. They must do everything possible to maintain a mood of 'public calm'. He thought it inevitable that they would be required to broadcast 'a certain amount' of official propaganda. All countries did that during national emergencies. Even though, as colleagues, they 'might not be very pleased about it', they had a duty to carry out instructions.

The members of the meeting spent the rest of their time together working through what was to be done to ensure the security of station staff, studios, and equipment. Only authorised station staff were to be permitted 'to approach a microphone'. Announcers who were in the habit of ad-libbing during their sessions were to be 'extremely careful' about what they said in future. There was to be absolutely no mention of 'soldiers, or troops on the march or in camps etc'.

If the war were to spread to the Pacific, station directors might find themselves having to deal with the 'extreme situation' of an enemy attack on the country by sea or air. In such an event, the chiefs of the defence forces would use 2YA to broadcast a message to all stations to close down, and 'the men on the spot' were under instructions to close down 'within a second', without reference to anyone. That, Scrim emphasised, would be 'a very unlikely happening'.

The ZB stations worked well under these arrangements throughout the war years. There were a few occasions when some announcers had to answer for themselves to the official censor about ad-libbing. Ironically, as we shall see, Scrim would himself become the ZBs most persistent infringer of government instructions and wartime regulations.

There was good cooperation between the YA and ZB services. Scrim put aside any thoughts he had had about running a separate ZB news service. The ZBs took their news broadcasts from the YA stations. Both services broadcast the BBC's regular overseas news bulletins. Both services made a valuable contribution to the war effort by broadcasting official announcements issued by the Organisation for National Security, and through a steady stream of patriotic campaigns. At a time of national crisis, Scrim told his colleagues, there were to be no divisions between the commercial and national services, and 'no attempt to try to get things earlier or to get in on anything that is happening'. All that would be needed, he said, would be 'close cooperation' between the head offices of the two organisations. He did not see a need for points of contact between local ZB and YA stations, but anything that might be done locally 'could be mutually advantageous'.

The great public event in New Zealand during 1939–40 was the Centennial Exhibition, the impressive expression of national self-representation which opened in early December and ran for six months. The outbreak of war greatly reduced the number of visitors from overseas, but New Zealanders took it to their hearts.

Both national broadcasting services seized the opportunity to show how the new medium of radio broadcasting was enriching the lives of New Zealanders. The NBS set up a model studio which, with its large plate glass windows, allowed visitors to see what was going on in what became dubbed the 'goldfish bowl'. It originated a wide range of live studio programmes which were broadcast over YA stations. But interesting and innovative as it was, it was upstaged by 5ZB, the NCBS station.

Scrim had retained the mobile station for use as the NCBS flagship before decommissioning it as a radio station. 5ZB became the voice of the Exhibition. Each afternoon the station broadcast commentaries and interviews based on the Exhibition's offerings. It produced its own passing parade of entertainments. It regularly transformed moments in the life of the Exhibition, such as, for example, the arrival of the millionth visitor, into celebratory broadcasting events. Its report of each day's highlights was broadcast by all ZB stations every evening at 10pm. 5ZB did not broadcast any feature programmes itself. Ian Mackay was again in control, and he again lived in the carriage. After the Exhibition closed at 10.30 each evening he was the only person left on the Exhibition site.[27]

5ZB was one of the Exhibition's most popular highlights. A viewing platform alongside the carriage made it possible for visitors to see everything inside. Large crowds gathered on it each afternoon and evening, craning their heads to see what was happening inside the studio.[28] An early celebratory event was the prime minister's visit to the Exhibition during which he visited 5ZB and made a broadcast to the nation's schoolchildren.

Outdoing even that event was the public welcome to Fred and Maggie Everybody and Daisy Sproggins, aka Edward Howell and Therese Desmond and their daughter Madeline Howell. Edward had written and produced, and he and his wife and daughter were leading actors in the much-loved radio serial 'Fred and Maggie Everybody' which had been broadcast over the ZB network for a year or more. The Howells were the first of the ZB's visiting celebrities. They made a triumphal tour of the country in early January, visiting Auckland, Dunedin, and Christchurch, filling theatres wherever they went, and ending it in Wellington as the guests of honour at two wildly enthusiastic public functions. Scrim and 40,000 people welcomed them to the Exhibition for what was said to be the largest crowd ever to come together in New Zealand. That evening in a packed Majestic Cabaret, they were farewelled by the deputy prime minister, Peter Fraser and other cabinet ministers and civic dignatories. The Royal New Zealand Air Force band delighted everyone present with its musical entertainment. It had been a great day for the NCBS and for Scrim. But the *Dominion*'s stand-off continued. Next morning it published a full account of the evening function but did not mention

Public reception for Fred and Maggie Everybody, New Zealand Centennial Exhibition. (*New Zealand Listener*, 19 January 1940)

the midday function at the Exhibition nor the fact that the Howells had donated the total proceeds from their tour to the King George V Memorial Health Camp Fund.[29]

Even more impressive as an outside broadcasting event was the ZB relay broadcast of the national celebrations at Waitangi that Scrim and his colleagues organised and broadcast on 6 February. This called for prodigious feats of cooperation, organisation and timing from amateur and professional broadcasters.[30] Radio was adding new dimensions to people's lives. Scrim and the ZBs were leading the way.

The publication in December of Lee's 'Psycho-pathology in Politics' was a sensation. The *New Zealand Herald* published a transcript of the piece. Other newspapers quoted from it or summarised it. Savage was not named but the piece was unmistakeably an attack on him. To senior members of the Labour Party it was an unforgivable attack. Some members of the Auckland East Labour Party moved to have Lee expelled. The piece was brought formally to the attention of the party's national executive. Walter Nash asked Lee to resign as Parliamentary Undersecretary and, when he refused to do so, cabinet sacked him.[31] During the next three and a half months Lee and his

supporters were locked in a grim contest with the party leadership which ended with his expulsion from the Labour Party during its 1940 annual conference.

Members of the Parliamentary Labour Party were by this time anxiously concerned about Savage's health. He had belatedly had an abdominal operation in early August. The *Standard* reported that he was making a 'wonderful recovery', but Gervan McMillan, himself a medical doctor, was clearly sceptical. Members of caucus knew officially only what Fraser told the public: that the prime minister was making good progress and would soon resume his full responsibilities. Lee had been told by Kelliher a year earlier that Savage had a cancerous stomach ulcer, but he had not taken it seriously. He callously thought that it was 'Johnny Lee' who was the 'bad pain in the PM's belly'.[32]

Fraser was overseas from mid-October until Christmas Day. Politicians with long memories knew what had happened in 1906, when Seddon died, and in 1925, when Massey died. On both occasions the deputy leader of the party, and the man expected to become its leader, was overseas and was thus unable to be present in the party caucus for the election of the new prime minister. In 1906 the Liberals made what in effect was an interim appointment until Ward returned to the country, when he became prime minister. In 1925, with Downie Stewart overseas, the Reform Party caucus voted in Gordon Coates to replace Massey.

Fraser's absence added more spice to Lee's ruminations about a challenge for the leadership. But Lee's support within caucus, particularly from some ambitious new members, was not as firm or as wholehearted as he assumed it to be. There was widespread dismay in caucus over the publication of his piece on 'Psycho-pathology in Politics'. His dismissal as Parliamentary Undersecretary left him with things to explain to all his caucus colleagues. Savage was still alive though evidently mortally ill when Fraser returned on Christmas Day, and any possibility of an upset in the process of appointing a new leader of the party disappeared.[33]

Whether to expel Lee remained the focus of Labour Party attention. Lee's opponents argued the case for expulsion in the Auckland Labour Representation Committee, in the national executive, and at the 1940 party conference. Lee's supporters fought them all the way.

As the days rolled on toward the Labour Party annual conference, everyone knew that Savage might die at any moment. Each day, Lee noted in his diary, Savage's life expectancy was extended by twenty-four hours. On Saturday, 24 March, Lee and what he refers to in his diary as a majority of caucus met to discuss tactics for the annual conference which would open on the following Monday. During the meeting, a message for Lee was brought into the meeting room. It said that Scrim had rung to say that Savage had died. This was distinctly unwelcome news. It 'blew tactics to hell', Lee noted. It meant that the issue for caucus would be 'an election for PM in the fact of death'. 'The meeting decided,' his diary entry continued, 'that we had to allow ourselves to be nominated. We had brandies, three each, to celebrate Savage's death.' Lee thought he would emerge at least as a cabinet minister from a caucus vote. He later wrote that he 'never thought there was a chance of defeating Fraser'.[34]

But Lee soon realised that he 'got the report wrong'. We cannot be sure what it was that Scrim had said. Lee's diary entry for 23 March contains more than he included in the published version, which telescoped events. He corrected the entry to read that Scrim had rung up to say that his 'Man in the Street' programme had been put off the air, and that 'he was ready to go berserk the moment we desire it of him'. But Scrim's 'Man in the Street' session was not suspended until 2 April. It is clear from Lee's reference to Scrim's being ready to go berserk that he was in an emotional state when he rang. It is probable that he was wanting to tell Lee of the possibility that he would be put off the air as soon as Savage died.

The first day of the Labour Party Annual Conference was dominated by an acrimonious debate on a motion for Lee's expulsion from the Labour Party. Sick as he was, Savage had hoped to be able to be present to vent his anger at Lee, but was unable to do so. He was, however, represented by something that, in the circumstances, was even more powerful than his presence. Copies of his annual report had been distributed to conference members. But, as they discovered when the conference convened, Savage had added a handwritten addendum to his report. This he had intended to use in his conference speech, but he arranged for it to be sent to Fraser a few days before the conference. At what Fraser judged to be an appropriate moment in the debate, the statement was read to the conference.

'Regret to say,' it began, 'internal conditions had not changed since last conference.' For about two years, he wrote, his life had been a living hell. For the last year, 'in spite of last conference's decision', Mr Lee had attacked him through the 'public press with all the venom and lying innuendo of the political sewer'. These attacks had emphasised 'the worst points and said nothing about the strong ones'. Lee had spoken of him within the hearing of others as 'the silly old bastard up on the hill, the pathological case'. Savage then referred to Lee's articles in *Tomorrow* which, written for the most part during his illness, had tried to 'destroy me as a political force'. Were these, he asked, the acts of a loyal Labour supporter? And where did Lee's challenge leave him as prime minister? Was he to 'allow himself to be cast aside by a few conspirators in the ranks'? Or was he to face his challengers on the floor of the House, and if he is defeated go down in full view of the people?[35]

Wilson, the general secretary of the Labour Party, declared that the issue before the conference was not one of democracy but of party discipline. Did a member have the right to defy rulings of the conference and the national executive and attack the party leader in 'an anti-Labour paper'? The prime minister, he assured the conference, had been making a remarkable recovery before Lee published his article. Whether or not it was coincidental, Wilson asserted that Joe Savage had suffered a relapse since that time, and was dying. 'Jack Lee had stabbed him in the back.' Fraser took up this theme. 'It would have been more decent and honourable,' he said, 'for Mr Lee to have taken a revolver and shot the prime minister dead than to have tried to destroy him by spreading the idea that he was physically and mentally a wreck.'[36]

Lee defended himself forcefully, and his main parliamentary supporters – Barnard, Nordmeyer, McMillan, O'Brien, Barclay, and Catherine Stewart – argued against his expulsion. The motion was passed by 546 to 344.[37]

Lee returned to Auckland where, with some thirty or forty supporters, he held a meeting to discuss the formation of new political party. This evidence of personal support was very important to him. But he had not yet dismissed the possibility that the Labour Party might offer him an olive branch that he could accept. In the weeks and months to come he had some conversations that suggested that reconciliation might be possible. But the emotions that had been stirred by his dissident actions and his expulsion meant that he had placed himself beyond the pale. It would be nearly three years before Fraser exchanged words with him again.

Savage died in the early morning hours of Wednesday, 27 March. The news, announced to shocked conference members, brought proceedings to an early end. The nation mourned. Savage had come to be loved as a man of the people. A solemn requiem mass was celebrated in the Basilica of the Sacred Heart. An estimated 50,000 people filed reverently past his body while it lay in state in the vestibule of Parliament.

Shelley took personal charge of arrangements for the broadcasting of all events associated with the lying in state, the progress of the funeral train to Auckland, and the burial service. The funeral train carried the coffin on the main trunk line to Auckland, taking twenty-eight hours to do so and providing opportunities at twenty stopping places for thousands of people to pay their last respects, hear speeches, sing hymns and listen to solemn music played by local bands. The day of the funeral, Sunday, 31 March, was sunny and warm. An estimated 200,000 people lined the route taken by the cortege from the railway station to Bastion Point. Tributes of flowers and wreaths covered the burial site, 200 yachts and launches rode at anchor in the bay below. Bishop Liston conducted the committal service.[38]

Scrim was thinking about what he would say in his weekly 'Man in the Street' session from 1ZB that evening. Fraser, he remembered, spoke briefly to him as he was leaving the grave side. 'If you're broadcasting on Joe Savage, no politics.'[39]

# CHAPTER 10

# Testing the Limits

Fraser's warning to Scrim did not become public knowledge until 1971, when it appeared in *Scrim: Radio Rebel in Retrospect,* Les Edwards' biography of Scrim.[1] There is no way of knowing how accurately Scrim remembered what Fraser had said at the time or how accurately Edwards recounted what Scrim had told him. But the statement has the ring of truth and is consistent with the relationship that soon developed between Scrim and Fraser.

As acting leader of the party, Fraser was treading carefully during the week after Savage died. With Savage interred at Bastion Point, he had brought four days of public mourning to a successful conclusion. But it would not be until the following Thursday that he would know whether, as he hoped and expected, his caucus colleagues would elect him leader of the party. Fraser knew that some members would make a stand of principle, and he and his backers were doing everything they could to keep that number small. He was determined to ensure that Lee did not get favourable headlines during the interregnum. He knew that a great many listeners would be deeply impressed by what Scrim said in his Sunday evening radio broadcast. His warning to Scrim at the grave side was a reminder, should Scrim need reminding, to make Savage the sole focus of his talk. Fraser was letting him know in the clearest terms that he was now answerable to a new political master.

It is probable that Fraser's warning only strengthened Scrim's determination to link Lee with Savage in the talk he was about to broadcast. Scrim was second to none in his grief for Savage. But he was also convinced that the Labour Party had blundered in expelling Lee and should move quickly to repair the damage.

Taken at face value, the peroration of Scrim's eulogy was a soft-spoken appeal to the Labour Party to heal the rift that Lee's expulsion had brought about, to live and let live. In a way that listeners had come to expect, he grounded his remarks in his own personal experience. He wove Lee into his tribute by recalling that Savage had used Lee as his 'messenger' during the discussions with him in 1936 about taking charge of the government's commercial broadcasting service. Then Scrim appealed to New Zealanders to 'rise above the merciless bludgeonings of misunderstandings and not lose the services of two men who desired to serve the nation – one by death, the other by dissension'.[2]

Members of the cabinet were on their way to Wellington on the Limited, the overnight express train, when Scrim gave his Sunday evening broadcast and did not hear it. But they heard enough at stopping places to conclude that something would have to be done about it. At its meeting on Monday, 1 April, the cabinet suspended Scrim's 'Man in the Street' session until further notice. Fraser does not seem to have announced the decision. It was left to Scrim, answering a question from a journalist, to say that the prime minister had suspended the session.[3]

The suspension became a talking point throughout the country. Reports in the press generally thought Scrim's remarks were ill-judged. The *Dominion* – no friend of Scrim or the Labour Party – thought that, even by the standards of Scrim's 'not infrequent political utterances', he had 'gone too far'. He should have found another 'time and place' if he wanted 'to make a statement about Mr Lee's position'. The *Observer* said that Scrim must have known that 'any allusion to Mr Lee' would have been 'construed only as a deliberate gesture of defiance towards those members of cabinet whom he knew to be unfriendly to him'. The heading of the *Observer*'s piece struck a note of foreboding: 'Radio's Stormy Petrel. Mr C.G. Scrimgeour's Remarkable Past. What Will His Future Be?'[4] The only criticism of Fraser's decision came from the *People's Voice*. Almost the first decision of the new prime minister, it said, was to follow the example of Adam Hamilton and put 'Scrim off the air'. It 'was another milestone on the path to a Coalition' government.[5]

The 'Man in the Street' session was back on the air on Sunday 15 April. Three and a half decades later, Scrim claimed that he ended the suspension by simply putting himself back on the air. He was rewriting history. Fraser had been firmly in control throughout the episode. The suspension was discussed at the caucus meeting on Tuesday, 3 April, and the *Taranaki Herald*, briefed by Frost, the local Labour member, reported a summary of that discussion. Caucus, it said, decided to let the matter rest after a discussion that included a full consideration of the right of free speech.[6]

Scrim, however, was not prepared to let the matter rest. Ian Mackay, who was Scrim's closest associate during the last year of Savage's life and during the years he served Fraser and Wilson, later wrote that 'Scrim would not or could not accept that the Savage era died with him'.[7] An experienced head of a department would have deplored his bad luck in being landed with a minister he disliked but would have done what he could to establish a satisfactory working relationship with him, hoping for better luck next time. But Scrim was not an experienced public servant and he could not curb his emotions. He would not 'submit' to Fraser's authority'[8] and later heaped his criticisms of the Fraser government on Fraser himself. But that was a sign of his mistaken sense of his own importance. Fraser, unlike Savage, had no interest in commercial broadcasting and involved himself in its administration only when there were problems that required his attention. As wartime prime minister he had more important matters to attend to.

Fraser was well known for his ability to keep his private thoughts to himself. Scrim was never able to cite evidence of Fraser's malice toward him. When in 1975 Scrim and Lee were writing their joint memoir and would have happily made use of any scraps of information that would have vilified Fraser, Scrim accepted that there were none.

Wilson, who had day-to-day responsibility for broadcasting, remains a shadowy figure. Savage had brought him into the cabinet in November 1939 with some other Labour Party and trade union stalwarts he was relying on to frustrate his critics in caucus.[9] Wilson was not, and had never had been, an elected member of parliament. He had none of the political ballast that his parliamentary colleagues had built up over many years. His office in the legislative chamber building isolated him from his other cabinet colleagues. A large file of memoranda dealing with Scrim provides ample evidence of his frustrations.[10]

As the party president Wilson had led the charge against Lee at the 1940 Labour Party Annual Meeting. That was reason enough for Scrim to be very wary of him. But Scrim had even deeper reasons for resenting the transition to the Fraser government. He was entirely out of sympathy with the changed political leadership. Apart from the polite formal letter of congratulations he sent to Wilson when he was appointed minister in charge of broadcasting there were no signs of warmth in Scrim's dealings with him.[11]

Scrim saw himself as the decision-maker on all operational matters. Discussions between minister and controller – meetings which Wilson came to refer to as 'interviews' – seem typically to have taken place *after* Wilson had found it necessary to write to Scrim questioning or objecting to something he had done. It was not until April 1942, for example, that Wilson finally succeeded in getting Scrim to acknowledge that he must have prior ministerial approval for any broadcast he proposed to make that could raise questions about national security.

Their frosty relationship took its toll on both men. Wilson believed, with good reason, that Scrim was setting traps for him. His suspicions of Scrim's friendship with Griffin and Dyer intensified when he became aware of talk about communist infiltration of the National Commercial Broadcasting Service (NCBS) and about the setting up of a freedom radio station in New Zealand. When Wilson challenged Scrim over his friendship with Griffin and Dyer and said he was concerned that he might become a communist, Scrim replied blithely that he was just as likely to convert them. As late as November 1942, however, Wilson told the executive members of a Labour Representation Committee that he had 'no enmity toward Mr Scrimgeour', although he was 'unable to trust him'.[12] Scrim dismissed Wilson as 'a complete idiot'.[13]

The ZB stations adapted well to wartime conditions. Currency restrictions meant fewer American and more Australian programmes. Announcers on the early morning sessions became more careful with their ad-libbing. Aunt Daisy and Catherine Parr, with their unscripted sessions, earned cautions from the director of publicity. Kenneth Melvin, the popular 1ZB broadcaster, was criticised for not keeping strictly to his scripted talks in his commercially sponsored talks on international affairs and his programme was taken off. But it was Scrim himself who became the main offender. When the war broke out he had told his senior colleagues that they must obey government instructions even when they did not agree with them. But he exempted himself from that advice when Fraser became prime minister, and would be cautioned several times for breaching the wartime regulations. His first transgression, however, was a controversial 'Man in the Street' session which he broadcast without prior consultation with Wilson.

During his Auckland years Scrim had got to know some of the people in the health professions who were stressing the importance of preventive medicine and good eating habits in the cause of healthy living. With their advocacy went also criticism of the medical establishment in New Zealand. Scrim had criticised the New Zealand Branch of the British Medical Association in 1938 when it opposed the provisions for doctors in general practice under the Social Security Bill. He criticised it again when it resisted the government's proposal to extend the provisions of the Social Security Act to include the services of specialist doctors. When the Social Security Amendment Bill was about to be introduced in the House in 1941 there was some nervousness in government circles that Scrim might use his 'Man in the Street' sessions to attack the doctors' organisation. But Scrim's mind was moving in a very different direction.

In the early months of 1941 he launched a series of talks over the ZB stations on what modern medicine had to say about eating wisely and keeping fit and well. The talks usually went to air sometime between 11am and midday two or three times a week. They were given by Dr Muriel Bell, the recently appointed nutritionist in the Health Department, and by Dr Guy Chapman, whom Scrim had come to know in Auckland.

But Scrim had a message of his own about healthy living, and the 'Man in the Street' session gave him his platform. Without any advance notice, he began his session on Sunday, 4 May by saying that he was going to talk about 'Sex and its Contagious Diseases', and launched into his subject. Answering children's questions, he said, was the main part of sex education, and parents and teachers should deal with them in the same way as any other knowledge: truthfully, without being 'emotional or dogmatic'. What he went on to say would probably have been endorsed by parents with progressive views on child rearing, but the overwhelming majority of his listeners would have felt affronted that he should broach such an embarrassing subject in a session that had for many years been family listening in homes throughout the country.

There was a strong public reaction, and many listeners wrote letters of protest to Wilson. Scrim claimed that only a very small proportion were letters of protest, but Ian Mackay thought that little of the comment was favourable.[14] Wilson reprimanded Scrim for making the broadcast without his prior agreement, and instructed him not to make any more broadcasts on sex education.[15]

One thing that will have pleased Scrim was his inclusion in the fourth edition of Dr G.H. Scholefield's *Who's Who in New Zealand*. In the years since the publication of the first edition in 1908, *Who's Who* had become the authoritative compendium of the country's elites in public life. Scrim's inclusion at the age of thirty-eight was a clear sign of recognition. The men and women invited to be included in *Who's Who* wrote their own entries within guidelines set by the editor. Scrim took the opportunity to promote himself to Gisborne School for his schooling.[16]

It became a sore point with Wilson that, although the NCBS was playing its part in broadcast campaigns supporting the war effort, Scrim had not added his voice in support. He asked Scrim to do his bit. But Scrim's first response added another source of tension between them. Scrim's stand-offish attitude to the war changed when Hitler invaded Russia in June 1941. He immediately became one of the founders of the Society for Closer Relations with Russia, spoke approvingly of the Russian people at the society's inaugural meeting in Wellington on 21 July, and spoke enthusiastically about the Soviet Union on his 'Man in the Street' session.

Scrim had not informed Wilson beforehand of the role he was playing in the formation of the Society for Closer Relations with Russia or of what he intended saying about the Soviet Union in his 'Man in the Street' session. Nor had he submitted a text to the director of publicity to be censored before he broadcast it. Wilson was affronted. Scrim had ignored his clearly enunciated instruction that he must have ministerial authority for any talk he intended to make. He had also ignored the government's general directive that any broadcast that might have a direct or indirect bearing on national security must have the prior approval of the director of publicity. When Wilson learnt that Scrim planned to take a prominent part in a public meeting to launch the new society in Auckland, he banned the trip. Scrim retaliated in his 'Man in the Street' session by featuring a recording of the speech that his long-term friend, the Rev Percy Parris, had made at the Auckland meeting. He was provoking Wilson to take some form of disciplinary action.

Scrim cracked under the pressure of this battle of wills. In September he suffered what was referred to as a mild nervous breakdown, and was on sick leave for more than five weeks. His 'Man in the Street' sessions were suspended, and Wilson and Scrim gave different explanations for the decision. According to Wilson, Scrim had agreed with him that the sessions should remain in abeyance during his absence. Acting on their own initiative, however, Scrim's colleagues prepared a roster of speakers, headed by Lena Scrimgeour, to conduct the session in his absence. When this came to his notice, Wilson suspended the session.[17] It was also Wilson's understanding that, after his return to duty, Scrim had not asked for the session to be resumed. But Scrim was well aware of the public agitation for the session to be restored. It was in his interest to leave it for Barnes and Beckerleg and their supporters to be fighting against Wilson's ban. After he returned to work Scrim continued to be a regular speaker on the ZB morning 'reflections' session.

Wilson did what he could to help Scrim through his period of ill health. He 'sent him away for a holiday' and arranged for another public servant to accompany him and look after him.[18] Hal Pettit was probably the public servant who was taking care of him. In the absence of an official explanation of why Scrim was not at work, rumours began to circulate. One had it that the government wanted Scrim out of the way so that he could not make critical statements about the Social Security Amendment Bill while it was in the House. Another was that Scrim was about to be 'displaced by Mr Beau Sheil'. But the 'facts', the *Observer* reported, were that Scrim had 'had a mild nervous breakdown and had gone on a fishing trip to the Bay of Islands'.[19]

Scrim appeared again in public on 6 October as a member of the official party at the opening ceremony for the new 1ZB station. It was his first day back at work. The reporter for the *Observer*, who like everyone else at the opening ceremony would have been observing Scrim closely, thought he looked far from well. Scrim's contribution was limited to a few words of welcome in his role as chairman of the meeting.

During the two years that it was being built, the 1ZB building had become a controversial addition to Auckland's central city landscape. The official view, set out in Scrim's annual report to Parliament for 1941, was that 1ZB had 'probably the most up-to-date and efficiently designed studios in the Southern Hemisphere' and compared favourably with the latest trends in the United States and Great Britain.[20] The *Observer* marked the official opening of the new radio station with a captious two-page spread. 'No one,' it pointed out, 'would ever have the view of the building that had been presented in the architectural sketch that had been published in the *NZ Listener*' two years ago.[21] Only by standing in the back stalls of the nearby Mayfair Theatre and looking through several brick walls could one have that view. 1ZB's concrete shaft rose more than one hundred feet from the street and was as tall as the Milne and Choyce building. The 'huge' 1ZB sign to be erected at the top of the slab, lit up with neon lights, was an 'unnecessary extravagance that would cost almost as much as a state house'.

These architectural flourishes aside, the *Observer* saw the building as an example of modernist severity: 'all straight lines and angles' with a lavish use of glass bricks. 1ZB's accommodation would fill the first floor and mezzanine floor and would be 'replete with every modern convenience'. The 'opulent elegance' of the 'handsome ground floor vestibule' would impress the world with the importance of the NCBS. The main studio, eighty-four feet long and thirty-four feet wide, rose through the height of two floors, and had a built in electric organ for which the *Observer* hoped that an import licence had been arranged. The reception office and staff offices were on the second floor, as were the broadcasting studios and rehearsal rooms. There would, it wrote, be no need for concern about the health or claustrophobic feelings of staff in their new surroundings.[22]

Scrim's supporters were doing what they could to mobilise support for a resumption of the 'Man in the Street' sessions. Several of the largest trade unions provided the sinews of organisation and publicity through their networks of district and workplace branches. Beckerleg, Scrim's comrade from his Auckland days, mobilised support among 'people of progressive opinions'. With the suspension of the 'Man in the Street' session, he said, freedom of expression had been sadly reduced. A dominion-wide organisation was needed to 'protect what democratic liberties we have left' and extend them.[23] Wilson received a deputation from the Waterside Workers' Union early in 1942 to respond to their arguments for reinstating Scrim's session.

For Wilson, however, any thought of restoring the 'Man in the Street' session had been replaced by the more pressing issue of whether Scrim should be retained in his post or dismissed. In preparation for the meeting he wrote an aide-memoir for himself which listed the arguments for and against retaining him. There were more reasons for dismissing him than for retaining him, and they were more compelling. Scrim, Wilson wrote, was undoubtedly the best radio voice in the country. He professed to be helpful to the war effort. If he honestly did his best he would be a great asset to the government. But Scrim had filled the NCBS with his friends, with the object of tightening his control. Mrs Scrimgeour was 'fomenting trouble in the Happiness Clubs'. It would have been to Scrim's credit if he were to agree to 'a subordinate position under Shelley', but having said he would do so on £1000 a year, he had since refused.

The case against Scrim was much more compelling. He could not be trusted. He 'must to a great extent be responsible for the present state of affairs'. He was doing little for his £1500 a year. He was always obstructive if he did not agree with what was being required of him. He did things and then asked for approval. His management was incompetent, as illustrated by the service buying feature programmes through local agents instead of by direct purchase. 'If we are going to get rid of him, *now* is the time.'[24]

In March 1942 Scrim was in further trouble for breaching wartime regulations. Tens of thousands of American marines had recently arrived in the country and gone into camps near Warkworth in North Auckland and Paekakariki north of Wellington, where they completed their training for active service in the Solomon Islands. Their presence was a matter of national security and not to be mentioned in the press or over the radio. Scrim broke the embargo, urging listeners to 2ZB to offer hospitality to American servicemen they might meet. As controller of the NCBS, Scrim entertained the commanding officer of the contingent of marines, receiving in return ample gifts of American petrol. Petrol was strictly rationed but he does not seem to have had any qualms about retaining it for his personal use.[25]

Scrim had not cleared his announcements with the director of publicity. Wilson discussed the incident with Fraser, who authorised him to tell Scrim that he would be dismissed if he failed again to comply with the war regulations. 'How many times,' Wilson asked himself in a minute on his copy of his letter to Scrim, 'do we have to threaten him with dismissal before we do it?'[26]

Wilson was preparing the ground for the amalgamation of the two broadcasting services. In March 1941 he had directed officials of the National Broadcasting Service and the NCBS to consider possibilities for rationalising the two services and let him have their recommendations. They were also to report on the pressing matter of releasing radio technicians for war service. Their report, which he received in July, confirmed the view which, he said, he had long held, that the two services should be amalgamated 'under one Head'. That 'would release redundant technicians and clerical staff and would result in considerable financial economies'.[27] He took a paper to cabinet in November, and was authorised to consult Shelley and Scrimgeour with the aim of amalgamating their services. As a first step, all radio technicians were placed under the control of the NBS.[28]

Wilson thought that Scrim was initially in favour of some form of amalgamation. When, however, he raised with him the question of senior management positions in an amalgamated service, Scrim reacted angrily. Wilson asked Scrim how he would respond if Shelley or some other person were to be appointed director of the new organisation. Scrim, according to Wilson's notes, expressed the strong opinion that he should be director and was emphatic that he would not serve under Shelley at any salary, whether it was £1000 or £1500. He said 'in a threatening manner' that he would 'go to work on the wharf' if not appointed. If the government 'wanted a fight we could have it'. Later in the meeting he 'toned that down' and said that he would 'drop out of radio altogether' if he were not appointed director. The understanding was 'director or nothing'.[29]

Scrim's account of the meeting, written thirty years later, recorded the same conclusion but was more explicit about the options he believed to be available to him. He had told Wilson, he wrote, that he would not accept a subordinate role under Shelley. Wilson then asked him what he would do if the government dispensed with his services and he lost his 'highly paid position'? He was an ex-watersider, he answered, and he would go back to his old job. Wilson reminded him that the Waterside Workers' Union was a closed union, to which Scrim replied that he would have the choice of another 'very strong union'. There was the Freezing Workers' Union, of which he had once been a union delegate, or the Seamen's Union, 'for which even your friend Walsh wouldn't vote against me, or the Miners' Union'. Scrim added that he was quite sure that he would have been able to find work as a journalist in Australia at four times his New Zealand salary but had deliberately withheld that from Wilson.[30] Scrim thought he had won a victory over Wilson. But with his 'Man in the Street' session in abeyance he had lost his vital regular link with his supporters.

Scrim rang Barnes, president of the Auckland branch of the Waterside Workers' Union, applied for membership of the union, and was admitted at the next union meeting. Answering an inquiry from the *Herald*, Barnes explained that his union, together with most other working-class organisations had been agitating, without much success, for the return of the 'Man in the Street' sessions. The union was clearly happy to have Scrim as a member. Scrim also fielded questions from the *Herald*. He would not take up membership of the union 'straight away, but there is nothing like being prepared'.[31]

The Auckland watersiders' decision irritated the government. Webb, as Minister of Labour, told the *Herald* that he was 'surprised' that the union should 'block' applications from hundreds of Auckland men with young families who had been waiting for years to join it, yet give preferential treatment to a 'high-salaried officer of the broadcasting service'. The government was 'looking into the matter'.[32]

Pamphlets calling attention to the principles at stake were printed and distributed. Copies of two of these found their way into Scrim's personal archive. Both were anonymous productions. One marshalled quotations from various sources in defence of freedom of expression. The other was an early New Zealand example of a commentary based on the results of a survey of opinion. It expressed, it said, the opinions of a sampling of the opinions of 'a hundred people in trade unions, professions, and other walks of life'. Of those surveyed, it said, 70% believed that Scrim had been right to seek a renewal of his membership of the Waterside Workers' Union if his radio programme was to be discontinued, but 11% thought his decision would prejudice his future in radio broadcasting. A further 10% thought Scrim's concerns should take second place 'in the world today, when we are struggling for our very existence', and 9% had no opinion.

Of particular interest was the range of opinion expressed in the ten responses that were published. A returned soldier thought that if Scrim was looking for a change in occupation he would be better suited to a post as a radio director broadcasting regular propaganda to 'counter the poison that is coming over from Tokio'. A shop assistant thought that Scrim was 'the most genuine man in New Zealand, and should eventually stand for Parliament'. A cleric thought Scrim a showman, and he didn't like showmen. A theatre usher thought that perhaps the suspension of the 'Man in the Street' session was because Scrim was resisting the terms that were being offered him for its resumption. A charwoman 'agreed with Paddy Webb'. Why should Scrim be allowed into the union when hundreds of other men who need a job were kept out? An old-age pensioner 'loved listening to Uncle Scrim'. 'Please can anything be done be done to bring him back?' A postman said that though Scrim was earning £1500 a year

All Quiet on the Waterfront. (Gordon Minhinnick cartoon, *New Zealand Herald*, 13 March 1942, Alexander Turnbull Collection B-100-034)

he would now be earning a fortune under the terms of his initial contract. Are there many men, he asked, who would be so generous as to accept the lower salary.[33]

To counter criticism that its public campaigns on behalf of the war effort were not focusing sufficiently on the contributions of ordinary citizens, the government launched the We Work For Victory campaign early in 1942. The ZBs broadcast a series of programmes based on interviews with men and women in workplaces. Scrim saw the campaign as an opportunity to put together some programmes on a project that was close to his heart: the response of the Liberal and Labour parties to the rise of the Labour movement during the previous half century. Pember Reeves' industrial legislation had been a credit to the Liberals, and Harry Holland's advocacy during the 1920s had done credit to Labour. But the party under Fraser's leadership had lost its commitment to reform. Scrim's political intention was clear.

The first programme, on Pember Reeves, was broadcast over the ZB network. The second programme was to have been an ambitious thirteen-part series on Harry Holland. But only the first episode was broadcast. F.P. Walsh objected to it and complained to Wilson, who stopped the series after consulting Fraser. The director of publicity, Paul, was also consulted and agreed that the rest of the series should not be broadcast. The 'serial', he wrote, had 'no direct relation to the war but would not be helpful to morale'. It did not do justice to the man who made a very deep impression on our country' and it 'lacked dignity in places'.[34]

While interviewing for the We Work for Victory campaign, Sheil found an old miner in Waihi who, like Fraser, had taken part in the Waihi mine strike in 1912. Scrim and Sheil returned to Waihi, plied the old man with liquor, interviewed him, and Scrim made a recording of his graphic account of Fraser trampling on the Union Jack. The swear words that laced the old man's account meant that the recording could not be used in radio broadcasting. Scrim later wrote, however, that it had been enjoyed by groups of trade unionists he had played it to.

Wilson became aware of the recording and thought that it included an 'attack on the Prime Minister'. Asked for an explanation, Scrim wrote that he 'was at a loss to understand the allegation'. The offending record, he said, had been destroyed. It had been played once 'in the presence of Trade Union officials to illustrate the difficulties to be overcome in compiling the "Work for Victory" series'. It contained 'some very common but quite unbroadcastable swear words'. The prime minister might have been mentioned but Scrim did not remember anything 'that could be regarded as disparaging'.[35]

Fraser was seemingly unperturbed when he became aware of what the miner had said about him. Fifteen months later, after Scrim had been dismissed, he recalled the incident in the House. The miner, Fraser said, had not known that he was 'speaking for posterity'. Asked for his opinion of the 'Prime Minister, he had given quite an inaccurate but interesting and picturesque description, using some words that would not be found in the usual dictionary'.[36]

Scrim would play the record as one of the highlights of the final public meeting of his election campaign against Fraser for the Wellington Central seat in September 1943. He had deceived Wilson when he told him that the record had been destroyed.

A new sequence in Scrim's dramas began in November 1942 when, with other men in the forty-year age group, he was called up for military service. There was a regular procedure for deciding whether appeals should be made on behalf of public servants who were called up. Officers whose services were deemed to be essential were given the option of accepting the call-up or being exempted from military service.

When the public service commissioners received notification of Scrim's call-up, they discovered that, because of the unusual nature of the conditions of his appointment, a decision to retain him in the public service would have to be made by the government, not the public service commissioners. They referred the matter to the Wilson. Scrim called on Wilson during the ten days allowed for an appeal to be lodged against his call-up notice. Wilson told him that it was not government policy to appeal for public servants and he would not be appealing for him. He told Scrim that he could appeal on his own behalf but Scrim said that he would not be doing that. Scrim called on Wilson only once during the next two months, on 28 January 1943, and Wilson recalled that he said nothing about an appeal.[37]

Members of the cabinet were no doubt surprised to find that the government was required by the conditions of Scrim's appointment to decide whether he should be retained as an officer whose continuing service as a public servant was essential to the war effort. But they will not have had any difficulty reaching their decision. They had already decided that the NCBS would be amalgamated with the NBS in a reorganised broadcasting service and that Shelley would head it up. Wilson knew that Scrim would not serve under Shelley. The only matter still to be resolved was whether he should be offered a lesser position in the new organisation or have his employment terminated with a payment of six-months' salary. They expected that the military authorities, in consultation with Scrim, would assign him to duties in the armed services that would allow them to make the best use of his experience as the head of a government department.

Scrim decided to appeal on his own behalf. His senior colleagues knew what was afoot, and they made a submission to Wilson. It would emerge later in the year that most if not all of them had personal grievances against Scrim. But they knew that more than his call-up was at stake. The government's proposals for broadcasting transcended personal feelings. They needed Scrim as their bulwark against amalgamation and the loss of commercial broadcasting's separate identity. Their submission to Wilson expressed their concerns. Scrim's call-up, they told him, would have a 'seriously deleterious effect' on the efficient running of the National Commercial Broadcasting Service. They urged Wilson to appeal on his behalf. But Wilson was unyielding. He had told Scrim, he replied, that he did not think his services were 'essential to the success of the Commercial Broadcasting Service', and the government had not appealed.[38]

Scrim conducted his own appeal before the Military Service Appeal Authority on 23 February. Wilson, Barnett for the public service commissioners, and Elliott and Bullivant appeared before the board under subpoena. Walsh, president of the Federation of Labour, had also been subpoenaed but was not called.

Scrim told the appeal authority that he had expected the government to appeal on his behalf, and had been surprised when he received his mobilisation order early in February 1943. Wilson replied that it was not government policy to appeal on behalf of public servants. He had himself lost the services of two secretaries to military service. The second of these, however, had been replaced by an over-age man who was giving good service.

Scrim's animosity toward Wilson was clearly evident in their exchanges during the hearing. Scrim submitted that it was in the public interest that he continue to occupy his senior position in the NCBS instead of serving as a private in the army. Wilson countered by saying that neither the public interest nor the war effort would be affected if Scrim was released for military service. He said, too, that Scrim's alternatives were not as stark as he was presenting them. There were a number of positions in the army that could make good use of Scrim's experience. A broadcasting unit that the army would be setting up in the Pacific was one possibility. When Scrim asked Wilson if he would put in a good word for him, Wilson said that, as a Minister of the Crown, it would be inappropriate for him to do so.

The second arm of Scrim's appeal was that he should be exempt on grounds of hardship. His elder brother had recently died, leaving his sister-in-law to care for four children, and Scrim had a duty to help her out. The appeal authority dismissed the appeal, but responded to Scrim's plea of hardship by deferring his call-up until 15 May.[39]

As soon as the hearing was over Scrim began marshalling his supporters. He sent telegrams to Barnes and Matthews at the Trades Hall in Auckland and John Roberts at the Christchurch Trades Hall.[40] He told them that the appeal had failed because Wilson, hiding behind the military call-up, was trying 'to bring the ZB service under Shelley and get rid of me'. The fight 'was only beginning'. He told them that the Otago Trades Council had already pledged to take joint action against Wilson. He appealed to them to join in combined action.

Then he launched his own attack through an interview with a *Truth* reporter. *Truth* responded with an editorial alleging that Scrim had been 'railroaded' into military service. For six years *Truth* had attacked him unremittingly. Now it entered the lists as his defender against an oppressive government. Lee was also quick to assail the government over its handling of the call-up. It had not acted even-handedly, he said. It had used Scrim's appeal to exact vengeance on him. It should have dealt with Scrim's case on quite different grounds. No forty-year-old man with three children should be called up for military service. Lee agreed with the editor of *Truth* that Scrim had been railroaded.[41] That would be at the heart of the allegations that Scrim and his supporters would make against the government during the next six months.

★

Before the dust settled on this episode Scrim provoked a showdown with Wilson. There was nothing controversial in the programme he planned to broadcast on the evening of Sunday, 1 March. It was, in his words, an innocuous selection of scenes from English pantomimes strung together by a commentary. But he had deliberately not gained Wilson's prior approval to make the broadcast, and in applying for the director of publicity's approval he had not disclosed who would be presenting the programme. Paul had a standing instruction that the script of any programme to be broadcast by Scrim was to be submitted to him for his personal attention. But one of his officers cleared the script, thinking that it raised no problem. When, after the programme had been broadcast, Paul discovered what had happened, he immediately informed Wilson.[42] Wilson reported the incident to cabinet, which suspended Scrim for flagrant breaches of instructions.[43]

Wilson then made three decisions that caused shock waves for Scrim's senior colleagues. He suspended Scrim, changed the locks on his office, and instructed him to keep away from it. He appointed Greenberg acting controller. He gave a direction that Griffin was to be restricted to the public spaces of NCBS premises. He was taking no chances with Griffin. Wilson's distrust of Scrim had burgeoned into a belief that Scrim and Griffin were plotting to set up a freedom radio station to broadcast anti-government propaganda. Restraining Griffin's freedom of movement was a necessary foil to any such plot. But there was no plot. Thirty years later Ian Mackay explained what had been afoot. In moments of 'administrative stress', he would say to his colleagues, 'We'll have to start a freedom station, as in Europe.' That item of black humour had grown legs by the time Wilson had come to hear of it.[44]

When, sometime on Tuesday, Scrim returned from Auckland he found that he had been dispossessed of his office and that Greenberg, his former colleague, now director of detention camps, had been installed as acting controller. Scrim was furious. Greenberg's return was a clear sign of Wilson's intentions. Scrim had come to distrust Greenberg and spoke aggressively to him. Then he sent a message to Bullivant, directing him to tell Greenberg 'to get his running shoes' on. Greenberg would need them when he returned to his post. Things were going well for him, Scrim told Bullivant. He would be back in his office 'very soon'.[45] Greenberg rang Wilson and reported that Scrim had threatened him with violence.[46]

Scrim moved quickly to mobilise his defence. He gave an interview to a reporter and expressed disbelief of what had happened. He was, he was reported, at a loss to know what his 'disobedience' could have been. Except for the suspension of his 'Man in the Street' session two years ago, he was not aware of any ban on his speaking over the air. He had applied for the approval of the director of publicity because he was 'curious' to know whether the script raised any problems under the national security regulations. He acknowledged that he had presented the programme. He also spoke about possible political developments in the run-up to the coming general election. The political situation was 'very unstable'. If Labour went to the country on a 'National government platform' he might stand against the prime minister. But there were other possibilities. His name had been associated from time to time with the Social Credit movement, with the Democratic Labour Party, and with the Communist Party. He would make up his mind closer to the election.[47]

Scrim privately deplored what he considered to be the damaging influence that the power brokers of the labour movement were having on the Fraser government. But he appealed to them for assistance and got it. A phalanx of union and Labour Party leaders led by Walsh, president of the New Zealand Seamen's Union, intervened with the prime minister on his behalf.

The government, as it happened, was having second thoughts. Fraser had not been present when the cabinet decided to suspend Scrim, and he thought it had overreacted. He was conciliatory when he met Scrim's emissaries and the matter was quickly resolved. He released a statement for the press saying that the suspension was a misunderstanding. That had been cleared up and the suspension had been revoked. He 'anticipated efficient, harmonious working relationships with the NCBS'.[48] The price for Scrim was to release a statement he had been prevailed on to agree to during the negotiation. He would do 'all in his power to further the harmonious working of the service'. 'An erroneous impression' had been created about the possibility of a National government. He would regret it if his remarks were interpreted to be an attack on the government, for that was not what he had intended.[49] Fraser and Scrim were signalling to each other in code. Fraser was telling Scrim that he was sorely testing the government's patience. Scrim was saying in return that he would be waiting for Fraser when he called the general election.

Newspaper editors scorned the government's handling of the affair. Scrim, the *Auckland Star* wrote, had been appointed for political reasons, and his 'Man in the Street' session was now suspended for political reasons. The *Press* saw the whole affair as evidence of administrative disorder and failure at the centre and at the top. The government had been slow to act, and when, belatedly, it did, it failed 'even to move with enough care to avoid political humiliation'. *Truth* said that a craven government had left it to the Military Appeals Tribunal to 'railroad' Scrim into the armed forces. The *Observer* said, 'No one comes out of it with credit. . . . How Mr Scrimgeour can accept reinstatement, after his public humiliation, is a monumental puzzle.'[50] Minhinnick in the *New Zealand Herald* sniffed the political breeze in a cartoon that hinted at the political dangers Fraser now faced from Lee, Scrimgeour and Langstone, who had recently parted company with the government over his grievances.[51]

The crisis had revealed strains in Scrim's relationships with his NCBS colleagues. The petition that Bullivant had addressed to Wilson at the time of Scrim's call-up had been an impressive display of loyalty. But it seems that Scrim's subordinates signed with varying degrees of conviction. At least a couple of his senior colleagues had not signed.[52] Scrim had subsequently told Bullivant that one of those who had

Three Live Ghosts. (Gordon Minhinnick cartoon, *New Zealand Herald*, 4 March 1943, Alexander Turnbull Library New Zealand & Pacific Collection N-P-1630-4)

not signed was 'not much use to me'. Loyalty to himself was always Scrim's litmus test.

Bullivant was one of Scrim's long-standing colleagues who now found himself with a conflict of loyalties. He had been living with a hurt. He had worked with Scrim from the early days of the Friendly Road. Scrim had promised that he would appoint him deputy controller but had not done so. Bullivant weighed up the pros and cons and decided that his commitment to the NCBS was more important to him than his loyalty to Scrim. He approached Wilson, who agreed to receive a confidential letter from him.

Bullivant's letter, when written, was dated 14 April, some six weeks after Scrim's suspension had been lifted. He did not discuss his personal situation. He wanted Wilson to be aware of a long-running saga at 3ZB that had centred on Harry Bell, the station director. He refrained from any comment on Bell. He was writing, he said, to 'indict Scrim's administration'. He had made Scrim aware of Bell's situation in February 1942 and Scrim had rebuked him for doing so. Scrim had said at the time that 'the matter was in hand'. It had resurfaced in head office in February 1943, when Scrim had again told him that 'the matter was in hand' and that 'he had talked to the public service commissioner about it'. But when Bullivant had raised the matter with the public service commissioner he found that Scrim had not made him aware of it. 'There was a story abroad,' Bullivant added, 'that Scrim would not act against Bell because Bell had something on him.'[53] Bullivant was letting Wilson know that he was prepared to testify should the government take disciplinary action against Scrim. He was also being careful not to compromise himself in Bell's eyes should Bell be subjected to disciplinary action.

Wilson had also washed his hands of Scrim. His earlier reports to cabinet had kept open the very slim possibility that Scrim might serve in the subordinate position of controller of commercial services The paper he took to cabinet in March 1943 no longer included that possibility. A note to the list of senior positions stated that: C.G. Scrimgeour's appointment would be terminated with six-month's salary on full pay.'[54]

Scrim's accord with the government held for not quite three months. On 31 May he wrote to Fraser to complain that, though he was acting in good faith and keeping to the agreed terms of the 'covenant', people acting for the government were acting as if they had not heard of it. It seemed to him that he had 'misplaced his trust', and he asked Fraser to confirm the understandings that the government had entered into with him. Specifically, he wanted Fraser to assure him that his military service would be limited to one month a year, that his services and the services of the NCBS would be 'fully utilised in the war effort', and that, if he complied with the conditions of the agreement, his appointment as controller of the NCBS would be renewed in November for a further three years.[55]

Because the letter raised matters that were new to him, Fraser informed Scrim that he was seeking comment from the Labour Party and union leaders who had intervened on his behalf. Fraser soon discovered, however, that Scrim had sent copies of the letter to the press and to the Leader of the Opposition before sending the letter to him. What had seemed to be private correspondence was in fact a public document. For their part, too, Walsh and his senior trade union and Labour Party colleagues were unimpressed with the case that Scrim was attempting to make out. Walsh replied to Fraser with a point-by-point rebuttal of Scrim's claims. At no stage in the discussions, Walsh wrote, was Mr Scrimgeour given an assurance that he would not be called up for military service. Nor was he told that, if called up, his military service would be restricted to one month a year. Walsh repudiated any suggestion that he or any of his colleagues had told Mr Scrimgeour that he would be given 'preferential treatment'. On one matter, however, they had given Mr Scrimgeour wrong information. But they later told him the correct position, which was that men with three children were eligible for overseas service.

Walsh pointed out that the terms of agreement to which Mr Scrimgeour had given his 'unreserved assent' were significantly different from the list of conditions set out in his letter to the prime minister. Mr Scrimgeour had told them that if reinstated to his position, there 'could be some complications because of his previous disagreements with the Minister of Broadcasting'. They had assured him that, if at any time he thought he had a grievance and was not being dealt with justly, they would be prepared to take the matter up with the government, in the same way they would for anyone else. But they had been careful not to offer to act as a disputes committee. That was the prerogative of the government. They told him that, so long as he worked to the satisfaction of the government, they did not 'know of any valid reason' why he should not be reappointed to the position of controller in November. They had also told him that under the Occupational Re-establishment Emergency Regulations he would automatically be entitled to resume that position after he had done his military service.[56]

Fraser referred Walsh's letter to Cornish, the solicitor general, and asked him to comment on the applicability of the Occupational Re-establishment Emergency Regulations. Cornish did not endorse Walsh's interpretation. In his opinion the regulations were complicated and in one important respect anomalous but did not bind the Crown. Under the terms of his appointment, Scrimgeour held his position during the pleasure of the governor in council. The governor in council could 'legally dispense with his services, and there was nothing more to be said'. Any obligations that the emergency regulations might impose were 'purely moral in character'.[57]

Since writing to the prime minister on 31 May, Scrim had actively pursued his concerns in other quarters as well. At his request, his solicitors had tried unsuccessfully to get the Military Service Appeal Authority to rehear his appeal. He had also made representations to his local MP, Walter Nash, who had taken them up with Fraser. This had been Fraser's 'first contact' with Scrim's case. He referred Scrim's representations to the military authorities, and asked them to take particular note of his family circumstances and to give him 'every consideration within the law'. The result was that the date for Scrim's mobilisation was deferred to 22 June.[58]

Then Scrim took the step that brought about his demise. He wrote a letter to the *Evening Post* attacking the minister in charge of broadcasting and the prime minister. His letter outlined his case against the government, and asked: 'Is this not a case of discrimination and victimisation at its worst?' A Minister of the Crown, he claimed, had 'railroaded' a public servant into the armed services 'on no grounds that would be supported by public opinion', and the army regulations would stifle his attempts to protest against the injustice he had suffered. He also asked if these actions against him were in any way influenced by his decision to stand for Parliament.

Scrim had crossed the line that no public servant can cross with impunity. He had very publicly accused the government of foul play. But his reasoning did not match the strength of his emotions. The *Evening Post*, knowing full well what it was dealing with, printed the letter prominently on its national news page, accompanied by rebuttals by the minister in charge of broadcasting and the prime minister.

Wilson was 'surprised' by Scrim's public attack on him. Scrim, he wrote, had undertaken to work harmoniously with him, and had not made any 'representations' to him since he entered into that undertaking. He was 'astounded' now to learn through the press that he had allegedly discriminated against Scrim and 'railroaded' him into military service. There was 'no truth' in these assertions.

Fraser explained that his only involvement in Scrim's case was to have the armed services consider the representations that Walter Nash had passed to him on Scrim's behalf. It was 'unfair and slanderous' to insinuate that 'senior military officials would be parties to discriminatory behaviour against Mr Scrimgeour'.

Wilson had been proceeding on the assumption that an acting controller would be appointed to replace Scrim. But the government was now presented with a wholly different matter. Scrim's actions were grossly insubordinate. He did not hold his position as of right but at the pleasure of the governor in council. There were compelling grounds for his dismissal. The solicitor general advised that, if Scrim were to be dismissed, he did not have a legal right to be reinstated as controller after he had completed his military service. But the government would have to act swiftly. If Scrim were still controller of the NCBS when he went into camp on 22 June he would have the right to be reinstated when his military service was over.

Fraser acted. On Friday 18 June, members of the cabinet meeting with the governor in council 'revoked and determined' Colin Graham Scrimgeour's appointment as controller of the National Commercial Broadcasting Service with immediate effect. Wilson then wrote to Scrim to inform him of the decision.[59] According to newspaper reports, Scrim received his letter of dismissal at ten minutes to five in the afternoon of his last day in the office before going into military camp.

Scrim responded with a call for a royal commission to inquire into all the circumstances surrounding his dismissal.[60] But there would be no commission of inquiry. The Federation of Labour had closed ranks behind the government. A meeting of Wellington Trades Council delegates overwhelmingly supported a resolution approving the government's decision to dismiss him.[61]

★

There was to be one last twist in the drama. Sometime before he was dismissed Scrim held a convivial party in his office for one of his public servant friends who was going into camp. Because it was one of Scrim's parties it included something out of the ordinary. He surreptitiously recorded moments of the party, intending to give his friend the recording of proceedings as a keepsake.

Sometime after the party, Scrim was surprised to discover that a recording he had made of the party – about an hour's playing time on a record player – had somehow found its way into Wilson's ministerial office. Scrim regarded this as an act of treachery. There is no record from the time of who Scrim thought might have committed this act. Thirty years later, however, when he was working on his autobiography he thought it might have been either Bullivant or Greenberg. Journalists had a field day when the news got around that the record was in Wilson's office. There were reports of a steady stream of church people and trade unionists being invited to the minister's office to listen to the record. Opposition MPs were all ears and attention. Rumours abounded.

More that a month after the party, the *Observer* discounted what it referred to as the 'more extreme interpretations' and gave its account of the 'facts about the Scrimgeour records'. Anyone, it wrote, who had been to a 'fairly alcoholic send-off' would recognise its tone. 'There was a good deal of robust masculine language, and some bacchic admonitions.' But, contrary to some speculation, there was not one derogatory reference to the government or the prime minister. In fact, neither was mentioned. There was nothing 'really objectionable' in what Mr Scrimgeour had to say, which was 'modest enough'. The *Observer* thought that more questions might be raised for the government by the place where the party was held than by the nature of the party itself.[62]

When, on 10 August, the broadcasting estimates came up for consideration in the House of Representatives, Polson led the debate for the Opposition. He wanted to be informed about the 'mysterious record' that seems to have been made of a function in the NCBS and was now held by the minister of broadcasting. With the general election not far off, Polson was hoping that the government's explanation would provide Opposition MPs with some good knocking copy for use on the hustings.[63]

Fraser saw Polson off. He was surprised, he said, that this matter had been brought up. It placed him in 'a delicate situation' now that Mr Scrimgeour had announced his intention to stand for Wellington Central. Drawing on his authority as prime minister and as the keeper of Labour's puritan conscience, he denigrated the maverick ex-controller to an attentive House. Thanks, too, to the popularity of parliamentary broadcasts and the power of 2YA's transmitter, he had a large radio audience throughout the length and breadth of the country. With a general election a little more than six weeks away it was good politics.

Mr Scrimgeour's dismissal, Fraser said, was simply a matter of public service discipline. The farewell party the ex-controller had run in his office was further evidence of his 'complete unsuitability to be the head of a government department'. The function, 'a drunken orgy', had been held in the head office of the National Commercial Broadcasting Service. Worse: for some 'strange psychological reason' that 'people were at a loss to understand' a recording had been made of the proceedings. No person who 'propagated the filth on that record was fit to be the head of a government department.'

Fraser accused the Communist Party for the part he claimed it was playing in Mr Scrimgeour's activities. Fraser's opposition to the New Zealand Communist Party was well known. For more than twenty years he had staunchly opposed allowing members of the New Zealand Communist Party to become members of the Labour Party. In more recent years the government had waged a campaign against communist infiltration in the industrial movement. Communists, he claimed, had been trying to infiltrate the NCBS, and the prominence of 'certain communists' in Mr Scrimgeour's electorate campaign committee persuaded him that they were being to a degree successful. It was all, he said, 'deeply disturbing'.[64]

No one challenged the prime minister's statement. Lee made a restrained speech which raised no points that called for a reply from government speakers. Doidge hoped that, with the controller's dismissal, the two separate broadcasting services would be brought together under Professor Shelley's control.[65] Government and Opposition were largely agreed.

The Wellington Trades Council passed a motion approving the government's action in dismissing him. The *Observer*, which in the past had balanced its criticisms of Scrim with some acknowledgement of his success as controller of the NCBS, confined itself to the political consequences of the decision.[66] Scrim's senior colleagues kept their heads down. It would have been improper for any of them to make a public comment.

The government disbanded the NCBS and integrated it into the National Broadcasting Service. Shelley made regular visits to the NCBS head office, where he presided over a committee comprising Duff, Kilpatrick, and Mackay. Mackay wrote in his unpublished memoir that they all got along well together. He believed that Shelley's own operation 'had something of a Reith atmosphere about it . . . But he was quite different on our premises and would concern himself with our problems with a great deal of chivvying and joking – we scored some notable successes.'[67] The government included clauses in the Statutes Amendment Bill, 1943, to enact the necessary legislative changes. Mackay was appointed to the senior position in the commercial division of the National Broadcasting Service. He enjoyed Shelley as a person, but he and his commercial colleagues 'felt themselves to be very much the junior partners in the amalgamation'. He chafed under what he thought of as an unimaginative organisation.[68]

Nearly forty years later, Ian Mackay recorded his thoughts about Scrim in his unpublished autobiography. From Mackay's early years in the Nelson Radio Club until Scrim's dismissal, the 'chief' was the dominant presence in what Mackay wrote. Scrim 'had that indefinable "something" that made him stand out in the crowd', Mackay wrote. He was 'the most influential man in the country' during the depression and the early years of the Labour government. He revolutionised New Zealand broadcasting. During the early days of commercial broadcasting his staff 'worshipped him'. They found him 'stubborn, not short of courage, a born salesman, a good organiser, and a complete enigma'. He would be 'all sweetness and light' with his soft spoken voice, and then, without warning 'shout like a bullocky'.[69]

He showed himself to be a poor judge of character. Some of his appointees performed 'rather poorly', and by condoning their poor performance he allowed resentments and opposition to build up among 'young ambitious' colleagues. His willingness to 'take on lame dogs' was also resented. 'Near the end of his time,' Mackay wrote, Scrim 'was standing almost alone'.[70]

Mackay asked himself if it had been from a lack of good advice that Scrim had failed. 'That, he thought, was not quite the right question to ask. He doubted if anyone 'really "advised" Scrim'. Sometimes Scrim sought advice, more, however, to be polite than because he was interested in the reply. He was seeking 'endorsement of his own views rather than expressions of opinion'. Those conversations could be frustrating because 'he did not place all the facts on the table'. Mackay did not think that Scrim deliberately set out to deceive his friends. It was 'just that he was singularly confident in his own ability'. Mackay's sense of disappointment was palpable. Scrim 'built the commercial broadcasting service', then 'he destroyed it'.[71]

# CHAPTER 11

# 'Fighting Frazer'[1]

Scrim was the only permanent head of a government department ever to be dismissed from the New Zealand public service. There had been faults on both sides. Wilson had not been able to manage a less than cooperative Scrim, but Scrim had provoked the government into dismissing him. Clearly, too, he had alienated the influential members of the Labour Party and the Federation of Labour who had rallied to support him in May but did not assist him in August.

Nor did Scrim do anything to smooth his transition into the armed forces. It was well known that there were non-combatant positions in the armed services that senior public servants were well qualified to fill. Wilson was grandstanding when he told the Military Service Appeal Authority that it would be improper for him to be in any way involved in facilitating such an arrangement for him. But ministerial intervention would not have been needed. The military services had procedures for matching the expertise of skilled recruits. Scrim's colleague, Sheil, had recently been called up and was serving as a squadron leader in a non-combatant position.

Behind the scenes Scrim's solicitors were doing what they could to have the military service authority's decision revoked. For his part, Scrim played the role of victim, likening himself to Lawrence of Arabia, the legendary figure of the years between the two world wars. Lawrence had been spurned by the British authorities despite his celebrated successes during the First World War and, by his own decision, had ended his days as an AC2, the lowest rank in the Royal Air Force. Scrim, in his own opinion, had also been spurned. He would do his war service. But he, too, would insist on being an AC2 in the Royal New Zealand Air Force. Scrim was being driven by his anger.

It was a mark of Scrim's egotism that he should expect other people to see his world and his concerns the same way that he saw them himself. He had never been able to stand outside himself and try to imagine himself as others might see him. By what stretch of imagination did he equate his situation with Lawrence's?

Scrim had been required by the decision of the Military Service Appeal Authority to report to Linton Camp in early June. It had been open to him to apply to serve in some other military service should he not want to enlist in the army. He had not done anything to exercise his choice before 8 June when he received his call-up papers directing him to report to Linton Camp, a date that was soon after rescheduled for 22 June out of consideration for his personal circumstances. Sometime after that he sent an undated application to the Air Department to join the RNZAF. The Air Department informed him on 21 June that his application was out of time. He needed the written consent of the army authorities before the Air Department could consider it.

Fraser was monitoring Scrim's enlistment. On the evening of 23 June he rang Air Commodore Isitt, who told him that he had spoken to Scrim in terms of the Air Department's advice to him of 21 June. He also told Fraser that he had informed Scrim's solicitors that the Air Department would enlist Scrim if the army released him.[2] Fraser had a reputation for ringing officials and challenging them to justify administrative decisions, but in this instance there was no scope for prime ministerial intervention, even if that was what he might have had in mind. Scrim's future in the armed services was at that moment in the hands of the army department, which was yet to make a decision on his belated application to be transferred to the air force.

In recollections written some thirty years later Scrim said that an 'unidentified colonel' rang one of his solicitors and said that he was to proceed to camp. That, Scrim wrote, was Fraser's last ditch attempt to get him into the army and posted for active service in the 10th Reinforcements after a short period of training.[3] He recalled that he went immediately to see Air Commodore Isitt and told him that he wanted to enlist in the air force 'on the lowest rank'. Scrim and Isitt had known each other since Scrim's flying days in Auckland, and Isitt had examined him for his pilot's licence. Isitt's offices and the offices of the NCBS from which Scrim had just been dismissed were both in the Government Life Building. According to Scrim's account, Isitt swore him in on the spot and rang Scrim's solicitors and told them what he had done. But Scrim's account telescoped the sequence of events. The official record of Scrim's enlistment shows that he was not sworn into the air force until 5 July 1943.[4]

Scrim was in a heightened emotional state when an air force medical board examined him on 1 July. He told the board that he had been experiencing 'fits of shaking for no apparent reason', and was concerned about heart palpitations and his thyroid gland. The medical board's report noted that he had an enlarged thyroid but recorded that his heart and lungs were normal.

Scrim's later accounts of this period of his life emphasise the victimisation he believed to have been dogging him. He believed he was a marked man. Affixed to his personal file, he claimed, was a brightly coloured identification sticker which indicated that whenever he was to be transferred from one camp to another he was to be examined by a medical board and the results were to be sent to the prime minister. The unstated purpose, he claimed, was to have him reclassified A1 and therefore fit for active service overseas. Scrim also claimed, erroneously, that Dr Charles Burns was the doctor in charge of the medical board that reviewed his initial medical examination and, equally erroneously, that Burns was Fraser's personal physician, implying that Burns was part of Fraser's conspiracy against him.

None of these assertions is confirmed by Scrim's medical records. The first army medical board that examined him early in 1943 had classified him A1. There was some doubt about that classification, but a second army medical board re-examined him in June and confirmed the A1 classification. When, however, he was examined by an air force medical board on 1 July 1943 he was reclassified B2HS, which meant that he was not to be posted for active service overseas. The lower classification will have reflected Scrim's deteriorating emotional state. There is no sign on Scrim's personal file of anything having been affixed to it to distinguish it in any way. Dr Charles Burns' signature does not appear on any of his medical board reports. Scrim was examined by two medical boards during his time in the air force, one at the beginning of his service, the other in June 1944. While he was stationed at Levin he had two short spells of sickness and received medical care. His second medical board recorded that his cardiac and respiratory systems were normal and his heart was not enlarged. He had an enlarged thyroid but there were no signs of hypertension.[5]

*

In his interview with a journalist in February, Scrim had said that his name had been linked with a number of political parties, and he mentioned the social credit movement, Lee's Democratic Labour Party, and the Communist Party. He was trailing his coat. When, in July, he announced his candidature for Wellington Central, he stood as an independent. He was mounting a personal crusade against Fraser. He would not share it with any party or politician. Most of what he would say was in line with what Lee's party was advocating. But Scrim would not allow himself to be seen merely as one of Lee's associates, much less as one of his subordinates. Any sort of understanding with the Communist Party was out of the question. The Communists had thrown their weight behind the Labour government after Hitler invaded the Soviet Union. Scrim had turned to his mates for support, among them Dick Griffin and Jim Dwyer. Griffin chaired his organising committee and Dwyer was one of its members. That's what mates did for one another. They decided that their belief in Scrim was greater than their loyalty to the Party. The Party cancelled their membership. The Party also had a cut at Fraser for what he had said about Communists and Communist influence in the House. The prime minister 'well knew', it said, that the New Zealand Communist Party supported the government in fighting Nazism and fascism and was 'working for the return of government candidates in all electorates, including his own'. There were no members of the Communist Party on Mr Scrimgeour's committee. The Party did not 'admire' everything that the prime minister did or said, and instanced as 'nonsense' his recent allegation of a Communist plot to set up a so-called 'Freedom Radio'. But the Party's course was clear. It was mobilising support for the government's return to power.[6]

As a military serviceman, Scrim was allowed to be released from duty during the formal election period. One of the conditions of his leave prevented him from wearing military uniform when he was campaigning. Scrim infringed that restriction, and so also did other members of the armed services who were standing in the 1943 election. Lena Scrimgeour directed Scrim's campaign during the six weeks before he was released from camp. She entered the public lists with a firmly stated letter, which *Truth* published, setting out her response to the 'numerous rumours' which purported to show that her husband 'was a dreadful sort of person'. 'She could see the prime minister losing his prestige as well as his seat' unless he had 'ammunition more solid than rumour with which to fight my husband in the coming election'.[7]

On the eve of going into Linton Camp Scrim made a public statement giving his reasons for standing against the prime minister. He had intended to stand for Parliament, he now said, in 1935. But Michael Joseph Savage had urged him to continue his radio campaign 'for an enlightened public opinion'. The 'progressive policies' he wanted to promote had been 'constantly opposed' by Mr Fraser and his minister in charge of broadcasting. His differences with the government, however, were 'far more deep-seated than arguments about broadcasting policy'. He was standing against Mr Fraser because the principles he represented were national rather than local issues, and because Mr Fraser was incapable of providing the inspirational leadership needed 'to achieve a maximum war effort from all sections of the community'.[8]

Everything we know about Scrim in the months leading up to the general election and during his election campaign shows him to be living through a time of heightened emotional stress. For those closely associated with him his campaign was a month of memorable political theatre. For Scrim it was cathartic.

He remained in touch with Lee. Bill Sutch advised him on economic policy and foreign affairs.[9] He ran a vigorous, innovative campaign. For his headquarters he leased rooms in a Chinese laundry in Kent Terrace, from the roof of which he flew a long streamer announcing 'Scrim Will Fly In'. He made a personal appeal to 'Dear Friends' through a one-page handwritten letter which was widely distributed in the electorate. He made good use of handbills and flyers to publicise his campaign messages. He circulated mimeographed typescripts of his campaign speeches. He bought advertising space in the *Dominion* and *Evening Post*, presenting readers with a relaxed photograph of himself framed with pithy political messages: 'Vote for Scrim and let the Labour Movement Live Again'; 'Split Fraser off from the Labour Movement'; 'Only This Man Can Do It'; 'Don't Let the Labour Party Peter Out. Put Peter Out'; 'Scrim Will Fly In'.

Scrim had a stroke of luck during Eleanor Roosevelt's short, unscheduled visit to Wellington at the beginning of the election campaign. While she was in the city, the *Dominion* published the

'Yes, Mr Fraser, but who IS Mr Scrimgeour?' (George Searle cartoon, *Dominion*, 1 September 1943, Alexander Turnbull Library New Zealand & Pacific Collection N-P 1625-3)

first of a series of cartoons disparaging Peter Fraser. George Searle drew a smilingly imperious First Lady saying to the nonplussed prime minister: 'Yes, Mr Fraser, but who IS Mr Scrimgeour?'[10]

The government turned down Scrim's application for broadcasting time. It had allocated broadcasting time to Labour and National speakers and to two independents, Harry Atmore, the veteran Nelson independent, and John A. Lee. Scrim would not have been surprised not to have been added as a third independent. The *Observer* could not resist a comment in its 'Free Lancings' column. 'Why can't "Uncle Scrim" have an election broadcast? He had plenty in 1938.'[11]

Scrim launched his campaign to a packed meeting in the De Luxe Theatre on Sunday, 9 September at 3pm. The date and time were innovative. No other candidate held election meetings on Sundays. He had decided on the date and the timing of the meeting, Scrim said, so that servicemen could attend the meeting and get back to camp before the evening curfew. The De Luxe and Paramount theatres were packed and overflowing for the meeting and were linked by a landline so that Scrim could speak simultaneously to both audiences. He gave a slashing speech under the heading: Why I Fight Frazer.[12] He addressed four evening meetings in church halls in or near Kent Terrace during the next fortnight.

Even for political warfare, Scrim's inflammatory attack on Fraser was extreme in its personal venom. Fraser, he claimed, was a national calamity and a calamity for the 'Labour Movement'. Fraser held Labour Party delegates in a 'ruthless grip', controlling the old men 'while the young men are away fighting'. Fraser was 'the wet blanket' that the party was unable to throw off. The Labour movement had 'no heart' and, lacking leadership, was 'stifling progress'. In fighting Fraser, Scrim was fighting on behalf of all New Zealanders.

The people of New Zealand were disillusioned because the man in charge was a 'cunning, ruthless, scheming politician', 'a man without tenderness, or pity, or drive, or imagination'. Fraser must be removed from office. Until that happened, 'morale would never be good'. The Labour movement would not remove him. But 'the man in the street would'. The man in the street was 'exploited by high prices and vested interests'. He wanted 'a plan instead of muddle in the running of the war'. Fraser's 'defeat' would 'release the enthusiasm that was behind Mr Savage and which Mr Fraser killed'.

What 'liberal or progressive thing', Scrim asked, 'had Fraser done since he became Prime Minister?' What would Harry Holland or Michael Joseph Savage think of Fraser? What do Labour MPs 'really think of Fraser'? 'He was hated and reviled.' Fraser had introduced the Gestapo into New Zealand. He victimised people because of their political beliefs. He was responsible for the doctors' victory over the Labour Party. He had stamped on every piece of progressive legislation. He protected every vested interest in the country. He promoted monopolies. He 'sets aside labour laws about wives and wives and children'. He has held up the Education Bill for years. He terrorises the public service. Labour MPs would have fought against every one of these things if they had been in Opposition. But Fraser had done them all. Even the most conservative men in the Labour Party must see that there is something wrong with the leadership 'when able men like Barnard, Lee, McMillan, and Langstone are no longer in the fold'.

Scrim's message will have been very unsettling for Labour

voters. 'Working people,' he assured his audience, 'would remove Fraser.' Then the war would be fought 'efficiently'. Soldiers serving overseas would feel they had 'a New Zealand worth fighting for'. 'Fascism would be fought in all its forms.' There would be greater opportunities for workers to increase production. A more intelligent use of manpower would lower the cost of living and increase age benefits. The banking system would be reconstructed. The people would get the 'leadership that would make them enthusiastic about leadership'. 'Almost any leader would be better than Fraser.'

The war was not being waged 'efficiently'. New Zealand troops had done 'a magnificent job' in the Middle East. Domestic production had been impressive. But Fraser had overcommitted the country. The economy was under great strain. Essential industries were short of men. There were still too many people employed to make 'useless articles for sale'. But Fraser had been 'too much of a politician and too little of a patriot' to mobilise the full labour force. Too few 'women of leisure of all ages' were working full or part time. Not enough was being done to help 'mothers with babies and children'. 'Middle men' were not being mobilised. Fraser was more interested in keeping the friendship of the employers than in having 'a more progressive working class'. The government had failed to stabilise prices and control rents. It had sold out to doctors, and allowed workers' rights to be eroded.

The prospects for peace, when it was won, were no better. The government had done well to make Major Jerry Skinner the Minister of Rehabilitation. But Skinner would have Fraser 'on his neck' and would achieve little, and the country would be 'in the hands of the old gang again'.

Fraser had failed, too, on the diplomatic front. Unlike Churchill, he had failed to foster closer relations with the Soviet Union. He had failed to build on Harry Holland's work for 'the freedom and development of the Pacific peoples'. It was New Zealand's responsibility to right the record. 'It will be to our everlasting shame' if Fraser is not removed.

That speech, with variations from meeting to meeting, was Scrim's message to the electors of Wellington Central and to workers generally. It could not fail to evoke sympathetic responses from people who were weary of wartime restrictions and were finding it increasingly hard to make ends meet. It would not be until after the war was over that they would learn that, difficult as things had been, wages and prices had been controlled better in New Zealand than in perhaps any other country. Scrim's criticism of the government's efforts in education were quite simply wrong, although he was correct in saying that an amended Education Act was no longer a priority. A consultative committee appointed by the government was at that moment busily at work, and its report, when published later in the year, would be the blueprint for the transformation of post-primary education. So, too, with rehabilitation. The broad provisions of the Rehabilitation Act, passed by Parliament in July 1943 before the House rose for the general election, was a major political achievement. Fraser had himself singled out Skinner for the ministerial responsibility. Scrim was also off the mark over diplomatic relations with the USSR. Fraser had already announced the government's intention to establish the post in Moscow that opened in 1944. Scrim's criticism of the lack of interest in the future of people in the Pacific Islands by New Zealand governments was fair criticism. But Fraser's answer would come in 1945 with his successful advocacy at the San Francisco Conference of the United Nations of trusteeship arrangements that opened the way to political independence not only for people in the Pacific but for all peoples living under dependent colonial regimes.[13]

There is no way of knowing what, apart from giving Fraser a public drubbing, Scrim hoped to achieve by standing against the prime minister. Wellington Central was a Labour stronghold, although boundary changes had shed a block of Labour voters to Wellington North and its new eastern boundary included some National voters. A victory for Scrim was out of the question but there were two other possibilities. If he polled less than 10% of the vote he would lose his deposit and his fight against Fraser would be judged to have been quixotic. Or he might poll well enough to split the vote and let in Will Appleton, the National candidate. Appleton was a well-known businessman who was prominent in local government and would be elected mayor of Wellington in 1944.[14] He had stood against Fraser in 1938. In 1943 he mounted a vigorous campaign, portraying Fraser as a captive of Trades Hall. The Communist Party may or may not have feared that Appleton might take the seat on a split vote, but it was taking no chances. It warned that a vote for Scrim was a vote for National.

Fraser conducted his election campaign the way he had conducted all previous campaigns. He spent the last week in Wellington, held meetings in small halls in the electorate, and ended with an enthusiastic packed public meeting in the Wellington Town Hall on the Wednesday evening before the election. He did not dignify his opponents with responses to their criticisms. 'Messrs Appleton, Scrimgeour, Griffin and Dyer and others,' he said, 'had done their worst and could do their worst, and when they were done they would still be defeated in Wellington Central.'[15] The president and secretary of the Labour Party and the president and secretary of the Federation of Labour tidied up for him with a resolute joint statement that was published on the last day of the campaign.[16]

Whispering campaigns played an important part during the election. The Labour Party circulated stories about the drunken orgy Scrim was alleged to have held in his office while he was controller of commercial broadcasting. Scrim dealt with that line of attack in his last public meeting by playing excerpts of the recording he had made at that party and, no doubt to rile Fraser further, he also played excerpts from his interview with the old Waihi miner.[17] Scrim's supporters launched what would become the standard left-wing smear of Fraser as the failed Labour leader. Fraser, it ran, had been a conscientious objector in the First World War but had conscripted young men to fight in the second. He had trampled on the Union Jack during the First World War but wrapped himself in it during the second. Les Edwards would give that canard a renewed lease of life in 1971 with the publication of his biography of Scrim. But the facts were altogether different. As a sixteen-year-old, Peter Fraser had been caught up in the patriotic fervour that gripped Scotland during the Boer War, and had joined the Ross branch of the Seaforth Highlanders territorials. He had become a socialist before he emigrated to New Zealand, and it was as a revolutionary socialist that he had rallied the Waihi gold miners during their strike in 1912. His stand in 1916 had not rested on the ground of private conscience but on political principle: if conscription were to be imposed, wealth must be conscripted as well as men. It was for sedition that he had been arrested, tried, and gaoled.[18]

Scrim did not unseat the prime minister. He did not lose his deposit. He did not get enough votes to let Appleton in on a split vote. He won 15% of the votes, and Fraser retained Wellington Central with 47.4% of the vote, his smallest share since he first won it in 1918.

Scrim got most of his support from the poorer parts of the electorate. His best booth was the Boys' Institute, where he received 23% of the vote.[19] Elsewhere in the country the political tide also ebbed away from Labour. The party unseated Sir Apirana Ngata in Eastern Maori, Lee in Grey Lynn, and Barnard in Napier, but it lost seats in rural areas and provincial centres and faced the new parliament with forty-five members.[20]

Scrim began his military service at the air force induction camp at Linton. He then spent four months at Levin, for four weeks of which he was on leave conducting his election campaign. He was transferred to Delta station in Marlborough in December, served there until July 1944, and then did a two-month stint at the nearby Woodburne station.[21]

In his political campaign against Fraser, Scrim had hammered away at inefficiency and low morale in the armed forces serving in New Zealand. His recollections of his time in the air force give the impression that he, and no doubt others, were able to 'work' the system. He wrote, for example, that, because he was 'a crack shot', he regularly stood in for other recruits on the firing range to ensure that they received good scores.[22] A report on his work written near the end of his service by his commanding officer was clearly appreciative. Serving as a welfare officer, Scrim organised concert programmes, community sings, 'fun sessions' and quiz sessions, and organised weekend recreation activities. He put in a lot of time outside his regular hours of duty and was helpful to men with personal problems. He had the 'confidence of the men'. He never worried about the hours he worked, he had good informal relations with senior officers, and was 'most valuable' to the station.[23]

Towards the end of his time in the air force, however, Scrim found himself in conflict with air force decision-makers in Wellington. He had been in correspondence with Australian newspaper and broadcasting interests with a view to arranging employment for himself in Sydney. He applied for leave to return to Wellington to pursue this personal interest, but it was refused. On 21 June his solicitor addressed a firmly stated complaint, claiming that his client was being discriminated against. The last item in Scrim's personal file makes it clear that he was disciplined as a result of the incident, after which, according to the station wing commander, he had lost all interest in the station and 'desire to work on it'. The wing commander requested the Air Department to give 'prompt attention' to his demobilisation.[24]

A matter to be settled was the extent of the government's financial indemnity to Scrim for his summary dismissal. Mr H.J.V. James, the senior partner in the legal practice of Chapman, Tripp, Watson and James, initiated negotiations with David Wilson in July 1943. The issues, James wrote, could be solved amicably 'without recourse to legal proceedings', but Mr Scrimgeour reserved all his rights. The claim was for salary in lieu of untaken leave, £577 13s 9d, and six month's salary in lieu of notice, £750.[25] Wilson replied that Scrim would receive whatever he was entitled to. He did not think that Scrim had 'any moral or legal claim' to any payment in lieu of notice' but he would nevertheless consider it further.[26] Further exchanges of letters followed, Wilson kept his cabinet colleagues briefed, and the solicitor general and the secretary of the Treasury provided memoranda of advice.

Cornish firmly believed that the government was under no moral or legal obligation for any salary in lieu of notice. The state of Scrim's record of service as controller of the NCBS raised questions for Ashwin. There was no formal record in his personal file of Savage's decision that he was to have four weeks annual leave. There seemed to be large amounts of untaken leave during his more than six years in the job, but it was not clear that Scrim's claims for annual leave gave an accurate, complete record. Ashwin recommended that Scrim's leave record be accepted as valid, but that his entitlement to untaken leave be on the same basis as for officers in the public service. That would give an entitlement to six weeks' leave accumulated over the previous two years: £172 8s 11d. On the recommendation of the minister of finance, the cabinet approved that amount as its legal obligation for untaken leave.[27]

The matter was resolved in January 1944. The cabinet approved the payment of £500 provided that Scrim was prepared to accept it 'in full settlement of all claims whatsoever', and James accepted it on Scrim's behalf.[28] Wilson would have been justified in concluding that the government had negotiated a satisfactory outcome.

There is no record of any further negotiations between the government and Scrim's solicitor, but it emerged later in the year that

Scrim's solicitor had negotiated some additional concessions. Despite the prohibition in the wartime regulations of the sale of property, Scrim was allowed to sell his house in Lower Hutt for a market price. He was granted a place on the official flying boat service to Sydney, a service normally available only to officers in the armed services with the rank of colonel and above. Lena Scrimgeour and their children were granted free passages on the Tasman steamer service. For the man whose provocations had brought about his dismissal from government service, the settlement seems to have been far from ungenerous.

In 1978, when Scrim talked to Michael King about the settlement, he gave the impression that his solicitor had succeeded in getting everything he asked for.[29] By then, however, as we shall see in chapter 16, Scrim had added a Machiavellian backdrop to the negotiations. It never became known at the time, he told people, but Fraser masterminded the negotiation and insisted on his deportation from his 'native land' for twenty-five years.

## CHAPTER 12

# The Offshore Years

This chapter, like chapters one and two, is an account of Scrim's life seen largely through his own activities and correspondence and his selective and haphazard collections of personal papers. Apart from the year he spent in China in 1959, as an adviser to the Chinese government, he lived in Australia, mostly in or near Sydney, from the end of 1944 until early 1968 when he returned to New Zealand. Lena and Gary, their seven-year-old second son, soon joined him. The two older children, Joan, aged sixteen, and Graham, aged twelve or thirteen, remained in New Zealand until 1946, when they rejoined their parents and Gary.[1]

Scrim was one of the steady flow of journalists and radio people who criss-crossed the Tasman during the thirties and forties. He quickly established himself in Sydney as one of the leaders of the New Zealand media people living there. One of his former colleagues left an account of a supper party that Scrim and Lena hosted for people with New Zealand connections 'in their delightful flat' in one of the inner harbour residential areas. Among those present were Dorothy Wood, Beau Sheil, Bob Pollard who, as well as being a 3ZB announcer had played the male lead in the centennial feature film, and the financier Bill McArthur.[2]

Scrim got his foothold in Australia in the newspaper and radio chain controlled by Sir Keith Murdoch. He was based in Melbourne to begin with, then he moved to Sydney, where he broadcast from 2UE, the *Sydney Sun* station. He had two regular programmes, one on moral and philosophical issues, the other on new developments in science. His programme on moral and philosophical issues did not last long but his science programmes won a large following and remained on the air for several years.

Scrim had much larger ambitions. He was convinced that

television was the mass medium of the future, and set about laying the foundations for a sea change in his fortunes. He kept a close eye on developments in television broadcasting in the United States and the United Kingdom and saw himself as the man who would lead the way in developing a yet-to-be-established television industry in Australia.

He found an influential backer in Sir Ben Fuller, the legendary entrepreneur who for more than half a century had promoted tours by theatre and opera companies and distributed films in Australia and New Zealand. Scrim managed the New South Wales leg of the tour by the Old Vic Theatre Company which Fuller sponsored and which brought Sir Laurence Olivier and Lady Vivien Leigh to Australia and New Zealand in 1948. More important for the longer term, Fuller took the largest shareholding in the company which Scrim set up to buy Pagewood Studios from the British film-maker Ealing Studios. That gave him the base for his venture in film-making and, he expected, television broadcasting.[3]

Scrim's move into film-making was one more example of his ability to branch out into an entirely new direction and win the backing of influential people. Television was sweeping all before it in the United States and had a voracious appetite for well-made feature and documentary films. He was quick to spot a marketing opportunity.[4] Film-making was an essential adjunct to broadcast television. Television would inevitably come to Australia and would create endless opportunities for Australian film-makers, technicians, actors and performers. The market for Australian film-makers was by no means limited to Australia itself. The market for film was becoming global. Scrim was convinced that export earnings from films made in Australia would become second only to wool as earners of foreign exchange, especially in American dollars.

The first sign of this ambition came in 1948 when he launched his company: Associated TV Pty Ltd. The twenty-four acres of land that the company was proceeding to hold under a government leasehold would with some upgrading of buildings and plant be a satisfactory base for its initial operations. There was plenty of unused land on the site that could be built on to house a much larger operation when the company was operating a television service. The state government had assured the company that it would be able to freehold its holding when that day arrived. At that time, too, the company would reconstitute as a new commercial entity with a much larger capital base and safeguards for the financial interests of its shareholders.

Associated TV soon notched up successes. It produced a suite of well-produced, eye-catching films that highlighted appealing features of Australia and contemporary Australian life. Equally important, it cemented working arrangements for the sale of Australian films to American and British distributors and for the purchase of films and television programmes for use in Australia. Scrim never passed up an opportunity to draw attention to the meeting he had had in New York in 1939 with David Smirnoff, the president of RCA. From that meeting he would routinely claim his 'continuing involvement' in television. Regardless of the accuracy of that claim, he eased the way for some leading Americans to invest talent and money in film projects in Australia. One of these was Joseph Kaufman, an independent Hollywood producer. Kaufman spent £500,000 making a cinemascope feature film *Long John Silver* which was screened in the United States as well as in Australia, and followed that up by spending £1,000,000 making twenty-six half-hour television programmes for American television. Australians provided more than 90% of the talent and technical services for Kaufman.

Scrim was also forging good working relations with British film and television makers. When he visited London at the end of 1953 to complete the purchase of Pagewood Studios he negotiated Australian screening rights to 150 British feature films. With his penchant for headlines he referred to this agreement as the biggest deal ever made in show business. His visit coincided with the launch in Britain of high-definition electronic cameras which transformed the shooting and editing of television film. He signed up Pagewood Studios to be equipped with these cameras. This gave Associated TV the most advanced film-making equipment in South East Asia. The company emulated Hollywood by renaming its Pagewood plant Television City.[5]

Scrim also hoped to build on his relationship with Sir Laurence Olivier, and offered him the lead role in a feature film on Robert Louis Stevenson's life in Samoa. Olivier declined the offer, as he would Scrim's later overtures. But Scrim kept him on his visiting list and met him from time to time in London.[6]

Scrim played an important role in Cecil Holmes' successful

transition into the Australian film industry. Holmes was a talented film director who had quickly earned his reputation with the films he made for the New Zealand National Film Unit soon after the war. He was also a member of the Communist Party and an activist in the Public Servants Association. He was the focus of a political scandal in November 1948 when his satchel containing his party card and some other personal papers were clandestinely removed from a car parked in Parliament grounds. The government sacked him, and although he was reinstated after successful action by the Public Servants Association, he resigned from the film unit and moved to Australia. Scrim employed him to direct what became the highly successful feature film *Captain Thunderbolt* and other feature films and documentaries.[7]

Scrim had not lost his ability to make the most of unexpected happenings. On his visits to London he stayed at the Connaught. On one occasion he found himself talking to Clark Gable. They found that they were both bound for New York, booked on the same flight (and both were travelling first class), and they began a conversation which, with flight delays and an overnight stay in Gander, lasted many hours. It was important enough to Scrim to merit a mention in one of his autobiographical jottings.[8]

Scrim knew in his bones how important it was to create good public relations for his company and for the yet-to-be-established television industry in Australia. Building a network of people and organisations who were informed about what he was setting out to achieve and were sympathetic to it was a key feature of his strategy. He sent promotional bulletins to a select list of politicians, church leaders, government administrators, editors of newspapers and magazines, business leaders, and business organisations. There were 125 names on his distribution list. Scrim had become a master of the short, carefully crafted publicity statement. His mimeographed bulletins were between 650 and 1250 words long. They gave accounts of television as a revolutionary medium of communication, summaries of developments in television in the United States, Britain, and other countries, descriptions of the sorts of programmes that were being broadcast, and reports of innovations in the making of television programmes.

Scrim emphasised that, regardless of whether television services were operated by public or private organisations, their programmes must be informative as well as entertaining, with standards of production that were recognised internationally. That applied to commercial advertisements as much as to feature films and documentary programmes. It was a point Scrim was happy to illustrate by instancing commercial spots that were inserted in feature films (which in Australia in 1953 could be seen only in cinemas). Commercial spots, he insisted, must be up to the standard of the features they appeared in. With the aim of lifting standards, Associated TV became actively engaged in making commercial spots. Some of Scrim's bulletins dealt specifically with topics which he knew to be of concern to church people and church organisations.[9]

Scrim used press releases to publicise milestones in Associated TV's progress, such as the company's purchase of high-definition electronic cameras. He spoke to rotary clubs and other social service organisations. In 1953 and again in 1954 he addressed the annual convention of the Australian Association of National Advertisers. He still knew how to charm birds out of trees.[10] Early in 1953, coinciding with the government's announcement of the royal commission on television, he organised public screenings in Sydney and Melbourne of films made by Associated TV which were intended to show off their range and quality. The Sydney screenings were held in an upmarket hotel.[11]

Public opinion in Australia was very divided over the possibility of introducing television. There were concerns that it would undermine public morals. The big, American-based film distributors, facing the prospect of reduced advertising revenue, were alert to a threat to their interests. All the political parties included supporters as well as opponents of television. But official party policies were sharply divided on the central issue of whether television should be operated as a state monopoly or be open to commercial competition.

In 1949, in what would be its last year in office, the Chifley Labor government had decided to introduce television services as a state monopoly but had not begun to give effect to its policy before it was defeated in the 1949 general election. The Liberal-Country Party coalition government led by the Rt Hon R.G. Menzies favoured television services based, as with radio broadcasting, on a mixture of publicly and privately provided services. It foreshadowed its policy in February 1953. It would amend the Broadcasting Act to provide for the operation of competitive television services. Then it set up a royal commission to hear public submissions and give it policy advice for the introduction of television. The six-person commission heard submissions in the six states and reported to the government early in 1954.[12]

In its submissions to the royal commission, Scrim's Associated TV Pty Ltd presented a detailed case for a commercial television service based on Television City. In an important respect it was making a virtue of necessity. Scrim knew that his company would have to add very significantly to its share capital if it was to gear up for television. His bargaining chip was part of the land the company leased. There was more than enough land at Television City for the company's needs, and there would be enough for other providers of television services to base their operations there as well. A concentration of television production services at Television City seemed to Scrim to be in everyone's interest. Associated TV included that suggestion it in its submissions. We cannot say if his offer was received favourably by other organisations that saw a future for themselves in television. But we do know that Scrim became the object of a whispering campaign impugning his integrity while the royal commission was conducting its inquiry.

In public statements about himself and in formal descriptions of his background as chairman of Associated TV, Scrim routinely referred to himself as the founding permanent head of the New Zealand Commercial Broadcasting Service. That was a factual statement as far as it went but it concealed the associated fact that it was a position from which he had been dismissed. From this time onwards Scrim's statements about his years as controller of New Zealand's commercial broadcasting service would be economical with the facts.

In Australia in 1953 Scrim was a public advocate of television, and his company had declared its interest in operating a television service. He will have known that he was at risk. He had been subjected to whispering campaigns in New Zealand. Now he had to cope with one in Australia. In July 1953 Associated TV issued a special bulletin to alert its friends and supporters to the 'McCarthy smear tactics' that were being employed against 'Mr C.G. Scrimgeour'. Australia's 'international reputation' for fair play was being put at risk, it said. 'Do you know' it asked, that the man who for the previous five years had spent most of his time and about £100,000 of his company's money 'to advance the cause of commercial television in Australia', the man whose 'record of public service and commercial success' was matched by few others, was 'being subjected to a campaign of vilification and abuse'? It was being variously said that Mr Scrimgeour was 'a member of the Communist Party' and a 'fellow traveller', and that the Australian intelligence organisation held 'secret information' on him. C.G. Scrimgeour issued 'an open challenge' to anyone hearing such information to 'name the source' of their information, and he would 'institute an action for slander'.[13]

If Scrim gleaned any information from this appeal there are no traces in his personal papers and it left no trace in his folders of correspondence. Allegations against him were made during the hearings before the royal commission, and in later hearings before the public broadcasting commission for a television licence. His briefing notes for these hearings include suggestions about how he might handle 'personal attacks'. He would 'deny, as grossly false', any charge that 'he was recalcitrant and defied the authority of the Minister of Broadcasting'. He would affirm that he had been in charge of the National Commercial Broadcasting Service for seven years during which time 'there was never one complaint about his administration'. His 'only refusal' had been 'to refuse carrying out an instruction' which would have required him 'to use a public utility to further the interests of a particular political party'. To any mention of the party in his office at which intoxicating liquor was consumed he would say first that the allegations were made by the prime minister in the House under the cover of parliamentary privilege, second that they were made at a time when he was in the military forces and debarred by military regulations from replying, and third that during the election campaign that followed soon afterwards, at which he was a candidate, he challenged the prime minister to repeat his allegations in public but he never did.[14]

Here we have Scrim contemplating himself as the blameless head of a government department who had been put upon by his political masters and hounded out of his post. It was a fantasy that would have been dispelled in any serious examination of the breakdown in his working relations with the Fraser government and his dismissal. What Scrim would never acknowledge was any fault or shortcoming on his own part in bringing about that breach. That aside, his company, Associated TV, was pitting itself against large, powerful commercial organisations. Writing to his friend Allan Martin many years after the broadcasting board hearings, he recalled the 'powerful array' of power politics arrayed against him. 'Radio, Cinema, Newspapers, the Church . . . it was all evidence of the Devil. Really it was not [Macquarie] and that array of legal talent that beat me – it was the CIA.'[15]

The royal commission reported in March 1954. The government adopted its recommendations in June, soon after its re-election, authorising the establishment of publicly funded television services in Sydney and Melbourne, and arranging for the Australian Broadcasting Control Board to consider applications from private organisations for the right to operate a commercial service.[16] To Scrim's chagrin, the Macquarie chain were awarded the licence.[17]

Scrim's folders of correspondence include only the sketchiest information about his application to the broadcasting board, his failure to win the commercial licence, and his subsequent sale of his shares in Associated TV. The key facts are set out in what we can assume to be the last of the information bulletins he wrote for friends and associates of the company. It was Scrim's answer to 'fictions' that were circulating against the company.

Associated TV claimed that it had done 'twenty times' more than any other company or group of Australian companies to develop Australian television. The company had never failed to meet its obligations. It was not broke. It had not been taken over by American film interests On the basis of valuations of the company made two years earlier, its shareholders would make a profit on their investment if they decided to sell it. He repeated the offer the company had made in its submissions to the royal commission and the broadcasting board. Its plant and associated facilities were available for use by other organisations intending to become actively engaged in television, including the Australian Broadcasting Commission.[18]

Instead, Associated TV wound up its affairs, but there is no mention of that in Scrim's papers.

In 1962 Scrim had one more momentary flutter of interest in running an Australian television service. When the government called for applications for the third television licence in Sydney he said he was sounded out for the chairmanship of a group in New

South Wales comprising returned servicemen's leagues, sports clubs, and entertainment bodies. Tempted at first, he decided not to become involved.[19]

While Scrim was engaged in Associated TV's ambition to win the right to operate a commercial television service he was also living through a major change in his private life. As with everything about his private life, the details are sketchy, but it seems that from sometime in 1953 he was living with Pamela Gates, whom he would marry in 1958 after he and Lena were divorced. Twenty years younger than Scrim, Pam was an attractive woman employed by the Australian Broadcasting Commission.

Scrim had been cheating on Lena from at least the late 1930s. In a later brief mention of his divorce in a letter to his son Gary, Scrim acknowledged that it was he who had decided to divorce Lena. The divorce greatly undermined Lena's self-confidence and she went through years of depression. But by the time she talked about her marriage with Gary some twenty years later she seems to have regarded it in a spirit of forbearance.[20]

Sometime in the mid-1950s Scrim left Sydney to live on a ninety-six-acre block of land at Kurrajong, near the Blue Mountains. Included in the land were two residential sections with a cottage on one of them. Bowen Mountain, Kurrajong, was his postal address for the rest of the time he lived in Australia. In his correspondence for those years he sometimes referred to himself as a farmer and sometimes as a business consultant. His correspondence includes his replies to some British and American publishers and film-makers about his possible involvement in projects that would include Australian contributions, but none of these seem to have come to anything. His main source of funds may well have been the money he received for the sale of his shares in Associated TV. He told Dick Griffin that he had come out of the TV business with assets worth £30,000, and had made more money 'in failure than most people get out of success'.

A new chapter in Scrim's life opened in 1958 when he and Pam began exchanging letters with his second son Gary. The correspondence continued until 1979, and included Gary's second wife Helen after he remarried. Pam typed all of Scrim's correspondence, so we cannot say how much he contributed to their joint letters. In later years he added no more than brief postscripts to them, but he made some audio tapes which were sent to Gary. Between 1981 and 1987 Pam and Gary wrote regularly to each other.

The letters between Gary and his father record a slow easing of the resentments and tensions that Gary had grown up with and had been exacerbated by the break-up of his parents' marriage. As a small boy Gary had formed a very close relationship with his mother. He was the only one of her three children living at home during the crisis in her marriage and was one of her mainstays. It is clear from the early letters in the correspondence that in Scrim's mind Gary is 'mother's boy'.

Gary had been only seven when Scrim's New Zealand broadcasting career ended, but he grew up believing without question that his father was a good, public-spirited man who had dedicated himself to helping people in distress. His personal experience as Scrim's son was unsettlingly different. Lena had come to understand that although Scrim 'liked youngsters and was generally very good with them', taking responsibility for his own children was something altogether different. He kept his family on a tight rein. He insisted that the house remain quiet during the evenings so that he could concentrate on his work. Gary remembered Scrim's anger with anyone who broke that rule. He grew up with deeply ambivalent feelings about his father.

Gary was a clever boy. He graduated from Sydney University, and went on to Washington University, and then Princeton, where he completed a PhD in English literature in the mid-fifties. His academic success became an additional source of tension between him and his father. Scrim was proud of Gary's success but admitted to feelings of an 'inferiority complex'. Gary, for his part, was proud of what Scrim had achieved from very modest beginnings. In the course of their correspondence, Gary's feelings of admiration came to the fore, particularly after the publication of Les Edwards' biography in 1971 and *The Scrim-Lee Papers* in 1976. But his underlying fear still remained. As late as 1977, when he was forty-three years old, he would write of his anxiety at not hearing from Scrim, fearing that the gap in correspondence was sign of Scrim's displeasure.[21]

Like his father, Gary was opinionated and prone to sound off, and he did not hesitate to criticise what he assumed to be Scrim's beliefs. This was very evident in the early letters in the series, written in 1959, when Scrim was providing expert advice on television to the Chinese government. Sometimes, too, Gary was unprepared for the anger that even a friendly question could trigger. In particular, he would learn that only his father had the right to talk about his mother, Gary's grandmother. Scrim had spoken of her in one of their long-distance telephone calls. When Gary incautiously added a comment of his own about her in a follow-up letter, Scrim rebuked him and did not write to him again for several months.

Not much can be said about the background to Scrim's invitation to visit the People's Republic of China to be its sole foreign adviser when it was planning the establishment of its national television broadcasting system. All we have from his files of correspondence is his comment that his friends in Actors' Equity had been helpful and that Vic Wilcox, the president of the New Zealand Communist Party, had written to Peking on his behalf.

The ground had clearly been prepared for him by December 1957 when he wrote to the management of Peking Radio setting out his experience of radio and television broadcasting. He wrote, he said, in the knowledge that others had already vouched for his experience and contributions. Should, however, the Chinese authorities wish to corroborate that experience or confirm 'his devotion to the cause of socialism' he offered the names of the Rt Hon Dr H.V. Evatt of Australia and the Rt Hon Walter Nash of New Zealand, 'the political leaders in their own respective countries and both of whom are my lifelong friends'. Scrim's letter was not so much an application as a reply to a job offer.[22]

Scrim was invited to be a specialist in the work that the Chinese Broadcasting Administration Bureau was doing in television. He and Pam travelled to Peking in December 1958, and he was formally appointed on 1 January 1959. In comments on his work in China he was careful to point out that he was engaged not as a political cadre but as a technical expert. He and Pam travelled widely in China and met a great many Chinese and foreign nationals who, like himself, were working for official Chinese agencies.

Scrim's appointment was for one year, renewable for another year if both sides agreed. His task was to lead the comrades in the relevant departments who were working to establish the national television service. This he was to do 'in accordance with the needs of our television work and in conjunction with your own opinions'.[23] Scrim being Scrim, he did not leave a connected account of his task. He had always been a man for the short episode and the telling anecdote, and at fifty-seven he showed no sign of changing. It was Pam who, through several circular letters, kept some of their Australian and New Zealand friends informed of what they were doing. Only one or two of these seem to have been dictated by Scrim, who did, however, write a few letters to former colleagues and business acquaintances.

Scrim kept in touch with Gary by including him among the addressees of his circular letters. Gary did not like this arrangement. Though pleased to hear from his father, he protested at being 'treated as a member of a mass audience to an Eleanor Roosevelt travelogue'. He thought it naive of Scrim to write so enthusiastically about the achievements of the Chinese people.[24]

Scrim arrived in China thinking he would be one of several overseas specialists working on the television project, and was surprised to find himself the only foreigner, working in a team which in total numbered fifty-six men and women. The size of the operation, he told Beau Sheil, was in scale very similar to the one they had been part of in New Zealand when they were establishing the commercial broadcasting service. The differences were the complexity of television and the scale of an operation that, in a short time, would provide a service for one fifth of the world's population.[25]

It was the second attempt by the Chinese to establish a national television service. The first, which would have depended entirely on Russian expertise and equipment, had been abandoned when the Chinese realised that, when completed, China would get a national television service that depended entirely on outsiders, with Chinese expertise relegated to subordinate roles. That approach to development was now deplored. The mood of all the Chinese that Scrim met was that their country was moving steadily ahead through a series of Great Leaps. They had done it in film production. The Chinese film industry in Scrim's opinion was the equal to if not superior to the best work being done in the USA and Britain. Now television was making its Great Leap Forward.

Two years before Scrim had arrived, no Chinese had seen television. By the time he arrived the first television transmitting station was ready to be commissioned. Using Russian plans and specifications, all the equipment had been built in China by Chinese, with equipment devised by Chinese expertise.

The men and women Scrim worked with were confident, able, enthusiastic, and adaptable. They were not hampered by preconceived ideas, nor were they doctrinaire. They had unquenchable self-belief: they knew they were transforming their country and their goal was 'more, faster, better'.[26]

Scrim seems to have had the role of the seasoned outsider who would involve himself in the work of his Chinese colleagues, enter into countless discussions with them to assess what they were doing, and discuss their responses to his ideas and suggestions. No stranger to discussion and argument with colleagues, he was nevertheless surprised by the expectation of his Chinese colleagues that he tell them exactly what he thought, even if it was critical. They saw criticism, he said, in positive terms.

As a man long used to being a decision-maker, Scrim may have come to have misgivings about the advisory role he was playing. In a letter he wrote to Rex Mason halfway through his consultancy, he said that the work he was doing was 'in itself . . . rather routine' but it gave him 'a great opportunity of seeing at first hand a most exciting and gigantic experiment in . . . social reconstruction'.[27]

Scrim found his China venture unbelievably uplifting. He was greatly impressed with the people he had worked with. He maintained and deepened some of these relationships through correspondence after his return to Australia. He had a new mission: to open up channels of communication between Chinese and Australians and other English-speaking broadcasters and traders. The correspondence preserved in his papers for the next five years is very largely taken up with that mission. He made four or five return visits to China during those years, some of them paid by for wholly or partly by the Chinese government, some by the Australian Wool Board and other corporate sponsors.

It was uphill work. Public opinion in Australia reflected the Cold War. The Liberal governments that ruled the country had not followed Britain's lead, and had not formally recognised the People's Republic of China, but they did not ban trade relationships. Practical difficulties on the Chinese side were harder to overcome. Working closely with his senior contact in the Chinese television service, Scrim spent five years fostering the co-production of a non-propagandist television documentary on life in contemporary China only to end up empty-handed. He seems to have been approached by broadcasting authorities in Vietnam, Indonesia, and Singapore for advice about the setting up of national television services, but nothing came of them.

Some Australian corporate interests were, however, interested in opening up trading relations with China. Acting as a go-between during the early stages of consultation, Scrim played a part in opening up channels of communication between the relevant Chinese authorities and the Australian Wheat Board, the Australian Dairy Produce Board and some other national organisations. Once, however, initial working relationships were established, there was no further role for him to play.[28]

Scrim's innate optimism was regularly put to the test. A letter he wrote to one of his Australian exporters dispirited by the downturn in negotiations with the Chinese showed his public face in such circumstances. His experience in a long, varied career, he consoled his associate, was that 'disappointments are eventually the stepping stones we need to cross rivers without getting our feet wet'.[29]

One of the last items in his file of China correspondence shows that Scrim was having to lower his sights. Writing to Mai Yi, the director of Peking Radio with whom he had worked in China, he said he was disappointed that no progress had been made on the long-delayed film project. But would the Chinese authorities look favourably on 'a large Australian tour party' for which he and Pam would be 'tour managers'?[30] The profoundly disruptive effects of Mao's Cultural Revolution seem to have brought Scrim's Chinese ventures to an end.

Another letter in his folders of Australian correspondence is a reminder of Scrim's inveterate determination to have things done his way. It is a short, stiff letter from Scrim's solicitor recording the sundering of their working relationship. His solicitor informed Scrim that he was convinced that 'till the end of your time you must go your own way, regardless of anyone's advice, or anyone's wishes . . . your way is not my way Scrim, and I've gone as far as I can with you.'[31]

Scrim made a short visit to New Zealand in October 1967. He would soon be old enough to be eligible for New Zealand superannuation, and he no doubt wanted to be assured that Pam would also be eligible as his wife. But he would not be returning to New Zealand to retire.

He had business plans to promote. He had long been interested in converting grass into protein by industrial processes, and the Australian scientists with whose work he was familiar had reached the point where their research could be commercialised. Now was the time to get the ear of the New Zealand government. Sir Henry Kelliher arranged a meeting for him with the prime minister, Rt Hon Keith Holyoake.

Scrim spent more than an hour with Holyoake and the deputy prime minister, Marshall, and was very pleased with their interest in the protein project. He was pleased, too, and no doubt relieved, to find that they showed no sign of wanting to hark back to his controversial broadcasting career in New Zealand. No doubt he told them what he had already told Kelliher, that he 'was determined not to get caught up in the crossfire of politics'.[32]

Back in Auckland he gave an interview to Michael Brett, who wrote a favourable personality piece on him in his weekly 'Auckland Diary' column in the *Auckland Star.* 'A new role now for Uncle Scrim' was how Brett presented him to readers. Uncle Scrim would be returning to New Zealand as the 'link man' for a group of Australian university scientists who had discovered how to produce proteins biochemically. He would be explaining the potential of their discovery to leaders of New Zealand primary industries.

Brett realised that Scrim needed an introduction to a new generation of New Zealanders. Thirty-two years ago, Brett wrote, Scrim's name was one of the two names 'on the lips of every man and woman', Michael Joseph Savage's being the other. He was the 'slim, intense, spellbinder', who was 'later to be known as the man who put Labour into power'. In a few sentences Brett touched on the highlights of Scrim's career in the thirties: Methodist city missioner, founder of the Friendly Road, the man put off the air in the 'jamming incident' just before the 1935 election, the first director of the National Commercial Broadcasting Service, and the man sacked by the Labour government in 1943. 'The rise and fall of Uncle Scrim makes fascinating reading now.'[33]

As an exercise in anticipatory public relations, Scrim's visit could scarcely have been bettered.

# PART 3

# Creating the Myth

# CHAPTER 13

# Second Coming

The *Sunday Times* interviewed Scrim on his arrival in Auckland in February 1968 and carried a photograph of him and Pam on page one. Scrim was back, it told its readers, and he would soon be 'on the road again'.[1] Scrim and Pam were guests of Sir Henry Kelliher for a few days at the Royal International Hotel in Auckland before they set up home in Waiwera, fifty kilometres north of Auckland, where they would live for the next four years.

Scrim and Pam were an effective husband and wife team. Pam ran the household, acted as his secretary and typist, and coped happily, it seems, with his quietly spoken, dominant personality. Scrim set about renewing his contacts and forming new associations as he relaunched himself as a public figure. He was keen to promote his scheme for the industrialised production of protein, and he wanted to get back on the air with his own programme. His view of himself was that he was an international authority on radio and television broadcasting and a media personality in his own right. By returning to his homeland he was giving New Zealanders the opportunity to reclaim him as a national personality.

Kelliher already knew of Scrim's plans. Scrim talked to Jim (Sir James) Wattie who was sufficiently interested in them to commit his board to consultations with other parties. Wattie was prepared to back Scrim for three fifteen-minute radio sessions a week for an annual fee of $10,000. But Scrim mismanaged his consultations with the NZBC and with Wattie's general manager, and the Wattie board backed off from both his broadcasting proposal and his protein proposal.[2] There were indications in the background papers to the board's decision that Scrim had tried to bulldoze his NZBC contact and, separately, Wattie's general manager.

Scrim turned his attention to television. There was a growing public expectation that New Zealand would soon convert to colour television and introduce a second channel. Issues surrounding colour television were soon resolved, but the prospect of a second channel raised the much-contested issue of whether, like the existing channel, it should be publicly owned or operated by private enterprise. The Holyoake government established the New Zealand Broadcasting Authority in 1968 to make that decision.[3]

Scrim was quickly out of the blocks. He enlisted the interest of Jim (Sir James) Weir and Sir Fred Doidge, who, with Kelliher and Wattie, backed his proposal for a national television network. Scrim was able to tell Gary that, for the first time in ten years 'he was on someone's payroll as a consultant'. No doubt it was for tax purposes that he was giving his time free of charge, but he received $500 a month for expenses. With that level of support and perhaps the possibility of greater remuneration before long, he could see himself remaining in New Zealand 'for some time, if not permanently'.[4]

Working on what he referred to familiarly as the 'four knights proposal' brought Scrim into a working association with Gordon Dryden, with whom he was soon impressed. In Scrim's mind it was

Scrim at Waiwera in 1969. (Photographer unknown, *Scrim: Radio Rebel in Retrospect*)

a case of the old dog and the young dog. When Gary asked Scrim how much of the four knights proposal was his work and how much Gordon Dryden's, Scrim replied that Dryden was 'so good in fact that at forty he is better than I was at thirty'.[5] That was clearly a statement for family consumption only. The record of the four knights proposal makes it clear that Dryden managed the project, undertook the extensive investigations that were called for, oversaw the preparation of numerous detailed submissions, and fronted up to the Broadcasting Authority.[6]

Scrim's active work on the four knights proposal was cut short in the middle of 1970 when he suffered what he referred to as a 'complete heart attack'. In the course of the next year or so he had a series of heart operations before his heart specialists at Green Lane Hospital declared him healthy and unlikely to have further attacks. He was fitted out with a pacemaker which ensured that his heart maintained a regular beat. Scrim was unstinting in his praise for Dr Barratt-Boyes and his team who, in his opinion, were running 'the most famous heart place in the world'.[7] But Scrim's campaigning days were over. On the advice of his medical specialists, he started to think of things he might do that would be less of a danger to his health.

The four knights bid for the second channel ended in disappointment. The Broadcasting Authority recommended the introduction of colour television and the setting up of a second television service, but left it for the government to decide whether the second channel should be operated by the NZBC or by a private provider.[8] After much debate in cabinet and in the National Party caucus, the government authorised the NZBC to operate both channels, and the four knights folded their tent. But neither Scrim nor Gordon Dryden were prepared to capitulate, and they separately made out applications to the Broadcasting Authority for the right to operate a commercial television company. For Scrim it was a matter of principle. He was opposed to monopoly providers whether they were state owned or privately owned.[9] But both major political parties were committed to a state monopoly. National awarded the second channel to the NZBC. Labour kept both channels in public ownership when it returned to power at the end of 1972.

★

All his life Scrim had enjoyed opportunities to yarn with his mates and make new acquaintances. His home at Waiwera was always open to people who wanted to talk about old times and to others from a younger generation who were interested to know what he might have to say about their present-day concerns. But he never kept diaries, and we cannot say how many of his visitors came and went without leaving a trace in his records.[10] From some of his visitors, however, we can get impressions of their meetings with him.

Some of Scrim's visitors were old left-wing mates, of whom Bill Sutch and Bert Roth get mentions. Some were Methodists of the younger generation who wanted to talk to him about his work at the Auckland Social Service Centre and how it related to their commitment to the church's social gospel.

The Rev Les Clements, and his adult son Kevin visited in 1968. The piece that Kevin Clements published in the *Methodist Times* in 1969 was the first of several newspaper articles which presented Scrim's view of himself to the public. It was the story of a young man who turned his back on the wild ways of his youth to become successively a Methodist home missioner, the first director of the Auckland Social Service Centre, the founder of the Fellowship of the Friendly Road, and the creator and controller of the National Commercial Broadcasting Service (NCBS) from which, after seven years, he had been sacked because, as he put it, 'he refused to be the mouth piece of Peter Fraser'. Scrim would have been back on the air again after his recent return to New Zealand, Clements wrote, but the NZBC had refused to broadcast a new series of his 'Man in the Street' programme. Scrim could not have hoped for better publicity.[11]

Two Methodist ministers, Rev Russell Marshall and Rev Barry Jones, spent an afternoon with Scrim in January 1972.[12] They arrived unannounced on the off-chance that Scrim might be home. Scrim spent several hours with them reminiscing about his years as a home missioner and linking his pioneering work at the Auckland Social Service Centre with his vistors' commitment to the social gospel.

The journalist Gabrielle David added a new dimension to Scrim as a subject of public interest with a pen portrait of him in the *Evening Post* in March 1973. Scrim, David wrote, looked much younger than his seventy years. His handshake was as firm as that of the timber miller he had been in his youth. He was 'wiry' and he had 'an alert, facile brain'. He talked 'with studied nonchalance, weighing his words carefully'. There was 'still a glint of battle in his piercing blue eyes'.

David noted that Scrim had not spared himself in 'his blunt criticisms of youthful indiscretions'. These to him were among the things that had made his life distinctive. He spoke of the chance circumstances that had led him to become a Methodist home missioner, his years as the first Methodist inner city missioner in Auckland, his founding of the Friendly Road, and of his broadcasting years.

There were moments in their conversation, David thought, when Scrim had 'the look of a man' who felt he had received much less recognition from his countrymen than he deserved. He did not appear to be bitter, but he had not forgotten. Scrim said that he did not envy his contemporaries who had become millionaires or knights, but he was sure that he could have become one or the other. He let David know that his universal superannuation was his only source of income, adding with a characteristic flourish of exaggeration that he could not remember the time when he did not have to pawn his insurance policies. He was writing his autobiography, he said, and was thinking of calling it 'I Died Broke'.[13]

Sympathetic newspaper articles were good for publicity. But nothing could match a biography written by a sympathetic writer. The three booklets that Harry Bell had published in the early thirties on Scrim's early life had been a launching pad for his career in broadcasting. Les Edwards, a left-wing Labour activist, offered to assist in relaunching Scrim's broadcasting career by writing his biography. Scrim had come to know Edwards during his NCBS days. Edwards had been a reporter for the *Standard* and, later, an editorial writer for the *Southern Cross*. Scrim gave Edwards open access to his scrapbooks of correspondence and newspaper clippings.

Edwards later said that his motives in writing Scrim's biography were 'entirely political'.[14] He wanted to invent 'a politically useful' legend. He and other left-wing members of the Labour Party had become distinctly out of sympathy with the leadership of the Labour movement. A biography defending Scrim and discrediting Peter Fraser would serve notice on Norman Kirk's leadership.

*Scrim: Radio Rebel in Retrospect* began dramatically with the police batoning of Jim Edwards in front of the Auckland Town Hall on the night of 14 April 1932 and the riot that followed.[15] Then it narrated the main political events in which Scrim was involved during the depression, reaching a climax with the jamming of his 'Man in the Street' session and the Labour victory of 1935. The second part of the book dealing with Labour in power was a sustained attack on Fraser. Politicians and trade union leaders figured prominently. Edwards was not interested in Scrim's career as a Methodist home missioner, but he included a reference to the Rev Seamer and some laudatory comments on Scrim's activities as home missioner and the first director of the Auckland Methodist Social Service Centre.

The book's message was that Labour failed to convert its sweeping electoral victories of 1935 and 1938 into 'social creativity and venturous civilisation', leaving a legacy of 'disappointed hopes'. Scrim could have 'contributed a lot' to a genuinely progressive government, but became merely 'a footnote' to those disappointed hopes.[16]

Edwards presented Labour's broadcasting policy as a victory for Savage and Scrim over opposition from Fraser and Nash.[17] To Edwards, Fraser and Nash were antiprogressive no-sayers. Most newspaper proprietors, he claimed, thought that Scrim's 'political dynamic' was potentially greater than the Labour Party's. Fraser also 'sensed and feared' it. [18] Fraser and Nash regarded Savage as an 'innocuous mascot', and they used the government's popularity as a 'weapon' against Jack Lee and other left-wingers. Fraser had been 'cravenly sensitive' to newspaper opinion when, during Savage's absence overseas, he had to deal with Scrim's public spat with *Truth* and other newspaper owners. The entire episode had shown how much Fraser had in common with Adam Hamilton.[19]

The art was in the telling. Few people reading Edwards' book in 1971 would have known that it was Scrim in his 'Man in the Street' session on 1 April 1937 who had provoked the public row Edwards was writing about. There, as elsewhere in his book, Edwards was skilful as an advocate but economical with the facts.

Savage's death and Lee's expulsion are the book's political climax. Edwards sketched in enough of the fraught background to present Lee in a favourable light but not enough to let readers know what was going on. Fraser was the grey eminence and intriguer whose trade union 'bouncers' were always at his beck and call. Scrim was a quick-thinking left-winger with a subversive sense of humour.[20] The 'consummate' broadcasting professional now faced Fraser, the 'consummate politician'.[21] By identifying himself so publicly with Lee, Scrim knew he was in danger. The 'unwritten' terms of his appointment under Savage would not necessarily bind Fraser, 'who could alter the rules to suit himself'. But 'Fraser was not just another Adam Hamilton', and there was no way of avoiding confrontation.[22] The question to be settled was whether Scrim had enough support in the Labour movement to remain an independent voice in broadcasting. Only an open clash with Fraser would decide that, the sooner the better.'[23]

Fraser, as Edwards presented him, 'was determined to eliminate Scrim' and was equally eager to force the issue. Gaining office had been the 'limit of his ambition'. His 'natural enemies' were not the Tories but the people of his own party 'who wanted to exercise real political power and achieve fundamental social changes'.[24] The rest of the book is Edwards' account of an internecine party power struggle. Fraser, supported by Wilson, F.P. Walsh, and other 'gangsters' were pitted against Scrim, their victim.[25]

Edwards gave a brief account of the fallout from Scrim's broadcast following Savage's funeral. 'The broadcast', Edwards wrote, was 'an intriguing climax to a politically remarkable week'. He recorded the government's suspension of the 'Man in the Street' session and its reinstatement two weeks later. According to Edwards, 'Scrim simply put himself back on the air.' That may be how Scrim wanted events to be remembered, but Fraser had suspended the session as a disciplinary act and it was Fraser who decided when it was time to relent. Edwards' account of the later incidents that ended with Scrim's dismissal in August also convey the impression that Scrim was in control of events. If, however, he had told the rest of the story he would have had to examine the episodes that Scrim had himself orchestrated in his relations with the government during his last year as controller of the NCBS. He would also have had to explain why Walsh and other union and Labour leaders who had held the ring for Scrim in April 1943 had withdrawn their support less than three months later.

To left-wingers in the Labour Party, Fraser had fallen from grace during the Second World War. Edwards presented the final months of Scrim's time as a public servant as a 'burlesque' in which he deftly circumvented Fraser and Wilson's clumsy attempts to railroad him into the army and have him slated for active service overseas.

⋆

*Scrim: Radio Rebel in Retrospect* was published in September 1971, and was noticed in the books columns of newspapers around the country and reviewed in the YA 'World of Books' programme. Most reviewers accepted without question that Scrim had been the victim of Fraser's relentless persecution. E.H. (Ted) Reynolds' full-page review in the *New Zealand Herald* was illustrated with a reprint of the Gordon Minhinnick sketch which, published in 1931, had been used by the publisher for the dust cover of the biography. The book, Reynolds claimed, had gone straight to the top place 'as the most outstanding book' published in New Zealand during the year.[26] J.N.M. in the *Christchurch Star* called it 'an explosive political biography', but left it for readers to decide if it was a 'fair appraisal' or an account 'of almost unprecedented vindictiveness'.[27]

Scrim sent Gary a copy of the book as soon as it was published, and was able to tell him in February 1972 that it was still selling well. 'So it should,' he wrote, 'with the number of helpful and provocative reviews it had had.' He was pleased that there was, so he said, 'no trace of political prejudice' in them, though he noted 'a lack of warm commendation from Labour members'. But he 'couldn't care less' about the views of Labour politicians because he could 'get on better with Bob Muldoon'.[28]

Gary's comments were the ones that Scrim was most eager to read. Gary felt sure that Scrim would have enjoyed reading 'all those unpleasant statements about Peter Fraser'. He was glad that the author had brought out Scrim's human dimension. Given Scrim's unwillingness to talk about what, for Gary, were the 'early days', it filled in some of the blanks. Gary was impressed, too, by the evidence in the book of Scrim's ability to bounce back apparently unworried and maintain a steady upward course.[29]

The publication of the tenth edition of *Who's Who* in 1971 was a reminder of Scrim's public status. His entry repeated what he had written for the fifth edition and ended with a mention of what he referred to as his 'retirement' from the commercial broadcasting service in '1944'.[30]

Scrim was well pleased with the public recognition he was getting as one of the leading figures of the depression years of the thirties, but he did not want to be pigeonholed. He saw himself as a visionary who had important things to say about life as New Zealanders were experiencing it in the here and now. He saw himself, too, as a man who was perennially young at heart. Significantly, two of his public speeches that attracted public notice were to audiences of young people.

His speech to Youth Yak, the 1972 conference of the Youth Branch of the Social Credit movement was acclaimed as one of the highlights of the conference.[31] The two sessions he conducted at the University of Canterbury later in the year also seem to have lived up to the organisers' expectations. *CANTA*, the student newspaper, talked up his visit in advance. Scrim, it told its readers, was, with John A. Lee, one of the 'two Rads' from the thirties. His radio broadcasts had been so controversial that a 'Conservative government' had used jamming equipment to prevent people from hearing them. When Labour came into power he 'was one of the most influential left-wing thinkers and propagandists'. But Labour 'went soft' and Scrim had been dismissed as a 'dangerous radical'. Scrim was not a man 'to pull his punches', *CANTA* declared, 'so don't expect to be bored, he's really worth listening to'.[32] The *Christchurch Star* carried a brief account of Scrim's public meeting. Scrim told his audience that New Zealand should learn the lesson of the Chinese cultural revolution and give youth a 'sphere of social and political responsibility'. Sixteen should be the age for all 'responsibility'. Scrim had been greatly disappointed to find on his return in 1968 that much of New Zealand's welfare state had been dismantled.[33]

Disappointingly for him, Scrim's first two opportunities to appear on television came to nothing. Partway through 1971, when the biography was published, Brian Edwards interviewed Scrim for a 'Gallery Special' current affairs programme. But Edwards conducted the interview in anticipation of a renewed contract with NZBC which did not eventuate, and the interview was not broadcast.[34] Never one to give up, Scrim kept at Edwards, hoping that he might work part of it into one of his later 'Gallery' programmes, but that did not happen.[35]

In 1974 Scrim was invited to take part in a high-profile current affairs programme that also came to nothing. Brian Edwards arranged for David Frost, the celebrated British television broadcaster to interview John A. Lee and Scrim for a programme during his highly publicised return visit. The three men were brought together but for whatever reason the interview did not take place or, if it did, did not go to air.[36]

Scrim was faring better on radio. James McNeish included him as one of the six people, five men and a woman, he featured in interviews for his 'Men of the Angry Thirties' series. The interviews were first broadcast over the Concert Programme early in 1974 and repeated on the National Programme during November and December 1975. Scrim took full advantage of McNeish's encouragement to his interviewees to tell their own stories in their own way. It had been to study television in the United States, he claimed, that Savage had sent him to the States in 1939, and had it not been for his feud with Fraser he might have introduced it to New Zealand viewers a decade before it became available here.[37] The *NZ Listener* review of the broadcast said that Scrim had spoken of what he called the 'genesis' of that feud but gave no detail of what he had said.[38]

Five years later Scrim spoke about that meeting in an interview with Michael King. He said that the meeting had taken place soon after Lee had been expelled from the Labour Party. Scrim had arrived in Fraser's office unannounced and, as he recalled the incident, was confrontational in the way he spoke to Fraser. He demanded that Lee be reinstated and made minister of defence and told Fraser that he would be 'a bloody idiot' if he didn't. Fraser went white and then purple, as Scrim thought, with anger. He warned Fraser that he was a professionally trained fighter and was giving him due notice. That is all that seems to have happened and Scrim walked off. 'Fraser,' Scrim told King, 'never forgot, never forgave.'[39] We cannot say whether the meeting took place or whether, as with some of Scrim's other recollections at the time, it was an invention. Whatever its provenance, the story became a marker in Scrim's accounts of his deteriorating relationship with Fraser.

It was a sign of Scrim's renewed celebrity that he was the guest of honour at the gala inauguration of colour television in October 1973. But Scrim was no friend of the state broadcasting service and was privately scathing of the function. The large audience of personalities, he wrote in an autobiographical note, had to sit through endless delays. Billed to start at 7pm, the show finally got under way at 10pm. The minister of broadcasting, Roger Douglas, who was expected to inaugurate the service, failed to show up. Nearly everyone, Scrim thought, was left wondering why such a fuss was being made about colour film which every cinema in the country had been screening for years.[40]

Much more pleasurable was Scrim's involvement in the official function that Radio New Zealand held in August 1975 to acknowledge fifty years of radio broadcasting in New Zealand and to celebrate its own emergence as a distinct corporate identity among the state broadcasting services. The chairman, Patrick Downey, invited Scrim and Pam to be Radio New Zealand's guests, and they accepted, although Scrim was experiencing one of his bouts of ill health. In the course of his opening remarks, Downey welcomed Scrim by name, and the audience acknowledged his presence with a spontaneous round of applause.[41]

TVNZ marked radio's jubilee by screening a programme on the history of radio in New Zealand. It was a cavalcade of pioneers, and Scrim made his first appearance on television in the company of popular announcers from John Gordon and Clive Drummond to the currently popular John Clarke. It was a once over lightly programme. Scrim spoke about his beginnings in radio broadcasting at 1ZR, of his use of biblical quotations during the depression to make political comments against the Coalition government, and of his campaign, as he put it, for the B stations to be allowed to become commercial operations.[42]

Scrim had told Holyoake that he did not intend becoming a focus of political attention after his return to live in New Zealand. Before long, however, he renewed acquaintances with some of the politicians he had known in earlier days and made himself known to some current politicians. He met Warren Freer again and remained in touch with him for the rest of his life. Through Freer he caught up again with Martyn Finlay whom he had probably not seen since their brief association as members of the executive committee of the Progressive Books Society in Wellington in 1941. We cannot say when he renewed his association with John A. Lee. Scrim's scrapbooks have correspondence between them from 1973, when they were providing information for the book Tony Simpson was writing on the depression. Scrim thought mistakenly that he had given Simpson the title of the book.[43]

Of Scrim's new acquaintances among politicians, Rob Muldoon was unquestionably the most important to him. Muldoon's seaside bach at Hatfield's Beach was only a few kilometres on the Auckland side of Waiwera. Scrim got to know Muldoon, and they and their wives exchanged visits from time to time. Muldoon and John A.Lee hit it off well when Scrim brought them together. Lee and Scrim both found that they had more in common with Muldoon than with the Kirk-Rowling government which, in their view, had fallen into the same timid conservatism as the first Labour government.[44] Lee was pleased when Muldoon took the trouble to thank him for suggesting that he lighten up his speeches with touches of humour.[45]

On Labour's return to power in 1972, Scrim took his opportunities to draw himself to the attention of ministers with responsibilities in fields of his interest. His scrapbooks of letters preserve carbon copies of letters he wrote to Bill Rowling, Martyn Finlay, Roger Douglas, and Matiu Rata.[46] Drawing on his long experience as missioner, popular broadcaster, and lobbyist, Scrim shrewdly began each letter with a personal touch. To Rowling as prime minister he began by mentioning that in 1939 Mr Savage had sent him to 'investigate something which did not exist at the time' – television – and that, fifteen years before that visit he 'had been studying at Auckland University the possibility of the cathode-ray tube as a possible means of adding vision to sound broadcasting'. He reminded Martyn Finlay of their discussion in 1968 during which he had told him of the part he had played in drafting the legislation for the commercial broadcasting service and of his role as the first controller of the NCBS. He began a letter to Roger Douglas by telling him that he knew his parents before he did, remembering very well 'performing the ceremony that made them man and wife'. He told Matiu Rata that he had been 'brought up in Gisborne among Maori people', and that he had been 'a rather controversial broadcaster' and was 'always in trouble'.

A chance encounter enabled Scrim to make the acquaintance of Hugh Templeton, Muldoon's minister of broadcasting in the National government that returned to power in 1975. Hugh and Natasha Templeton met him while they were holidaying nearby. Templeton was impressed with Scrim's grasp of the issues the government was dealing with, and kept in touch with him from time to time to bounce ideas off him.[47]

★

*Songs to Uncle Scrim* (Downstage 1976): Cathy Downes, Mervyn Thompson, John Banas, Garth Frost, Frances Edmond. (Photograph Di Robson)

History repeated itself for Scrim in March 1976. Forty years earlier Rudall Hayward, paying tribute to Scrim's humanity, had packed an Auckland cinema for showings of *On the Friendly Road.* In 1976 Scrim was the inspiration for *Songs to Uncle Scrim,* a late-night review presented by Downstage Theatre, written by Mervyn Thompson, directed by Catherine Downes and performed by a brilliant cast of actors. Sparkling with pithy lyrics, it was very well received during its short season. 'It was a marvellous piece of theatre,' the *Evening Post*'s theatre reviewer wrote. George Webby, writing for the *Dominion*, felt sure that all Wellingtonians, including a few politicians, would want to see it and urged Downstage to 'make this brilliant piece a regular part of its repertory'.[48] A short season in Christchurch followed later in the year. But *Songs to Uncle Scrim* has yet to have a return season.

Scrim had once again made his public mark and he revelled in his renewed celebrity. But the pleasure did not mitigate his abiding resentment at being, as he saw it, rejected by Fraser's Labour government. The journalist Gabrielle David had taken him at his word when he denied any resentment at not being a knight or a millionaire. But David had also noticed the anger in his eyes.

# CHAPTER 14

# In His Own Words

When, following his heart attacks, Scrim's doctors told him that he must give up his business activities, he began to think about writing his autobiography. He had long held the view that he had made significant contributions to the great broadcasting developments of the century, and that the time would come when he would tell his life story. The time had come sooner than he expected. A letter from Ray Richards, the publisher for Reed Books, encouraged him to try his hand, and he set to work.

Writing his life story was very much a solo performance. Pam was always present to take dictation from him and support him in various ways, but she had not been part of his life during the years he would be recalling and was unable to prompt him or correct his memory. His folders of correspondence and newspaper reports were sketchy and of limited use. But he prided himself on his memory and was happy to rely on it.

Scrim began with a heartfelt tribute to his mother, 'the secret source of any faith I might have had'. He narrated the sequence of events through which a country larrikin became an 'accidental Methodist', highlighting the Rev Edwin Cox's declaration that he was a 'natural' who, in his missionary work, must 'go his own way'.[1] He wrote for the first time about the embarrassing incident that had abruptly ended his service in the Putaruru circuit and could well have had him dismissed as a probationary Methodist missioner. There were lesser dramas in his second posting at Kaitangata, culminating in a serious illness which led the Rev Seamer to transfer him to a warmer climate.[2]

Living and working in the Bay of Islands brought him face to face for the first time with Maori as well as Pakeha church members. Among other things, this evoked more emotional memories of his mother, who for most of her life had lived among Maori. He recorded comments on Maori attitudes and Maori views on the history of the country since the arrival of Europeans. But it cannot be said whether these were views he held in the mid-1920s, an overlay of views he formed later in his life, or a mixture of both.[3]

He and his band of backers and supporters at the Auckland Methodist Social Service Centre had been engaged in a pioneering venture, working with people who were variously burdened down by despair, grief, bereavement and uncertainty. But he was soon struck by the limitations of social services that were provided separately by the various church communities.

What shines through is Scrim's sense of his mission and his determination to have things done his way. Winning the right to screen films free of charge in the Strand Theatre stemmed from his ability to find gaps in the fine print of the regulations governing the public screening of films, and persuade city council officers that they could give him the permission he was asking for. When he failed to get his fellow social workers to support a free boot repairing service he went to the Auckland Businessmen's Association, who took up the idea. When the Methodist Home Mission Board decided not to take up his proposal to establish a radio church, he won Lewis Eady's support, and station 1ZR became the first home of the Friendly Road.

He was, he wrote, working under great pressure. Only through quick changes of activity, he believed, had he preserved his sanity. Fulfilling his duty as a chaplain at the mental hospital, for instance, was his relief from 'the lunacy of poverty amid plenty'.[4] He acknowledged what Dr Hal Pettit and Harold Jones had done to get him to take up interests outside his work responsibilities. Fishing, wrestling, and flying figure prominently in his narrative. Sir Charles Kingsford Smith received honourable mention for his flying exploits and for his advocacy of trans-Tasman air and airmail services. It was as a lobbyist for Kingsford Smith that he first made the acquaintance of Gordon Coates and George Forbes in the Coalition government, and Michael Joseph Savage for the Opposition. He was, he wrote, an ecumenist before ecumenism had a name.[5] But he soon became convinced that more than the blurring of denominational differences would be needed to bring an end to the human suffering that the depression had brought. What in the past had been done by the churches and voluntary effort must become a responsibility of the state.

★

In other ways, too, he was seeing the need for state intervention. Several of his friends, including the Rev Edwin Cox and some other Methodist ministers, some of his acquaintances in the Farmers' Union, the businessman Harry Kelliher, and the poet Rex Fairburn convinced him that the reform of the monetary system was essential to the country's economic recovery.

He gave thirty pages to his first visit to Sydney to spread the good news of the Friendly Road. He wrote of the highlights of his broadcasting career. He spent, so he said, 'years organising the Federation of B Stations' and 'led scores of deputations to Parliament with no success'. His proposal for the future of the B stations would have brought them together in a network of separately owned commercial stations. He turned down Savage's offer of the position of director of broadcasting. He contributed, at Savage's request, to the writing of the Labour government's broadcasting legislation and was disturbed to discover how little cabinet ministers understood what they were doing. He mentioned what had happened in July 1939 to rescue the 1ZB building project and save Paddy Webb's bacon.

His account ended in a cloud of self-justification, and with some hard words for Fraser and his trade union 'gangsters'. Making the 'dream of commercial broadcasting true' had fulfilled an ambition. But 'creative men do not follow history, they make it. It was time to move on.' He had become a member of one of the strongest unions in the country. Without doubt, he could have been elected chairman of the Federation of Labour and 'used people power to wipe the slate clean'. Only the war 'saved Fraser's skin' and gave the first Labour government time 'to destroy themselves in a coalition with Forbes and Coates'. But a 'maverick' could not be 'left alone with a microphone'.[6]

He knew he faced impossible odds, but something he referred to as 'the extreme energy of patience' made far greater demands than 'force or anger'. It was the philosophy he had discovered in Jesus. Had Jesus not used that power he would have been quickly forgotten. Where, Scrim asked, 'were the monuments to Fraser, Nash, McLagan, Walsh, Young, and a dozen others who had tried every trick and used their power to destroy me'?[7]

Some of Scrim's recollections were a mixture of fact and imagination. Talking about his mother's association with Maori leaders on the East Coast, he mentioned a meeting she had had with

Te Kooti that could not possibly have taken place. His account of his acquaintance with George Bernard Shaw was another fiction. He recorded an apparently circumstantial account of crossing the Tasman with Shaw in 1934, dining with him at the captain's table, and taking a last-minute initiative to ensure that he would not be denied entry to New Zealand. (New Zealand at the time had the legal power, should a government decide to exercise it, to exclude anyone who had recently visited the Soviet Union, and Shaw had been a recent visitor.) But Shaw and Scrim had not travelled together. Shaw arrived in Auckland via Panama on 15 March and left Wellington for England via Panama on 14 April.[8] Scrim had left Auckland for Sydney a day or so later.

By June 1974 Scrim had completed 373 typed pages of an outline of his life until he left New Zealand for Australia in 1944. He called it 'Three Circuits and a City' and sent it to Richards.[9] Richards liked what Scrim had written and urged him to keep the flow going. He felt confident that Scrim was on the way to 'a publishable book that would have much to say about the spirit of the times, the state of the country, its politics, politicians, and personalities'. It 'would fill a gap in a period of the country's history about which not so much had so far been published'. Richards envisaged a 'first edition of not less than 5000 copies'.[10]

But Scrim was by then writing not one but two autobiographical accounts, and the second, which he was writing in association with John A. Lee, had first claim on him. That project had been propelled by the success of Tony Simpson's *The Sugarbag Years* which had been published early in 1974. Scrim and Lee had given Simpson a great deal of information about the depression years which he had used to good effect. They both liked the book and were pleased with its early success.

That had given Scrim an idea. He proposed to Lee that they work together on their own book of the depression years. Lee was at that moment between books. The text of his latest writing effort – his book written against Ernest Davis and the liquor industry – was with Alister Taylor, and was down for publication in 1975. He was working up a publication of his diary for the years of Michael Joseph Savage's government, but was happy for that to take its time. He leapt at Scrim's proposal. He was quite sure that they had a compelling story to tell of the seminal contributions they had made during the thirties and how they had been marked down for public assassination by Peter Fraser and his trade union henchmen.[11]

Lee and Scrim worked at a cracking pace. During the second half of 1974 Lee sent Scrim more than ninety handwritten notes about the book, few of them were more than a page long. He peppered Scrim with questions that only he could answer. Scrim responded by sending Lee scrapbooks of letters, newspaper clippings, and documents, and there were many telephone calls. They worked well together.

Lee soon began to see the shape of the book. They had both to be in it from the moment on Queen Street in the late 1920s when Pat Hickey, the veteran trade union leader, introduced Scrim to Lee. Then it would be into the 'hungry years' of the depression, the riots, their championing of the message that 'social change' must replace 'charity', Labour politics, the jamming of 1ZB, and Labour's victory in 1935. 'Yes, Scrim,' Lee wrote, 'we've got to show the advent of Scrim and how it suited the times.'[12]

Lee was not a self-effacing man, but it was clear to him that Scrim must have pride of place in the book. 'Lee comes in because you've got to be seen, as you were, against a background of real politic.'[13] Scrim was enjoying his trip down memory lane. He would never forget, he wrote, how, when they had discovered the jamming equipment at the Newmarket railway station, Lee had taken charge of the telephone, rung Labour Party headquarters in Wellington, and told them to get the message out to all Labour candidates. Going back over the Fraser years was, however, still as painful to him as it was to Lee.

In December Lee declared the task finished. 'It makes a good story.'[14]

Then it was a matter of finding a suitable publisher who would give them a good deal on royalties. Lee had to rein in his prejudices. Over the years he had had strong words of criticism for Reeds. He would have preferred a publisher with a radical reputation, but he already had two texts with Alister Taylor and, although he was satisfied with Alister's expertise, had reservations about his financial backing. Scrim had already opened a line to Ray Richards for the publication of his autobiography. Lee agreed to follow Scrim's lead, and they sent their manuscript to Reeds.

*

Richards favoured publishing the manuscript but the initial responses of his editorial colleagues differed widely. After some in-house discussion, however, there was general agreement that, by removing repetitions and adding some background information for readers who had not lived through the depression, they had a publishable book. There was agreement, too, that with Lee and Scrim's concurrence, Tony Simpson should be hired to edit the book. Scrim and Lee concurred.

Another question was the book's title. While they were working up their manuscript. Lee and Scrim had come to refer to it in ways that gave precedence to Lee's name. The title on the manuscript they sent to Richards was: 'The Lee-Scrim File'. But the Reed editors came to think that Scrim's name should come first in a title that gave equal standing to both authors. Lee agreed and the book was published as *The Scrim-Lee Papers.*

Tony Simpson, based in Wellington, kept in touch with Scrim and Lee through correspondence and occasional visits to Auckland. He knew that as editor and a very much younger man he was the junior member of the team. But he felt sure, too, that he had his own contribution to make to the book that would finally be published. Like Les Edwards, he was a left-winger. He set out to establish a context for the book by adding footnoted comments from some other left-wingers who had been actively engaged in the politics of the depression years.

When Lee read the first draft of Simpson's edited text, he decided that Simpson was exceeding his editorial role, and he would not have it. 'Tony had written some good material,' Lee wrote, but it was 'smothered by irrelevant comment'. He was particularly nettled by Simpson's strictures about the 'Psycho-pathology in Politics'. To Lee, that was 'one of the truest pieces' he had ever written. Tony was free to criticise his 'taste' in a publication of his own but 'not in a book that is alleged to be in part mine'.[15] Simpson won at least one important point, however. Late in the editing process Lee had a change of mind about the ending and wanted to add new material in a postscript. Simpson persuaded both authors to drop the idea.[16]

But Lee's intransigence was Simpson's overriding impression of the experience of working with him. Lee's mind was closed to any interpretation of the thirties but his own. This impelled Simpson to write *The Slump,* his own book about the Depression. Its central chapter is titled 'The Myth According to John A. Lee: Politics 1935–39'.[17]

*The Scrim-Lee Papers* was organised in two parts. Part I, 'The Lean Years', dealt with their work from the dark years of the depression in 1931 until the Labour electoral victory of 1935. Part II, 'After the Deluge', told their stories from the 'new dawn' until Lee's expulsion from the Labour Party in 1940 and Scrim's dismissal from the National Commercial Broadcasting Service in 1943.

Scrim sketched in the background of human distress that led him to organise the Auckland Businessmen's Relief Service. He was, he said, one of a 'diverse body' of monetary reformers who were convinced that only comprehensive state intervention could overcome the economic collapse that gripped the country. He explained that he had one great advantage. He was able to put his message across without flouting the broadcasting regulations which 'positively forbade political broadcasts – in fact forebade the use of the mike for any controversy whatever'. He based his message 'in the words of Jesus Christ', in particular the account of the scourging of money lenders from the temple.

> You made your mike the voice of history. You managed without advancing any political programme to state the simple truth of the times again and again. . . . We [in the Labour Party] were financial heretics. . . . You were saying night after night that what was materially possible and morally desirable was financially possible. We were framing the how, you were voicing the fact.[18]

Scrim wrote that he left school at the age of eleven to become a freezing worker, and 'the child had to become a man'. The only Sunday school he ever attended was a 'two-up school'. He was soon a militant unionist. His workmates elected him to be a job delegate and that forced him to 'know more and more about the workers' case'. He was an 'unusual type of blood-and-guts' slaughterboard hand. He was aggressive. He wore glasses. He dressed well.

He said he was 'never converted to Christianity'. But he 'liked the forthright character of the Carpenter of Nazareth', another worker 'who had known no education'. He became a probationary Methodist missioner and, over the years, preached the same moral message. 'Society as organised was immoral. I wasn't preaching any brand of politics other than the socialism of Jesus.' He had never met a Labour politician. But he was meeting far too many workers suffering unnecessary hardship for any missioner to remain silent.[19] That was Lee's cue to emphasise similarities in his own life. He regularly met people who, like himself, had been in an industrial school, or in jail, and who, sharing their experience with him, had begun to purge their feelings of shame.[20]

Scrim had set out to make the Methodist Social Service Centre 'a sort of humble tabernacle with a light in the window to invite and help hungry souls'. That, to him, was 'the politics of the Carpenter'. If he had 'presented anyone else's politics', he would not have 'rallied help'. He would have 'estranged many who wanted to help'. If he had mentioned radical politics he would have been 'put off the air'.[21]

The Queen Street riot had brought Lee and Scrim to each others' attention. Scrim's broadcast the next morning, Lee believed, calmed people's fears that the riot was the beginning of an organised rebellion. Scrim recalled walking down Queen Street after the riot, urging people to go home, and arranging, in a covert operation, for Dr Pettit to attend to Jim Edwards' battered head. Scrim did not add that he was one of the very few people who knew where Edwards was hiding during the months he was on the run. But he recorded that Ernest Davis knew of Edwards' whereabouts, and stood bail for him when he was arraigned in court.

Ernest Davis's behind-the-scenes networks of personal, business, and philanthropic interests had been very helpful to the Friendly Road and 1ZB. But Lee and Scrim had both become ambivalent about the wealthy brewer, Lee more than Scrim. From time to time Lee sounded Scrim out on his feelings about Davis, and Scrim's bland replies telegraphed an underlying lack of trust. 'Surely,' Lee asks in the book, 'Davis didn't want you to defend his hotels?' 'No,' Scrim replies. 'Ernest knew better than that. Why pay for something when you can get it for nothing?'[22]

The climax of Part I was the jamming of 1ZB which blotted out Scrim's 'Man in the Street' session on the Sunday before the 1935 general election. The whole country, Lee said, was 'wondering if you were going to endorse a Party'. Scrim denied that he intended to do that. 'What the government feared, be believed, was that he would broadcast the result of the poll he had conducted into the attitudes of the political parties to the B stations.' 'I had no intention of saying anything political which would have put the owners of the other small stations in jeopardy.'

Part I ended with the sequence of events that led to the discovery of the jamming device, Gordon Coates's denial of responsibility, Adam Hamilton's later acceptance of responsibility, and the findings of the inquiry that the Labour government conducted after it came to power. The last two sentences foreshadowed the end of Part II of the book. 'Peter Fraser did not pursue the matter after the [Labour] victory. Peter was the sort of fellow who would have been willing to engage in the same sort of tactic.'[23]

Part II, 'After the Deluge', began with Scrim's and Lee's jubilation over the Labour victory, but their comments are written in the knowledge of what would happen to them during the next few years.

Savage is presented favourably for his 'The Road is Open Again' speech, but Lee recalls what he believed to be the prime minister's resentment of him for pressing for the Labour Party to adopt monetary reform. From the moment Nash became Minister of Finance Lee doubted if 'the big things in our policy' would happen. He was also convinced that Savage came to dislike him under the influence of a 'millionaire crony [Ernest Davis]' and a powerful cleric, the 'Metropolitan of the Catholic Church'. Things began going bad for him from the first caucus after the election, when Savage was given the right to select his own cabinet. Scrim's account had the same shape but he has a looser grip on the facts of his case.[24]

By the time of the 1938 general election both men were looking out for each other. 'You were afraid that I was a little too far out,' Scrim wrote, 'and I was worried that you were. We were both too keen about seeing Labour's election promises fully realised.' That reference to being 'a little too far out' was as close as Scrim would get to saying anything about his 'Man in the Street' broadcast on Sunday, 7 August which had forced Savage to defend him against hostile editorials and the exasperated criticism of his cabinet colleagues. Scrim knew at the time, he said, that he was taking risks. It was, he said, part of a pattern that had started with his appointment as controller of the commercial broadcasting service. He had deliberately placed himself outside the power of the public service commissioner and, in so doing, 'thrown away a form of guarantee'. That was self-serving commentary.

Lee gave a dramatic account of his part in rallying back-bench support for Scrim during the crisis he had provoked. He had been visiting the West Coast at the time. He returned to Wellington to a flurry of trade union resolutions declaring solidarity with Scrim, and messages, he said, from 'half the union secretaries in Wellington' who had phoned in to ask him what they could do. Back-bench Labour MPs came to him for advice, and he believed that he had forced Fraser to back off. But he also believed that Fraser was biding his time. 'Peter was trying to do what Adam Hamilton had failed to do – jam Scrim. You (Scrim) had more friends than Fraser, if less power.' 'And though Fraser and his cronies hated you, they often needed you too.' 'If only [Fraser] had left letters, a diary, something which showed the inner workings of his mind,' Scrim lamented.[25]

That prompted Lee to mention the steady stream of visitors who regularly found their way to Scrim's office. 'All Labour voters wanted, if possible, to shake hands with the Prime Minister, and nearly all prominent Labour men and union officials were eager to be seen in your company.' Scrim concurred. But, he added, he now knew 'that there was a spy group which reported my visitors to my enemies. I'm sure that this goodwill was feared by Fraser.'[26] Thus were the themes of Part II brought into play: a brooding Fraser waiting for his opportunity; 'gangster' trade union bosses in league with a wealthy brewer; the backstairs influence of the Catholic Metropolitan; spies who were monitoring Scrim's friends and associates.

Nash was Lee's nemesis. Nash fronted for Savage in the bitter fights in caucus over pensions, the guaranteed price for farm products, and the takeover of the Reserve Bank. Lee made some sharp criticisms of Nash but was less censorious of Savage than he would have been had he been writing solely for himself. An example was his gnomic comment on Savage's public announcement of the government policy on social security. Lee knew better than anyone how determined Savage, Nash and Fraser had been to water down the proposal that caucus finally hammered out. Scrim, speaking first, said that in his opinion Savage had been very relieved that backbenchers had 'forced his hand'. He would 'never forget that great town hall meeting in 1938 when Savage announced the social security proposals. There was no half-heartedness that night.' 'To me,' Lee replied, 'it seemed humbug after his opposition.'[27]

Then it was on to the climax of their account. Lee narrated his expulsion for the drama that it was. Savage was dying but Fraser was issuing statements that he was on the path to recovery. Savage refused to bow to efforts to have Lee brought into the cabinet. Then in the face of much dissatisfaction in caucus, Savage appointed Wilson, 'who was being groomed to rid the Labour Party of Scrim as well as Lee'. Fraser had supported moves to have Lee in the cabinet, but later, so Lee believed, feared a challenge from him for the leadership if Savage died.[28] Lee was in no doubt that, if the caucus had been given a free vote, he and McMillan and Nordmeyer would have been appointed to cabinet. That was Scrim's view, too. He was, he said, 'informed of every move by the radical elements, [and] knew where the support lay amongst MPs until they were cowed by your assassination. The majority were behind you. That was the cause of your trouble. The majority couldn't be allowed to shape the future.'[29]

Lee acknowledged the importance of the 'Lee Letter' and 'Psycho-pathology in Politics' in his struggle with the party leadership. But he insisted that the Lee Letter had been written as a confidential document. It was the work of others that had made it 'the most circulated document in the history of New Zealand'. Writing 'Psycho-pathology in Politics''was the most courageous thing I ever did in my life'. It was published with his name on it.[30]

These publications rocked the Labour Party. Lee was censured at the party's 1939 conference. Then, standing for the first time for election to the national executive, he had topped the poll. The first of these votes, he said, reflected the power of the vote of the big unions, which for the first time had been able to cast 'card votes'. The second was evidence of his popularity among party members. His supporters staved off later attacks on him in the Auckland Labour Representation Committee and in the national executive. Finally, he was 'tried' at the 1940 conference for the 'murder' of the 'Prime Minister' and expelled. The Labour Party, he believed, 'should have been a great Party of Innovation. But it lost its chance and I went down with the lost chance'.[31]

Lee had been proud of Scrim for standing by him, and he quoted from what he had written in his diary at the time. 'Why was Scrim so full of courage last night when at the end of his tribute to Savage he paid a tribute to me. It wasn't at my request. This chap has rare courage allied to radicalism.' What an offence it had been 'to mention Lee in your Sunday obituary of Savage', he said to Scrim. 'I'd become a NON PERSON. Expelled from Labour, I was supposed to go away and die.'[32]

Scrim responded by saying that he 'knew then what most people know today. That you were assassinated not because of anything you'd written but because you had to be disposed of before Savage died. What was done was so indecent that I had to say something.' He also knew that 'what had been done to you would be done to me. Joe Savage had been my friend. You were my friend. Now my enemies were in power. I knew I was down for the slaughter. The question was when.'[33]

Scrim's account of his dismissal suffered from his prolixity. His anecdotes did not add up to a compelling narrative. He told the story of Mark Fagan's unexpected visit and what was done to save Paddy Webb from a breach of promise lawsuit. He also mentioned Webb's role in achieving the reversal of the cabinet decision to stop work on the rebuilding of 1ZB. But he did not mention the link between the two stories. He said nothing about his unsatisfactory working relationship with Wilson. There is no mention of Wilson's decision not to appeal against his military call-up, and no mention of the events that brought about his dismissal.

He chose instead to write about what he believed to be Fraser's determination to get him into the army and have him sent overseas only partly trained, and about his service in the air force as AC2 Scrimgeour. 'Fraser and his friends,' he said, 'had given me Hell.' To put an end to this harassment, he hired 'the top firm of solicitors in New Zealand to get me out'. When Fraser discovered what he was up against, he agreed with the solicitors' conditions for his discharge from military service. There was nothing to keep him in New Zealand. He went to Australia by air, and his family followed by sea. 'The great changes that I'd looked for never happened. The revolution was over before it had begun.'[34]

*The Scrim-Lee Papers* was published early in 1976. It was generously illustrated with newspaper extracts, political advertisements, election results, cartoons, caricatures and photographs. It included explanatory comments attributed to Jim Dyer and Bill Sutch, and anonymous comments written by J.P. Lewin, who was listed as 'a senior public servant'. Appendices to the book included abbreviated notes of Labour caucus minutes relating to cabinet selection, the Reserve Bank, and broadcasting, and the text of 'Psycho-pathology in Politics'.

All the men who had had any direct involvement in Lee's expulsion or Scrim's dismissal were dead, and there was no one to challenge the veracity of the case they had made out for themselves, but several of Scrim's broadcasting colleagues were alive and still living in New Zealand. The *NZ Listener* published a review from one of these, Stewart J. Duff. Under the heading 'Ousted Heroes', Duff thought the book 'slightly top-heavy with self-adulation', but welcomed it as 'a true record of a political game played for high stakes'. Only people who had lived through the 1930s, he wrote, would be able to recall the 'tense and angry feelings' that gripped the country when Lee and Scrim were 'axed'. Their book could not re-create the full drama of events as they unfolded, but it clearly revealed how important it had been for Fraser 'to make sure of his bid for total political power' by getting rid of them. *The Scrim-Lee Papers* showed 'that there are two sides to every story'. But the closest that Duff got to applying this dictum to the Scrim-Lee story was to quote an irrelevant sentence of Max Beerbohm.[35]

The most interesting review of the book was written by O.S. (Orton) Hintz and published in the *New Zealand Bookworld*. Hintz had represented the *New Zealand Herald* in the parliamentary press gallery for most of the time that the Labour government was in power and was later its editor. Many readers, he wrote, would be surprised to learn of the 'shabby intrigues' that went on in the Parliamentary Labour Party 'even in the first flight of victory'. Those who worked in the press gallery at the time knew that 'storm clouds hung ominously over meetings of the government caucus, but journalists were not expected to draw attention to them'. Scrim and Lee, he wrote, 'were and still are uncompromising individualists', and they had not written 'an objective account'. The picture they painted 'would doubtless be presented from a different angle if Fraser and Nash were still alive'.[36]

As with Les Edwards' book, Scrim was glad to receive Gary's praise. 'Congratulations on *The Scrim-Lee Papers*,' he wrote. 'How come you are a better writer than your professional colleague?'[37]

Scrim pressed on with his autobiography while he was making his contributions to the book he was writing with Lee. There were soon signs that he and Richards were at cross purposes. Over the lunch table Richards had enjoyed hearing Scrim's anecdotes but he thought less well of them when, at his suggestion, Scrim put some of them down on paper. That provoked an angry response from Scrim, and it seems from the letters they wrote to each other at the time that Scrim was determined to let Richards know who was running the cutter.[38] But Richards remained impressed with what Scrim was doing and encouraged him to send him more of his recollections.

Scrim soon realised that an account of his life that stopped at 1944 would leave out the post-war years which he had come to think of as the most productive and exciting years of his life. Another volume, perhaps even two volumes, would be needed to deal with them. But he made no attempt to fashion a narrative from the folders of his correspondence during the years he was living in Australia.

Then he made one of his characteristically unexpected changes of tack. Perhaps something had been triggered in his unconscious when Richards said that he preferred listening to Scrim's anecdotes to reading them. The spoken word had always been Scrim's preferred way of communicating, so why was he following convention by *writing* his autobiography? No: he would produce the world's first spoken autobiography. It would not, he told Lee, be a talking book of the sort that was now becoming available but something entirely new, something that was being done for the first time in a thousand years. Instead of dictating to Pam and sending typescripts to Reeds for publication, he began recording anecdotes on audio tapes that could then be played on tape recorders or broadcast over radio. He recorded more than sixteen hours on audio tape and sent them to Reeds.

Scrim's wilful nature undermined his intention. He ignored or swept aside Pam's suggestions. He refused to list items he would talk about in each recording session. He had no idea, he told her, what he would talk about when he began a recording session. He insisted that, except for poems and quotes, he never read from a text. He would keep his mind clear until he was seated in front of the tape recorder, when from past experience he expected his ideas to flow spontaneously. It didn't work.

He began with his birth, the ministrations of the Maori midwife who had brought him into the world, and the story of his father's registering of the birth. But from there on he switched disconcertingly from anecdote to unrelated anecdote. There were repetitions, part repetitions, and uncompleted episodes. He also had a recurring tendency to interrupt anecdotes with an interjectory, 'by the way' and then take up some entirely unrelated topic. His performances were undisciplined.[39]

There was a passing parade of prominent people, among them Queen Salote, Lawrence Olivier and Vivien Leigh, and Count Von Luckner. His freewheeling memory led him to Lawrence of Arabia. 'Why,' he asked were the British authorities so afraid of Lawrence? Why did they let him kill himself? Why did he take the lowest rank in the Royal Air Force?' 'Strangely,' he added, 'I made the same stipulation myself when I was railroaded out of my job of the principal person in commercial broadcasting.'

The incidents that still seem to have given him the greatest pleasure were from his flying days and from his association with the movers and shakers he met during his visit to America in 1939. Most of these recollections repeat or partly repeat what he had written in 'Three Circuits and a City': his first flight that cost him ten shillings; learning to fly under D.M. Allan; his flight to Hastings on the morning of the Napier earthquake; his associations with Kingsford Smith; meeting the 'great Sarnov' in Radio City; taking part in the world's first interview session on television; the honour of speaking at the UCLA commencement.

He said that there was 'no political intent' in his recordings, but he could not suppress his hatred of Fraser. Savage, 'his greatest friend', he mentioned not for himself but in relation to what he believed to be Fraser and Nash's deception of the public about the state of his health when he was close to death. He castigated Fraser for deporting him from his native land. Coates 'was honest and straightforward'. With Savage long since dead, Lee is Scrim's hero and is mentioned several times. He did not think that Lee 'hated' Savage. The article that led to Lee's expulsion from the Labour Party was a 'scientific' analysis of political leadership. John A. Lee was 'an independent intellectual, as I hope I am too'.

Scrim's comments on the Fellowship of the Friendly Road emphasised its role as an influence for religious tolerance, and he linked it to his later efforts through the Society for Closer Relations with Russia to foster understanding of the achievements of the Russian people. He recalled his contribution to the establishment of China's national television service.

It was inevitable from the way he was recording his anecdotes that there would be misses as well as hits. Of people he had worked with or known as acquaintances only the Rev Seamer, Hal Pettit and Harold Jones received incidental mention.

Pam was disappointed that Scrim was unable to give any expression to his emotions in his spoken recollections. She failed to persuade him to say something about how he felt when he was piloting the *Southern Cross*, one of the great moments of his life. She would have known that she was on dangerous ground when she asked him to tell how he met Lena. Scrim appeared to ignore her. Then a minute later he asked himself the question he thought Pam really wanted to ask: 'What was the truth about Scrim? Who were the women in my life?'[40] These were unprofitable questions, he said. 'He had nothing to hide. He would talk about anyone, male or female, who had influenced his life'. Except for his mother and Pam – and, when Pam prompted him, Lena – he could not think of any venture that may have had anything to do with women. Fraser and others had tried to discredit him, he said, but they had not found anything they could pin on him.[41] Scrim changed the subject and Pam let the matter drop. He was covering his tracks.

The feasibility of Scrim's idea of a spoken autobiography was not the only question hanging over his autobiography. Reed Books had entered a long period of internal reorganisations and crises in staff relations that ended in 1983 with a company takeover. Richards was an early casualty of the turmoil and resigned from the firm towards the end of 1975.[42] There is no record in Scrim's correspondence of what Richards thought of the idea of a spoken autobiography or what Reed editors thought of his tapes. All that can be said is that the tapes were returned to Scrim sometime in 1980.

Scrim had never been a man to give up. If Reeds were not to publish his autobiography he would have it published overseas, and he knew who would do it. One of his long-standing acquaintances was Trevor Constable, whose career he had launched in 1943. Constable had moved to the United States in 1953, and Scrim had been in touch with him from time to time. In 1980 he was working for the Matson Shipping Line in California. He had earned a reputation as a maverick UFO researcher, and he was also a published writer on wartime aviation history.[43]

Scrim sent him the typescript of 'Three Circuits and a City', and copies of *Scrim:Radio Rebel in Retrospect* and *The Scrim-Lee Papers*. Between September 1980 and July 1981 Scrim and Pam transferred Scrim's audio material from tape to compact disk and sent the disks to him.There is no record of any correspondence between Scrim and Trevor Constable during the years 1980–84 when he was involved in Scrim's autobiographical project. Scrim included messages to him a number of times on the audio tapes he was sending him, and perhaps Constable kept in touch by telephone or through audio tape messages.

Scrim had given up the idea of publishing a spoken autobiography. He hoped that Trevor would weave the first-person spoken material of the disks into a third-person publishable biography. He also hoped that Trevor would agree to being listed as the author of the book. Trevor was being cast as Boswell to Scrim's Johnson.

In comments to Trevor, Scrim said that he was self-conscious about the insistent use of the first person in the recordings. One of the things he disliked about autobiographies, he said, was the way they centred on the 'I' of the author. But his own autobiography was undoubtedly an 'I' book: the story of a 'man alone', written entirely around the first-person pronoun. No amount of editing could have reshaped Scrim's collection of anecdotes into a book that would have met the expectations that Ray Richards had initially held for it.[44]

Constable wrote to Pam in November 1984 to say that he would not be able 'to do the beloved old controller's biog'. To Gary he wrote that he was exhausted, having just completed a biography of a Second World War German air ace, and was not in the right frame of mind to take on another big project. There was a distinct tone of regret in his letter. 'I really do love your Dad,' he wrote. The recordings were a 'treasure trove'. 'Scrim's faults and failings' amounted to so little 'compared with his surpassing vision. All his life, he had to walk to his goals through shoals of impeding pygmies, including some of the most vicious humans living among civilised people.'[45]

Scrim accepted, how reluctantly we cannot say, that his autobiography would not be published. He was eighty-one and in poor health. He settled for the next best thing. He had said while he was working on it that he would lodge a copy of his autobiography with the Alexander Turnbull Library, and that is what happened. Much, but far from all, of what he had written was included in personal papers lodged with the Turnbull soon after his death. Another cache of papers, including typescripts of 'Three Circuits and a City' was added in 2001. Taken together, these deposits, with holdings of letters between Scrim and Pam, and Gary Scrimgeour, and a typescript of Gary's conversation with Lena Scrimgeour are a magpie collection of materials on Scrim's life.

# CHAPTER 15

# Last Years

To be closer to Greenlane Hospital, Scrim and Pam left Waiwera for Woodlands Park, near Titirangi in mid-1971. A few years later they moved to Laingholm, closer to the village at Titirangi and the Manukau Harbour. These changes of residence enabled them to garden, look after lawns, and tend fruit trees in ways that had not been possible at Waiwera. But Scrim still followed his own impulses and, for Pam, the change was a mixed blessing. Reading between the lines in Pam's letters to Gary from this time onwards it is not difficult to link the collapses and illnesses that dogged the rest of Scrim's life to accounts of his frenetic bursts of physical activity around their house and garden.

Scrim had probably slowed down somewhat after his first heart attack and the five operations that followed it, but his public life was developing a dynamic of its own. Men and women in radio and television broadcasting and in the media generally knew where to find him, and he was, it seems, only too ready to assist them in any way he could.

Scrim made his television debut on the commemorative programme that TV1 screened on the history of radio in August 1975. In April 1976 he was the subject of an extended interview which was screened a few months later. He was asked about his early life, his years as a Methodist minister, the depression, radio broadcasting, his contribution to television in China, and his views on socialism in New Zealand and abroad. Only the part of the programme dealing with China is held in the TVNZ Archive. It records Scrim's very general responses to the interviewer's unfocused questions.[1]

For these and later interviews the TV crews converted Scrim's home into a temporary studio and interviewed him in his garden. These were very demanding on Pam. After the visit in April 1976 she told Gary that she had been 'fantastically busy' providing food for forty-six people in the course of three weeks. But there were benefits as well. Scrim was obviously pleased to get a cheque for $150 for his contribution to that programme. He no doubt received honoraria for his contributions to later programmes.[2]

Working with John A. Lee on *The Scrim-Lee Papers* had firmly re-established their friendship. By the time of the book's publication in 1976 they were the popular embodiment of the dark days of the depression years. They kept in touch. Pam was surprised and delighted when Lee gave her an electronic typewriter, allowing her to discard her very old mechanical typewriter.[3] Scrim was present at the public launch of the Lee diaries.[4] He was preparing to chair a function to celebrate Lee's ninetieth birthday when Lee died. He was one of the cavalcade of speakers in the documentary of Lee's political life that the NZBC broadcast in April 1984. Two sound bites were his contribution: one of thirty-five seconds on Lee and the Labour Party, the other of twenty seconds on Lee's relationship with Savage.[5]

Scrim and Lee at Lee's 87th birthday party. (Photographer unknown, Alexander Turnbull Library Collection)

Scrim gave long interviews to two academic researchers who were interested in what he could tell them about leading figures in the first Labour administration. Michael King interviewed him in 1978 for the biography he was writing on Peter Fraser. Barry Gustafson interviewed him in 1981 for his biography of Michael Joseph Savage. Both men were in the early stage of their research and were interested in Scrim's impressions of the personal characteristics of the subjects of their research.

Michael King began by asking Scrim for his impressions of Fraser's appearance, demeanour, and personal characteristics. It was soon clear that Scrim had had virtually no personal contact with Fraser before he became prime minister. But that did not stop him from talking about him with great assurance. Vain about his own appearance, Scrim was disdainful of Fraser's lack of interest in his. Fraser dressed untidily, Scrim said. He never changed his spectacles all the time Scrim knew him. He wore 'very small steel spectacles' that 'reduced the size of his eyes'. As a speaker, Fraser was in no way to be compared with Holland, Semple, Lee or a dozen other members of the party who were all good speakers.

Fraser, Scrim said, 'was not an attractive personality in any way'. He was 'unscrupulous' in exploiting 'people's weaknesses'. He was a 'schemer' who had the reputation 'of being extremely devious in party matters'. He was incapable of giving credit where it was due. It was Fraser, Scrim said, who 'generated the split in the Labour Party'. He was absolutely without humour. When King asked Scrim if he thought Fraser was puritanical he replied adamantly that he was a sanctimonious hypocrite, and that, he said, was also the opinion of the permanent heads of the public service with whom he 'brushed sleeves' in the corridors of Parliament. The interview had given him an opportunity to exercise a hobby horse. Among other things he told King his story about assailing Fraser in his office and demanding that he take Lee back in as minister of defence.[6] He also rehearsed his romance about having George Bernard Shaw as his travelling companion when crossing the Tasman in 1934.

Barry Gustafson began his interview by asking Scrim when and in what circumstances he first met Michael Joseph Savage. Scrim quickly batted that away and then talked about his own commitment to socialism as a result of reading Tolstoy, whose books he said he had read before he read the Bible. Then followed some remarks on Nash's obstructive performance as Minister of Finance, a long digression on Ernest Davis along the lines of what he had written in *The Scrim-Lee Papers*, and some comments on the 'main trunk caucus' of Labour MPs of which Scrim had been an honorary member on weekly trips between Auckland and Wellington.[7]

When Scrim got around to talking about Savage his remarks were interspersed with some general comments that he had not previously made public. Savage was a 'very solid, generous man' though 'a lonely fellow'. He was 'a slow thinker' and was 'never a good talker or promoter of ideas'. He 'lacked a ruthless streak' and was not a 'good decision-maker'. But his intuition was usually sound. He was the right leader for Labour when it became the government in 1935. Without having the time to read about the Spanish Civil War, Savage was against Franco. He believed, as Scrim had, that Edward VIII should have been allowed to marry Mrs Simpson and remain on the throne. Savage was a pacifist but would not have 'made a good war time leader'. He made a serious mistake when he refused to take Lee into his cabinet for it left him without a 'credible Minister of Defence' when war broke out.[8]

It is unlikely that either King or Gustafson will have got any pay dirt from their interviews.

After a tetchy start in 1959, the letters that Scrim and Gary wrote to each other became warmer and friendlier. Scrim and Pam were proud of Gary when he completed his Princeton PhD in 1959. They counselled him when he was trying to make up his mind to leave his first wife. They warmly welcomed Helen, his second wife, to the Scrimgeour family. They endorsed his decision to transfer his academic commitments from teaching and English literature to research into road safety.[9] Their support was important to Gary, who knew that he shared many of Scrim's characteristics, including a tendency to branch out unexpectedly in new directions.

Gary was full of his latest enthusiasm when he and Helen made the first of their visits to New Zealand in January 1975. He had a notion that he could make a contribution to New Zealand political life and spent a lot of time talking to people who might back him in a campaign to be elected at the coming general election. He did not know whether he would offer his services to Labour or National, but was confident that he would be welcomed by whichever party he chose, and could win a seat. He persisted with the idea for several months before giving it away. His later decision to become a best-selling novelist was more productive. His first novel *The Magic Dragon* was published in 1976.[10] Others followed in later years.

But there was a recurring note of anxiety in Gary's letters to Scrim. Now in his early forties, he would write effusively of his anxiety that any delay in receiving news of Scrim might be the ominous sign that his father had died. Gary still had a fear, too, that some unwitting remark in one of his letters might spark Scrim's anger. Scrim's letters to Gary dealt almost exclusively with his own concerns and activities. Gary's were also about what he and Helen were doing, but they often included comments on the doings of other family members. With no children of his own, Gary was the self-appointed family uncle. He seems to have written regularly to Lena, and perhaps less regularly to Joan and Graham, and to his nephews and nieces. He visited Lena and Joan on trips to Australia.

Only once in his letters to Scrim and Pam did Gary venture a comment on anything of a personal nature in their lives. After his visit in 1977 he took them gently to task over their drinking habits. They had become addicted to Kelliher's regular supply of DB products. Gary wished that he could 'bully or bribe' them to give up alcohol for six months. They had forgotten, he wrote, how much better they would feel if they did not drink, and they would 'both be much more fun in the evenings if [they] weren't so befuddled'.[11]

We look almost in vain for any mention of family members or of other people in Scrim's letters or in his autobiographical notes. But he had played an important role in the lives of his brothers and sisters and perhaps of other family members in 1926 when he was in settled employment and they were not. He came to the rescue, too, in 1943 when his elder brother Gordon died, leaving a wife with a young family to care for. After his return to New Zealand in 1968, Scrim seems to have kept in touch with his brother Norman. When he was writing his autobiographical notes he called on his elder sister Jess for her to help in recalling the names of local shopkeepers for his chapter on his early years. It was through Jess's inquiries, too, that he was able to trace the fortunes of his Scrymgeour forebears. His younger sister Amy was the only sibling he mentioned in his autobiographical notes.[12] An incidental mention in one of Scrim's letters to Gary records that Joan and her husband had passed through

Auckland during a South Pacific cruise. There is a copy in one of his scrapbooks of a short letter he wrote asking her to take an interest in Pam's financial situation after his death. Graham, on the other hand, seems to have disappeared from his life.

Scrim went down with a mystery illness in July 1977. It was the first in what would be a sequence of illnesses that would plague him for the rest of his life. He was not so much ill as paralysed, Pam reported to Gary and Helen.[13] Simply helping him to sit up was a continuing challenge for her, for she was also in poor health at the time. After a series of medical examinations and fears that he might be suffering from a stomach ulcer or, worse, cancer, Scrim began to make progress, though he was not expected to 'be himself' for quite some time. But there were no more references to his health for two or three years. In 1980, however, he made a will.[14] He named Pam as the sole beneficiary of the residue of his estate after the payment of funeral and testamentary expenses and any just debts. Within his limited financial means he was protecting Pam's future.

Pam's letters to Gary continued in her usual matter-of-fact way until the end of 1982, when she wrote: 'Without rancour I must admit it has been a rather long haul in most of the thirty plus years Dad and I have been together.' That personal note aside, she assured Gary that Scrim was 'improving daily' and that his 'overall condition' was 'remarkably healthy'. They had been to Warren Freer's for Christmas Day, and Scrim's 80th birthday was 'quite an event'.[15]

Soon afterwards Scrim had 'a very slight stroke', from which he recovered.[16] But he went rapidly down hill after that. There were times, Pam told Gary, when Scrim was 'extremely disoriented'. She was finding it 'very demanding and trying'. 'It was a great shame to see someone fall apart before one's eyes.'[17] From the United States, Gary was watching with growing concern. He made a short visit to Auckland in September 1984. He visited again in October 1985 and, after discussion with Pam, made arrangements for Scrim to become a patient in Everil Orr House, the Methodist home for the aged.[18] The shift clearly brought great relief to Pam, who was then able to reduce her direct involvement in his care to a regular weekly visit.

Initially, living alone for the first time in more than thirty years, Pam had her 'down days' when she was 'sad' and felt 'stunned and adrift'.

Soon, however, she was aware of 'a sense of relief': she had coped with Scrim and covered for him for so long. She reorganised her living arrangements in the cottage. She played cassettes of music. She wore dresses and skirts more than she had. Sometimes she went out at night. She joined the Titirangi Senior Citizens' Association and took part in their weekly card evenings. But her greatest challenge was to be in control of decisions in her life. Scrim had always been the decision-maker. She became aware that the social worker who visited her once a week was unwittingly casting her into the same dependent role, and she was clearly pleased with herself when, summoning up courage, she was able to claim her own autonomy in this new relationship.[19]

Scrim was given the best bedroom at Everil Orr House, a sunny room on the first floor from which he had a view of the entrance hall and the path leading to the house. But he was living in a world of his own. He believed that Everil Orr House had been built specially for him. He talked incessantly as he lived out a succession of fantasies in which he was the man in charge of Everil Orr House, the director of a famous choir, and the chief executive of a corporate management team.[20] He had, as Pam had well known, episodes when he was very aggressive in what he had to say.

There was nothing that anyone could say or do. Scrim's rational life was over. He died on 16 January 1987, six days before what would have been his eighty-fourth birthday. The *New Zealand Herald* published an announcement of his death but there was no mention of funeral arrangements.

Ted Reynolds gave Scrim a half-page spread and a photograph in his weekly column in the *New Zealand Herald*.[21] He and Scrim had known each other at least since Scrim's return to New Zealand, and he had written a fulsome review of *The Scrim-Lee Papers* (see chapter 13). Under the heading 'Uncle Scrim had a Direct Line to the Heart of New Zealand' he gave Scrim a fond farewell. Reynolds wrote as if he had a direct line to Scrim. More than once in his piece, using the phrase 'on Scrim's telling of it', he presented himself as Scrim's mouthpiece.

Scrim's fame during the depression years, Reynolds wrote, and the affection that people had for him, were 'probably unmatched in

New Zealand history'. His Sunday sermons on his 'Man in the Street' programme 'did much to create the tidal wave that swept Labour into government in 1935'. The battle between a quick-witted Scrim and a 'vengeful Fraser' gave the piece its 'political' focus. That battle, Reynolds wrote, had its origin in what Scrim had said about John A. Lee in his broadcast tribute to Savage. In that tribute, Reynolds claimed, Scrim had said that Lee would have made a better leader of the party than Fraser. The rest of Reynolds' piece repeated the line that Les Edwards had developed in his biography of Scrim, and Scrim had repeated in *The Scrim-Lee Papers.*

It is probable that Gary will have flown to Auckland to attend his father's funeral. It is probable, too, that the heartfelt piece that the *NZ Listener* published a few weeks later was the eulogy Gary had given at the funeral. Under the title 'When Scrim Spoke', it was a two-page feature article, and it had a prominent place in the magazine together with a full-page portrait photograph of Scrim as he had been when he was conscripted in 1943.[22] The *NZ Listener* set the scene for the piece with its lead-in sentence, which announced 'Uncle Scrim' as 'the scourge of the establishment, the fabled New Zealand broadcaster who stood for irreverence, verve, and ordinary people'.

Gary's eulogy opened with an astounding assertion 'In 1944,' he wrote, 'a Prime Minister sought to have my father killed because he was the best-loved man in New Zealand. The Prime Minister was Peter Fraser.' We cannot say how this item of Scrim's propaganda became lodged in Gary's mind. He was seven years old in February 1943 when *Truth*, taking up Scrim's campaign against the Fraser government, claimed that he would be railroaded into the army and posted half trained to active service in the Middle East. But Scrim had had no further need of this fabrication after he enlisted in the RNZAF five months later. Perhaps Gary might have heard Scrim talking about his call-up at the time or in later years. But the railroading scenario, after serving a purpose at the time, may well have disappeared from Scrim's accounts of his hostilities with Fraser. Les Edwards' biography of Scrim was relentlessly hostile to Fraser but he spared readers the sort of embellishment that Gary now gave to the sequence of events.[23] The facts of Scrim's military deployment had been altogether different.

Having gained the attention of his readers, Gary gave his account of Scrim's career as an important public figure. Scrim, he wrote, was always valued more highly by 'outsiders than by the New Zealand establishment'. He met the 'Great Depression head on', taking the side of 'the person in the street'. He was 'the country's most popular social commentator'. He emphasised 'optimism in bad times'. He sometimes sounded simplistic, 'as humanism sometimes does'. But the support he enjoyed among ordinary people was enormous.

Scrim, Gary continued, 'created the art and structure of broadcasting in New Zealand'. Members of conservative elites thought he was dangerous but the support he enjoyed among ordinary people was enormous. In 1935 the United–Reform government jammed his regular broadcast 'because they thought he would swing the election to Labour'. In its turn, the Labour government censored him, fired him, and 'tried to railroad him' into the military firing line 'although he was forty and had a damaged heart'. Then they 'effectively exiled him' on the condition that he would not broadcast in New Zealand for twenty-five years. On his return 'the NZBC found it impolitic to let the public hear him'.

Gary's piece ended with an appeal. 'A voice so ardently silenced by governments,' he wrote, 'is worth listening to, especially when it spoke for ordinary people. It was a voice full of gentleness and humour, not rage.' There was an urgent need, he concluded, for Scrim's message to be heard at the present time 'when the establishment once more believes that ordinary people don't know what's best for them'.

Gary's admiration for Scrim was unquestionable. Nothing he now wrote about Scrim's broadcasting career, however, could have been based on personal experience. His image of his father will have been built up from his reading of Les Edwards' biography, *The Scrim-Lee Papers*, and his discussions in recent years with Scrim himself. He probably got the phrase about Scrim's gentleness and humour from Harry Bell's *Chats*. The story about an avenging Fraser was Scrim's make-believe. Writing about Scrim's controversial broadcasts and his guerilla campaign against Fraser and Wilson would have tested any eulogist. But Gary was writing propaganda and did not mention them.

There is no way of knowing what the generality of *NZ Listener* readers thought about the piece. Forty-four years after Scrim's dismissal, not many would have had memories of the events he was writing about. Only one reader, Denzil Ward, felt prompted to write a letter to the editor. Ward had been a parliamentary law draftsman who had worked with Fraser on legislative matters when he was prime minister. Ward would not comment, he wrote, on what Gary had to say about his father, but he was compelled to respond to his 'wild and unsubstantiated allegations' about Fraser. He 'had formed the highest opinion of Fraser's integrity and character' in his work with him, an 'opinion shared by my colleagues'.[24] It was an opinion that would have been endorsed by other senior public servants who had worked closely with Fraser. They grumbled with good reason about his undisciplined working habits, his unpunctuality, and about having to wait around for meetings with him late at night after Parliament had risen. But they were at one in agreeing about the quality of his mind, about his ability to get to the nub of issues, and about the reasonableness of his decisions.[25]

Gary claimed that Scrim was not being honoured in his own country. Scrim had suffered, Gary claimed, at the hands of the great New Zealand clobbering machine. Other countries treated their famous sons and daughters with greater respect, he wrote. But Gary was straining for effect and he was mistaken. Scrim's claim to public recognition had not been challenged. The public perception of Scrim in 1987 and for the rest of the century rested primarily on the Edwards' biography and *The Scrim-Lee Papers*. The outlines of their interpretations are clearly to be seen, for example, in the comprehensive biographical entry on Scrim that was published in 1998 in volume four of the government-sponsored *Dictionary of New Zealand Biography*.[26]

# CHAPTER 16

# What Did It Add Up To?

In the spring of 1936 few if any New Zealanders would have mistaken Scrim for the man sitting or standing next to him. He had become enormously popular, especially in and around Auckland. He was, with Michael Joseph Savage, John A. Lee, and Aunt Daisy, one of the most widely recognisable New Zealanders. His softly spoken broadcasting voice and the messages of comfort and hope he presented in his 'Man in the Street' sessions had made him so. He was becoming more visible as a public figure, and his popularity stemmed from what people could see as well as hear. He was not a commanding public figure but with his fairly tall, slim figure and wavy brown hair he was distinctive. He dressed stylishly. He had more than a touch of showmanship.

With the election of a Labour government, however, big changes were afoot in the country's broadcasting arrangements which, among other things, would transform Scrim's role. It is hard to believe that he and Savage were unaware that the bargain they struck was so deeply flawed. Public attention fastened first on the size of Scrim's remuneration as controller of a state-owned commercial broadcasting service. That was soon tidied up. But, cobbled together in private by Savage and Scrim, the essential features of Scrim's appointment were wrong in principle. Savage should have insisted that Scrim sever his relationship with the Fellowship of the Friendly Road when he accepted the role of organising the state's commercial broadcasting services. He should not have allowed Scrim to continue to broadcast his weekly 'Man in the Street' session. In allowing him to do so he should not have exempted him from the rules binding all other public servants in what they could say or write in public.

Perhaps Savage thought that Scrim would continue as he had begun, broadcasting weekly messages of comfort and hope. No doubt Scrim thought that he was still doing that but with the important difference that, with Labour in power, poor people should be encouraged to look for the light at the end of the tunnel.

New themes appeared in his 'Man in the Street' sessions alongside the older ones. When newspaper editors and National politicians accused him of taking political stances in what was supposed to be a Sunday evening religious session he retorted that he was speaking out as a matter of principle. When they replied with the all-too obvious point that he was the only civil servant who had been allowed the right of unfettered free speech and, furthermore, that he was exercising that right weekly on a state-owned wireless station, he had no convincing answer. When they asserted that he was the government's minister of propaganda, the local manifestation of Dr Goebbels, they had him in a political corner.

It seems likely that Scrim retained the loyalty of a great many supporters despite his occasional vituperative public attacks on people and organisations he perceived to be his enemies. But those outbursts provided a focus for people who were beginning to disagree strongly with some of the things he was saying and wanted him to be brought into line. Importantly, Savage's cabinet colleagues became uncomfortable with his broadcasts, and it was only Savage's backing in 1938 that saved him from being put off the air.

There are no signs that any of Scrim's opponents or any of Savage's cabinet colleagues had Father Coughlin in mind when they deplored the role he was playing as a public broadcaster. Their eyes were fixed on Germany and Dr Goebbels. Broadcasting as a man of the left, however, Scrim was performing the same role in New Zealand that the right-wing Coughlin was performing in the United States as an opponent of Roosevelt. In 1942 Wilson warned Scrim against becoming New Zealand's Father Coughlin, but he did so because he feared, mistakenly, that Scrim was about to set up a clandestine 'freedom radio station' to harry the government.

Scrim's moment of overseas recognition came with his visit to the United States in 1939. To have been discussed in the company of Dr Goebbels and Father Coughlin in a newspaper as reputable as the *Christian Science Monitor* was as unexpected as it was newsworthy. Not having seen the newspaper report I can only surmise what might have been written about him. But the fact, that the president of UCLA referred to the piece in a large meeting on campus at which Scrim was a guest of honour implies that it had painted his guest in a favourable light. Goebbels was Hitler's propaganda supremo and Coughlin was one of Roosevelt's most vociferous right-wing opponents. Scrim with his left-wing support for the New Zealand Labour government was probably presented as a contrast to them.

Scrim's other high-profile moments in the United States were his appearance in one of the very first interviews to be broadcast by the Radio Corporation of America (RCA) and his opportunity to discuss technical aspects of television with some of RCA's leading men. In later years he would date his active involvement in television from these incidents. But his involvement was slight, apart from his participation as an adviser in developments in Chinese television in 1959. In the early 1950s he made a significant contribution to the production of films to be used in television broadcasts. He made representations for the formation of television companies in Australia in 1953–54 and in New Zealand in 1970, but he was never engaged in the management, production or presentation of television broadcasting.

Scrim's unsuccessful bid for the control of Australia's first commercial television service was clearly deeply disappointing to him. Even without the questions that would have been raised at the time about the reasons for his departure from the NCBS, his bid would have had difficulty heading off the successful Macquarie bid. But he had left New Zealand under a dark cloud and it followed him across the Tasman.

On one occasion in the years of his retirement Scrim drew up a score sheet of his successes and failures in broadcasting. Successes there certainly had been. Establishing and building up the Friendly Road station in Auckland during the depression years was undoubtedly a success. He got state-controlled commercial broadcasting off to a bright start, but his occasional angry outbursts in his 'Man in the Street' session and his regular advocacy on behalf of the Labour government's policies tarnished his reputation. Away from public view, however, there were features of his day-to-day management that cost him the support of his senior colleagues as time went on.

A large part of his success during the depression years had stemmed from his success in winning the support of influential members of the Auckland community. But as controller of the NCBS he was very much his own master. He freed himself of day-to-day responsibilities but does not seem to have felt any obligation to inform his senior colleagues about his initiatives. It is clear from Ian Mackay's comments that this lack of accountability damaged Scrim's working relations with his colleagues. They found him overweening. He made decisions and took the organisation in new directions without informing his colleagues, much less asking for their advice. When he listened to them it was not to take note of their views but to allow them to be able to say that they had had their say. His unpredictable storms of anger were hard to take. In the end he was working in isolation from all but one or two of his senior colleagues and in opposition to his minister. He claimed that his dismissal was an act of victimisation by the Fraser government, but he had brought it upon himself. A career in broadcasting which began with such great promise came to an untimely end through his domineering personality.

# Notes

## Abbreviations

| | |
|---|---|
| *AJHR* | *Appendices to the Journal of the House of Representatives* |
| APL | Auckland Public Library |
| ATL | Alexander Turnbull Library, National Library of New Zealand |
| *NZPD* | *New Zealand Parliamentary Debates* |

## Chapter 1

1 MS-Papers-4104-73, n.d., ATL.
2 MS-Papers-4104-71, ATL.
3 Scrim to Jess, n.d., MS-Papers-4104-96, ATL; extract from Ian Moncrieffe of that Ilk and David Hicks, *The Highland Clans*, 1967; MS-Papers-4104-71, ATL.
4 MS-Papers-4104-73, n.d., ATL.
5 MS-Papers-4104-96, n.d., ATL.
6 Ibid.
7 Ibid.
8 MS-Papers-4104-71, n.d., ATL.
9 MS-Papers-4104-96, n.d., ATL.
10 Ibid.
11 MS-Papers-4104-107, n.d., ATL, Broadcasting History Trust interview with C.G. Scrimgeour, LCD-0444:7 Oral History Centre, ATL.
12 Ibid.
13 Lena Scrimgeour interview with Gary Scrimgeour, fMS-Papers-7289-1, n.d., ATL.
14 Ibid.
15 MS-Papers-4104-73, n.d., ATL.
16 MS-Papers-4104-109, n.d., ATL.
17 *New Zealand Radio Record*, 30 April 1937, p.31.
18 MS-Papers-4104-96 n.d., ATL.
19 Ibid.
20 MS-Papers-4104-71 and 73, n.d., ATL; Department of Internal Affairs, Register of Births, Deaths, and Marriages, No. 10235, 1920.
21 Gary Scrimgeour, note, 10 August 1986, fMS-Papers-7289-4, ATL.
22 MS-Papers-4104-96, n.d., ATL.
23 Department of Internal Affairs, Register of Births, Deaths, and Marriages, No. 4390, 1921.

24 MS-Papers-4104-96, n.d., ATL.
25 Ibid.

## Chapter 2

1 MS-Papers-4104-96, n.d., ATL.
2 C.G. Scrimgeour (Uncle Scrim) ed., *Hello Everybody: Life is a Friendly Road*, printed for Rev C.G. Scrimgeour, Auckland, Unity Press Ltd, n.d. [1933], 2, p.8.
3 Ibid.
4 Scrimgeour, *Hello Everybody*.
5 MS-Papers-4104-96, n.d., ATL.
6 Ibid.
7 Ibid.
8 C.G. Scrimgeour to Rev T.G. Brooke, 17 May 1923, 13 June 1923, Methodist Church of New Zealand Archives (Auckland).
9 C.G. Scrimgeour's telegram to Rev T.G. Brooke, 13 June 1923, Methodist Church of New Zealand Archives (Auckland).
10 MS-Papers-4104-96, n.d., ATL.
11 MS-Papers-7783-1, pp.53, 56, ATL.
12 Ibid, p.56.
13 Rosslyn J. Noonan; *By Design: A brief history of the Public Works Department and Ministry of Works, 1870–1970*, Wellington, Ministry of Works and Development, 1975, p.117; *AJHR*, 1929, Vol. II, D-1, p.iv.
14 Scrimgeour, *Hello Everybody*, 2, p.18.
15 Ibid, p.16.
16 MS-Papers-7783-1, p.73, ATL.
17 Ibid, pp.73, 75, 76, 77.
18 Ibid, p.78.
19 Ibid, p.84. The Kaitangata mine disaster happened in February 1879, killing thirty-five men; A.H.McLintock, ed., *Encyclopaedia of New Zealand*, Vol. 1, Wellington, Government Printer, 1966, p.484.
20 MS-Papers-7783-1, p.86, ATL.
21 Ibid, p.109.
22 Ibid, pp.103–8.
23 Ibid, p.110.
24 MS-Papers-7783-2, p.114.
25 Ibid, p.125.
26 Ibid, p.127.
27 Ibid.
28 Ibid, p.133.
29 Ibid, p.124.
30 MS-Papers-4104-130, n.d., ATL; Scrimgeour, *Hello Everybody, II*, p.21.
31 MS-Papers-7783-2, p.128.
32 Ibid, pp.129–32.
33 MS-Papers-4104-96, n.d., ATL.

34 Ibid; Diana Beaglehole, from 'Albert Ernest Davy' biography, in Claudia Orange, ed., *The Dictionary of New Zealand Biography,* Vol. 4, 1921–40, Auckland University Press/Internal Affairs, 1998, pp.132–4.
35 MS-Papers-4104-137, n.d., ATL.
36 Department of Internal Affairs Register of Births, Deaths and Marriages, 1926:2075.
37 Lena Scrimgeour, interview with Gary Scrimgeour, n.d., fMS-Papers-7289-1, ATL; *Standard*, 13 May 1937, Report of interview and photograph.
38 MS-Papers-7783-2, p.139, n.d., ATL.
39 MS-Papers-4104-138, n.d., ATL.

## Chapter 3

1 *New Zealand Methodist Times*, 5 May 1928, p.3.
2 Ibid, 5 September 1931, p.3.
3 Ibid, 18 April 1931, p.6.
4 Sir Gordon Edward George Minhinnick, Max Lambert, ed., *Who's Who in New Zealand,* 12th edition, Reed, 1991, p.440.
5 MS-Papers-7783-2, 'Three Circuits and a City', p.219, ATL.
6 Ibid, p.218.
7 Ibid.
8 Ibid.
9 Ibid, pp.211–12.
10 Ibid, p.105.
11 Ibid, pp.178–9.
12 Ibid, p.184.
13 *Sun*, 20 August 1927, p.1.
14 Ibid; Scrimgeour, *Hello Everybody*, p.3.
15 MS-Papers-7783-2, 'Three Circuits and a City', pp.172–3, ATL.
16 Ibid.
17 Anita Leslie, *Francis Chichester,* London, Hutchinson, 1975.
18 MS-Papers-7783-2, 'Three Circuits and a City', p.161, ATL.
19 Ibid., pp.225–40.
20 LCD-1082, Oral History Centre, ATL; 'Three Circuits and a City', p.78.
21 MS-Papers-4104-111, n.d., ATL.
22 Melville Harcourt, *A Parson in Prison*, Auckland, Whitcombe and Tombs, 1942, pp.211–12; Les Edwards, *Scrim: Radio Rebel in Retrospect*, Auckland, Hodder and Stoughton, 1971, pp.26–9.
23 MS-Papers-7783-2, p.163, ATL.
24 *New Zealand Observer,* 24 March 1932.
25 *Auckland Star,* 14 April 1932.
26 *John A. Lee's Weekly,* 10 December 1941.
27 *New Zealand Observer,* 22 April 1932.
28 *Auckland Star,* 26 April 1932.
29 C.G. Scrimgeour to Ray Richards, 19 June 1974, p.17, MS-Papers-4104-27, ATL.

30 *NZ Methodist Times*, 9 July 1932.
31 'The Call', No.8, Auckland Methodist Social Mission, MS-Papers-4104-102, ATL.

## Chapter 4

1 MS-Papers-4104, pp.185–6, n.d., ATL.
2 Hon A. Hamilton, postmaster general, *NZPD*, 2 November 1931, p.657.
3 Patrick Day, *The Radio Years: A History of Broadcasting in New Zealand*, Vol. 1, Auckland, Auckland University Press in association with the Broadcasting History Trust, 1994, p.119.
4 *New Zealand Radio Record*, 8 June 1931, p.23; *New Zealand Observer*, 5 October 1931, p.11.
5 *New Zealand Observer*, 3 June 1931, p.11.
6 *Truth*, 9 June 1937, p.15.
7 Asa Briggs, *The BBC: The First Fifty Years*, New York, Oxford, 1985, pp.92–3. For policy development in New Zealand, see Day, *The Radio Years*, chapters 5 and 6.
8 See for example *NZPD*, Vol. 226, p.403, Donald.
9 *New Zealand Observer*, 23 November 1933, p.24.
10 Day, *The Radio Years*, pp.119–20.
11 *New Zealand Observer*, 13 October 1932, p.22.
12 *New Zealand Observer*, 8 March 1934, p.10.
13 *New Zealand Observer*, 22 September 1932, p.26.
14 *New Zealand Observer*, 6 October 1932, p.22.
15 *New Zealand Observer*, 9 March 1933, p.24.
16 *New Zealand Observer*, 12 January 1933, p.24.
17 *New Zealand Observer*, 22 September 1932, p.26; 29 December 1932, p.22; 2 February 1933, p.24.
18 *New Zealand Observer*, 7 December 1933, p.24.
19 MS-Papers-4104-51, n.d., Scrimgeour Papers, ATL.
20 *New Zealand Observer*, 26 January 1933, p.24; 2 February 1933, p.23.
21 Another radio church, the Church of the Helping Hand, began broadcasting in April 1934. It was established by the Rev Leslie Neale, a Methodist minister. It broadcast from 4ZM, a low-powered station that could be heard only by listeners living within the radius of Dunedin. See Day, *The Radio Years*, p.201.
22 Harry Bell, *Chats: Talks on the 'Friendly Road' by Uncle Scrim*, Auckland, Unity Press Ltd, pp.41, 71.
23 *Church Gazette*, 1 June 1937.
24 Scrimgeour, *Hello Everybody*.
25 *New Zealand Observer*, 29 December 1932, p.22.
26 A.S. Fry, *The Aunt Daisy Story*, Wellington, A.H. & A.W. Reed, 1957; *New Zealand Observer*, 22 December 1932, p.24.
27 *New Zealand Observer*, 7 July 1938, p.7.
28 *New Zealand Observer*, 6 October 1932, p.22; 20 October 1932, p.22; 7

November 1932, p.22.
29 *New Zealand Observer*, 19 April 1934, p.23.
30 *New Zealand Observer*, 31 January 1935, p.23.
31 MS-Papers-7783-1, p.257, n.d., ATL.
32 *New Zealand Observer*, 18 May 1933, p.27; 10 August 1933, p.24.
33 *New Zealand Observer*, 25 June 1931, p.24.
34 *New Zealand Observer*, 29 June 1933, p.24.
35 *New Zealand Observer*, 29 June 1933, p.3.
36 *New Zealand Observer*, 16 November 1933, p.7.
37 *New Zealand Observer*, 29 June 1933, p.3.
38 *New Zealand Observer*, 29 June 1933, p.24.
39 *New Zealand Observer*, 29 June 1933, pp.3, 24.
40 *New Zealand Observer*, 8 March 1934, p.5; MS-Papers-7783-2, p.260, ATL.
41 *New Zealand Observer*, 19 April 1934, p.23; and 26 April 1934, p.23.
42 *New Zealand Observer*, 26 April 1934, pp.23, 24.
43 Scrimgeour Papers, MS-Papers-7783-2, p.292, n.d., ATL.
44 Scrimgeour Papers, MS-Papers-7783-2, p.325, n.d.ATL.
45 Scrimgeour Papers, MS-Papers-7783-2, pp.296–316, n.d., ATL.
46 Scrimgeour Papers, MS-Papers-7783-2, p.214, n.d., ATL.
47 Scrimgeour Papers, MS-Papers-7783-2, p.341, n.d., ATL.
48 *New Zealand Observer*, 24 May 1934, p.23.
49 MS-Papers-7783-2, 'Three Circuits and a City', p.343, ATL.
50 Peter Downes and Peter Harcourt, *Voices in the Air: Radio Broadcasting in New Zealand*, Wellington, Methuen in association with Radio New Zealand, 1976, p.95.
51 Lena Scrimgeour interview with Gary Scrimgeour, fMS-Papers-7289, n.d., ATL.
52 *New Zealand Observer*, 7 December 1933, p.5.
53 *New Zealand Observer*, 21 September 1933, p.24.
54 *New Zealand Observer*, 23 November 1933, p.24.
55 *New Zealand Observer*, 2 December 1933, p.3.
56 *New Zealand Observer*, 9 December 1933, p.3.
57 Ibid.
58 Ibid.
59 *New Zealand Observer*, 9 December 1933, pp.4, 14; 16 December 1933, pp.3, 16.
60 *New Zealand Observer*, 23 December 1933, p.5.
61 *New Zealand Observer*, 11 January 1934, p.5.
62 *New Zealand Observer*, 14 December 1933, p.5; 4 January 1934, p.4; 15 February 1934, p.23.
63 *New Zealand Observer*, 1 March 1934.
64 Wallace Stegner, 'The Radio Priest and his Flock', passim in Isabel Leighton, ed., *The Aspirin Age: 1919–41*, London, Bodley Head, 1950.

## Chapter 5

1 *New Zealand Observer*, 22 March 1934, p.3.
2 Day, *The Radio Years*, pp.110, 176, 226.
3 *New Zealand Observer*, 18 March 1933, p.24; 18 May 1933, p.27.
4 *New Zealand Observer*, 25 October 1934, p.23; 15 November 1934, pp.23; and 28 February 1935, p.23.
5 *Auckland Star*, 26 August 1935, p.5; *New Zealand Observer*, 29 August 1935, p.28.
6 *Auckland Star*, 26 August 1935, p.10.
7 See, for example, *New Zealand Observer*, 12 April 1934, p.3.
8 C.G. Scrimgeour to I.K. Mackay, 23 September 1935, Ian Keith Mackay Papers, MS-Papers-83-001-2/10, ATL.
9 'The Scandal of New Zealand Broadcasting', 1ZB Radio Club, Unity Press Ltd, Auckland, New Zealand, September 1935, Price 3d, 15 pp, ATL.
10 Ibid.
11 Ian Keith Mackay Papers, MS-Papers-83-001-1/15, ATL.
12 'More Scandal in New Zealand Broadcasting', 1ZB Radio Club, Unity Press Ltd, Auckland, New Zealand, November 1935, ATL.
13 *New Zealand Herald*, 2 December 1935, p.14.
14 *Auckland Star*, 29 November 1935; *New Zealand Herald*, 30 November 1935; Barry Gustafson, *From the Cradle to the Grave: A biography of Michael Joseph Savage*, Auckland, Reed Methuen, 1986, p.170.
15 *Auckland Star*, 30 November 1935; C.G. Scrimgeour to John A. Lee, MS-Papers-4104-19, n.d., ATL; C.G. Scrimgeour, John A. Lee, and Tony Simpson, *The Scrim-Lee papers: C.G. Scrimgeour and John A. Lee remember the crisis years 1930–40*, Wellington, A.H. & A.W. Reed, 1976, pp.44–50; Day, *The Radio Years*, pp.204–5.
16 *New Zealand Herald*, 27 November 1935, p.12.
17 *New Zealand Herald*, 27 November, p.12; MS-Papers-4104-19, n.d, ATL.
18 *Auckland Star*, 25 November 1935, p.3; MS-Papers-4104-19, n.d, ATL.
19 *NZPD*, Vol. 207, House, 10 July 1936, pp 807–8, F. Jones and A. Hamilton.
20 Scrimgeour, Lee, and Simpson, *The Scrim-Lee Papers*, p.51.
21 *New Zealand Herald*, 2 December 1935, p.14.
22 *New Zealand Observer*, 12 December 1935, p.3.
23 *New Zealand Herald*, 2 December 1935, p.14.

## Chapter 6

1 *New Zealand Observer*, 10 April 1940, p.7.
2 C.G. Scrimgeour to John A. Lee, 31 July 1936, MS-Papers-4104-19, ATL.
3 Ibid; MS-Papers-4104-092, n.d., ATL.
4 MS-Papers-7783-3, 'Three Circuits and a City', p.345, ATL.
5 C.G. Scrimgeour to Rt Hon M.J. Savage, 9 April 1936, MS-Papers-4194-019, ATL.
6 C.G. Scrimgeour to Hon M.J. Savage, 13 February 1936, Nash Papers-102-2281-0056-0170, Archives NZ; 'A Brief Survery of the Essential

Elements in Connection with Broadcasting and Television in New Zealand', compiled by Scott Ramsay, n.d., [1936], Nash Papers-102-1285-0359, Archives NZ.

7 MS-Papers-7783-3, 'Three Circuits and a City', p.357, ATL.

8 C.G. Scrimgeour to John A. Lee, 13 May 1936, MS-Papers-4104-19, ATL.

9 C.G. Scrimgeour to Rt Hon M.J. Savage, 3 April 1934 [sic], Nash Papers-2281-0182, Archives NZ.

10 *AJHR*, 1937–38, Vol. II, F3, p.8.

11 Fraser in *New Zealand Radio Record*, 26 September 1932, p.6; Nash in *Evening Post*, 3 September 1938.

12 *New Zealand Radio Record*, 5 June 1936, p.19.

13 C.G. Scrimgeour, telegram to John Lee, MP, 13 May 1936, MS-Papers-4104-019, ATL.

14 Gustafson, *From the Cradle to the Grave,* p.194.

15 Hon Adam Hamilton, *NZPD*, Vol. 249, 9 June 1936, pp.755 and 756.

16 Hon P. Fraser, ibid, p.771.

17 Hon Fred Jones, ibid, p.751.

18 Cabinet Approval, 30 June 1936, Nash Papers-2281-0142.

19 *New Zealand Observer*, 20 August 1936, p.4, photograph, p.5.

20 Ibid, 30 April 1936, p.11; Judith Bassett, from 'Leonard Poulter Leary' biography, in Claudia Orange, ed., *The Dictionary of New Zealand Biography*, Vol. 5, 1941–60, Auckland University Press/Internal Affairs, 2000, pp.281–2.

21 *On the Friendly Road* (1936), film credit.

22 L.R. Shelton, from 'Rudall Charles Victor Hayward' biography, *Dictionary of New Zealand Biography*, Vol. 4, 1998, p.229.

23 *NZPD*, Vol. 248, 4 November 1937, p.143.

24 Savage to public service commissioners, 5 October 1936, Nash Papers-2281-0164, Archives NZ.

25 H.H. Cornish, solicitor general, to Rt Hon M.J. Savage, Nash Papers-2281-0171, Archives NZ.

26 Public service commissioners to Rt Hon Prime Minister, 10 October 1936, Nash Papers-2281-0174, Archives NZ.

27 Note on Audit Office file, 12 December 1939, Nash Papers-2281-0170, Archives NZ; *AJHR*, 1937–38, Vol II, F-3, p.7.

28 *NZPD*, Vol. 247, House, Thursday, 29 October 1936, Urgent Question: 1071.

29 C G Scrimgeour to John A. Lee, 9 November 1936, MS-Papers-4104-19, ATL.

30 *New Zealand Observer*, 19 November 1936, p.7.

31 Ibid.

32 *Truth*, 8 December 1937, p.1.

33 *New Zealand Observer*, 19 November 1936, p.7.

34 Ibid.

35 *New Zealand Observer*, 29 April 1937, p.5.

## Chapter 7

1 When, with the passing of the Broadcasting Amendment Act in November 1937, the National Commercial Broadcasting Service and the position of controller were given statutory legitimacy, the public service commissioners aligned the term of Scrim's initial appointment and any renewals of the appointment with Shelley's. See Nash Papers-2281-0170, copy of note on audit file, 12 December 1939.
2 Fry, *The Aunt Daisy Story.*
3 *New Zealand Radio Record*, 25 March 1936, p.19, and 2 July 1936, p.7.
4 *New Zealand Radio Record*, 25 March 1936, p.19.
5 *New Zealand Observer*, 22 October 1936, p.5; *New Zealand Radio Record*, 5 November 1936, p.16.
6 *New Zealand Radio Record*, 6 November 1936, p.16, and 18 November 1936, p.7.
7 Staff Schedule, National Commercial Broadcasting Station 1ZB, Attachment to Beau Sheil, Advertising Department to Controller, National Commercial Broadcasting Service, 4 November 1936, Nash Papers-2281, unnumbered, Archives NZ.
8 *New Zealand Radio Record*, 18 December 1936, p.19.
9 *New Zealand Radio Record*, 6 November 1937, p.16.
10 C.G. Scrimgeour to John A. Lee, 9 November 1936, MS-Papers-4104-19, ATL.
11 *New Zealand Radio Record*, 5 February 1937, p.5.
12 MS-Papers-7783-3, 'Three Circuits and a City' p.360, ATL.
13 Ian Keith Mackay Papers, MS-Papers-83-001-2/01, p.9, n.d., ATL.
14 See, for example, Broadcasting of Gramophone Records, Shelley to Minister of Broadcasting, AADL, Box 424(a), 2/12/5, Pt 1, cabinet approvals 1936–47, Archives NZ.
15 Carter, Ian, *Gadfly: The Life and Times of James Shelley*, Auckland, Auckland University Press in association with the Broadcasting History Trust, 1993, p.228.
16 *NZPD*, Vol. 249, House, 4 November 1937, Rt Hon M.J. Savage, pp.148–9.
17 *New Zealand Observer*, 18 March 1937, p.6. Ian Carter, Shelley's biographer, wrote that Shelley and Scrim disliked each other and were 'continually at loggerheads'. But their respective broadcasting services were entirely separate with no overlapping responsibilities or interests, and their attitudes towards each other, whatever they may have been, were irrelevant. Carter, *Gadfly*, p.230.
18 MS-Papers-7783-3, p.352, ATL.
19 Carter, *Gadfly*, chapter 5.
20 Downes and Harcourt, *Voices in the Air*, p.104.
21 Ian Keith Mackay Papers, MS-Papers-83-001-2/05, p.44, ATL; Downes and Harcourt, *Voices in the Air*, p.104.
22 MS-Papers-7783-2, p.159, ATL.
23 *New Zealand Observer*, 18 March 1937, p.6; 9 December 1937, p.6.

24 *New Zealand Herald*, 5 April 1937; *Auckland Star*, 5 April 1937.
25 *New Zealand Herald*, 5 April 1937, p.6; *Auckland Star*, 5 April 1937, p.8.
26 *Truth*, 18 October 1928. My thanks to Redmar Yska for this item.
27 *New Zealand Observer*, 22 April 1937, p.6.
28 *New Zealand Observer*, 15 April 1937, p.6; and 22 April 1937, p.6.
29 *New Zealand Observer*, 15 April 1937, p.6; and 22 April 1937, p.6.
30 *New Zealand Observer*, 15 April 1937, p.6.
31 Lee, John A., *The John A. Lee Diaries 1936–1940*, Christchurch, Whitcoulls, 1981, 12 April 1937, p.19; and 29 April 1937, p.20.
32 Cabinet Schedule, 28 April 1937, Nash Papers-2038-0666, Archives NZ.
33 Lee, *John A. Lee Diaries*, 5 June 1937, p.23.
34 Friendly Road members had a small cardboard box in which they put donations that they would send to the Friendly Road every three months.
35 Lee, *John A. Lee Diaries*, 15 June 1937, p.23.
36 *New Zealand Radio Record*, 18 June 1937, p.17; *Truth*, 16 June 1937, pp.12, 18.
37 Bell, *Chats*.
38 *Standard*, 25 May 1939.
39 *New Zealand Radio Record*, 30 April 1937, p.42.
40 Ibid, 19 March 1937, p.9.
41 Ian Keith Mackay Papers, MS-Papers-83-001-2/01, ATL.
42 *New Zealand Observer*, 17 June 1937, p.5.
43 During the depression years Griffin had been convicted of sedition and imprisoned for eighteen months. Birchfield, p.100.
44 See for example, *New Zealand Observer*, 27 January 1938, p.5.
45 Lee, *John A. Lee Diaries*, 25 June 1938, p.76; 5 March 1940, p.203; see Lee's inscription on the inside cover of his copy of *The Scrim-Lee Papers*, John A. Lee Papers, APL.
46 See for example, *New Zealand Radio Record*, 25 April 1937, pp.34–5.
47 *New Zealand Radio Record*, 7 May 1937, p.3.
48 See for example, *New Zealand Radio Record*, 31 December 1937, p.17; 20 October 1938, p.24; *New Zealand Observer*, 20 June 1938, p.9; and 23 July 1938, p.28; 24 March 1938, p.29.
49 *NZPD*, Vol. 249, 10 November 1937, pp.147–8, 149.
50 Ibid, p.284.
51 *Truth*, 10 November 1937, p.1; 17 November 1937, p.1; *Evening Post*, 5 November 1937; *New Zealand Observer*, 11 November 1937.
52 Nash Papers-2281-0170, copy of note on audit file, 12 December 1939.
53 *New Zealand Observer*, 16 December 1937, p.5; *Truth*, 17 November 1937, p.17.
54 Nash Papers-2281-0073-0120 and Nash Papers-2281-0087, C.G. Scrimgeour to M.J. Savage, 11 November 1937.

## Chapter 8

1 Downes and Harcourt, *Voices in the Air*, p.112.
2 *New Zealand Radio Record*, 21 January 1938, p.20.
3 *New Zealand Radio Record*, 18 February 1938, p.32.
4 *Weekly News*, 16 February1938, p.1; Broadcasting History Trust Sound Recordings, LCD-0453-17, Oral History Centre, ATL.
5 Notes of interview between the public service commissioners and Mr C.G. Scrimgeour, controller, Commercial Broadcasting Department, Wellington, 6 May 1938, [43 pp.] Nash Papers-2281-0176, Archives NZ.
6 For the detail see AAFL 563, Box 1B, 1/30/- and Box 3B 1/31/-, Broadcasting Corporation of New Zealand, Archives NZ.
7 *Truth*, 14 April, p.1; *New Zealand Observer*, 21 April 1938, p.5; *Wanganui Herald*, 18 May 1938.
8 *New Zealand Observer*, 10 February 1938, p.8.
9 *New Zealand Observer*, 13 August 1938.
10 *Wanganui Herald*, 18 May 1938.
11 Ibid.
12 *Standard*, 11 August 1938.
13 *Dominion*, 11 August 1938.
14 *Standard*, 11 August 1938.
15 *New Zealand Observer*, 11 August 1938, p.6.
16 Lee to Savage, 10 August 1938, Lee Papers, APL.
17 Gustafson, *From the Cradle to the Grave*, p.217.
18 Ian Keith Mackay Papers, MS-Papers-83-001-2/01, p.15, ATL.
19 Lee to Savage, 10 August 1938, Lee Papers, APL. The italics are in Lee's letter.
20 *Standard*, 11 August 1938.
21 *Standard*, 18 August 1938.
22 *Press*, 18 August 1938.
23 *Auckland Star*, 18 August 1938.
24 Lee, *John A. Lee Diaries*, 5 November 1938, p.42.
25 *New Zealand Observer*, 6 October, p.15.
26 *Dominion*, 29 September 1938; *Auckland Star*, 3 October 1938.
27 *Auckland Star*, 3 October 1938.
28 *New Zealand Herald*, 3 October 1938; *New Zealand Observer*, 6 October 1938, p.5.
29 *New Zealand Herald*, 3 October 1938.
30 Ibid.
31 *Taranaki Daily News*, 4 October 1938.
32 *Taranaki Herald*, 3 and 5 October 1938.
33 *New Zealand Observer*, 13 October 1938, p.5.
34 Hon W. Perry, MLC, Open Letter to Rev C.G. Scrimgeour, *Evening Post*, 10 October 1938.
35 *Dominion*, 11 October 1938.
36 *New Zealand Observer*, 20 October 1938, p.5.

## Chapter 9

1 Lee to Savage, cited in Erik Olssen, *John A. Lee*, Dunedin, University of Otago Press, 1977, p.133; Gustafson, *From the Cradle to the Grave*, p.232, fn 13.
2 Lee, *John A. Lee Diaries*, 4 November 1938, p.101.
3 Lee, *John A. Lee Diaries*, 20 December 1938, p.115; 20 January 1939, pp.119–20; 13 December 1938, p.114.
4 Lee, *John A. Lee Diaries*, 6 February 1939, pp.124–5; 10 February 1939, pp.126–30.
5 *Standard*, 13 October 1938.
6 *New Zealand Observer*, 23 March 1939, p.8.
7 Ian Keith Mackay Papers, MS-Papers-83-00/2/01, p.68, ATL.
8 Ian K. Mackay, Report on North Island Tour of 5ZB, 22 August 1939, AADL 563, Box 19A, 21/9, Pt. 2, Archives NZ; Mackay Papers, 69; *Hawkes Bay Daily Mail*, Tuesday, 13 June 1939.
9 *Standard*, 25 May and 15 June 1939.
10 Scrimgeour Papers, MS-Papers-4104-73, n.d., ATL.
11 Ibid.
12 *Standard*, 27 April 1939.
13 Scrimgeour Papers, MS-Papers-4104, n.d., ATL.
14 Using Newspapers on Line, I checked out the *Christian Science Monitor* for the period 1 April–30 June 1939.
15 *New Zealand Observer*, 11 June 1939, p.5.
16 *Truth*, 27 October 1937, p.1; *Auckland Star*, 1 November 1937.
17 *Auckland Star*, 3 October 1938; *Workers' Weekly*, 13 November 1938.
18 *Truth*, 27 October 1938; *Auckland Star*, 1 November 1938; Lee, *John A. Lee Diaries*, 7 February 1939, p.125. For a discussion of *Zealandia*'s opinions on international relations in Europe during the Spanish Civil War and the Second World War, see Nicholas Reid, *James Michael Liston: A Life*, Wellington, Victoria University Press, 2006, pp.231–4.
19 *Auckland Star*, 2 February 1939.
20 *Dominion*, 29 November, 5 and 7 December 1939; *Evening Post*, 5 and 23 November 1939.
21 MS-Papers-7783-3, 'Three Circuits and a City', pp.364–6, ATL; C.W. Carrick, 'The £.s.d. of 1ZB Land Purchase', *New Zealand Observer*, 22 November 1939.
22 Scrimgeour Papers, MS-Papers-7783-1, pp.365–6, ATL.
23 Lee, *John A. Lee Diaries*, 1 July 1939, p.163; 5 July 1939, p.163; 8 July 1939, p.164. Lee Papers unpublished item, APL.
24 *NZ Listener*, 14 November 1939, p.1.
25 Ian Keith Mackay Papers, MS-Papers-83-001-2/05, pp.84–5, ATL; *NZ Listener*, 5 July 1940, p.20.
26 A widely supported anti-war movement was in full swing when Scrim arrived in Wellington in mid-1937 but there are no signs that he associated himself with it in any way. Quotations in this paragraph and the following

eight paragraphs are from Notes of Proceedings of Station Directors and Senior Head Ofice Executives, 2 September 1939, AAFL, 563, 3B 1/31/-, Broadcasting Corporation of New Zealand, Archives NZ.

27 Ian Keith Mackay Papers, MS-Papers-83-001-2/05, p.67, n.d., ATL.

28 Ibid.

29 Ian Keith Mackay, Miscellaneous Notes: Ian Keith Mackay Papers, MS-Papers-83-001-1/02, ATL; *NZ Listener*, 19 January 1940, pp.48–9 photograph; Day, *The Radio Years*, pp.253–5; Patrick Day, 'Broadcasting the Centennial', in *Creating a National Spirit: Celebrating New Zealand's Centennial*, ed William Renwick, Wellington, Victoria University Press, 2004, pp.80–82.

30 *NZ Listener*, 9 February 1940, editorial; 16 February 1940, editorial; and 23 February 1940, pp.47–9.

31 Lee, *John A. Lee Diaries*, 4 December 1939, p.181; 12 December 1939, p.192; 15 December 1939, pp.192–3; 19 December 1939, p.193; Olssen, *John A. Lee*, p.148; Michael Bassett with Michael King, *Tomorrow Comes the Song : A life of Peter Fraser*, Penguin, Auckland, 2000, p.180.

32 *Standard*, 10 August 1939 and 24 August 1939; Lee, *John A. Lee Diaries*, 9 November 1938, p.103; and 20 December 1938, p.115.

33 Lee, *John A. Lee Diaries*, 12 December 1939, p.192; 15 December 1939, pp.192–3; 19 December 1939, p.193; 21 December 1939, p.194; 8 January 1940, p.197.

34 Lee, *John A. Lee Diaries*, 23 March 1940, p.206–7.

35 Gustafson, *From the Cradle to the Grave*, p.267; Olssen, *John A Lee*, pp.158–9.

36 Olssen, *John A Lee*, pp.158–9.

37 *Standard*, 2 May 1940, p.7; Gustafson, p.269.

38 *Evening Post*, 27–30 March 1940; *New Zealand Herald*, 1 April 1940; author's recollection.

39 Edwards, *Scrim*, p.118.

## Chapter 10

1 Edwards, *Scrim*.

2 *Dominion*, 2 April 1940; *New Zealand Observer*, 4 April 1940.

3 *Dominion*, 9 April 1940.

4 *Dominion*, 2 April 1940; *New Zealand Observer*, 4 April 1940.

5 *People's Voice*, 12 April 1940.

6 *Taranaki Herald*, 6 April reporting an interview with F.L. Frost, MP.

7 Ian Keith Mackay Papers, MS-Papers-83-001-2/11, unpaged, ATL.

8 Ian Keith Mackay Papers, MS-Papers-83-001-2/11, unpaged, ATL.

9 Bassett and King, *Tomorrow Comes the Song*, p.179.

10 See the Nash Papers-2029 file, Archives NZ.

11 Nash Papers-2029-0248, Controller to Minister, 31 January 1941, Archives NZ.

12 Nash Papers-2029-0361, Wilson to members of the Executive of the North Canterbury L.R.C., 12 November 1942, Archives NZ.

13 MS-Papers-7783-2, p.367, ATL.
14 Ian Keith Mackay Papers, MS-Papers-83-001-2/11, unpaged, ATL; C.G. Scrimgeour, 'The Broad Problem of Venereal Diseases', in *Venereal Disease: The Shadow Over New Zealand*, Wellington, Progressive Publishing Society, 1942, pp.6–7.
15 Nash Papers-2029-0227, D. Wilson note 26 June 1941, Archives NZ.
16 G.H. Scholefield, ed, *Who's Who in New Zealand and the Western Pacific*, 4th Edition, Wellington, Rangatira Press, 1941, p.307.
17 *NZ Listener*, 5 September 1941, p.20; 12 September 1941, p.20; 19 September 1941, p.20.
18 Nash Papers-2029-0361, Notes on Exec. Meeting, North Canterbury Labour Representation Committee, 12 November 1942, Archives NZ.
19 George Bourne, *New Zealand Observer*, 17 December 1941, p.9.
20 Annual Report, National Commercial Broadcasting Service, F. 3:4. *AJHR*, Vol. 11, 1942.
21 See chapter 9, above.
22 C.W. Carrick, *New Zealand Observer*, 6 December 1939, p.6.
23 *In Print*, 15 December 1942.
24 Nash Papers-2029-0411, Notes for Meeting with Waterside W Deputation, 6.2.42, DW, Archives NZ.
25 C.G. Scrimgeour interview, LCD-04564-3, n.d., Oral History Centre, ATL.
26 Nash Papers-2029-0206, Minister to Controller, 10 March 1942, Archives NZ.
27 Nash Papers-2029-0251, Wilson to Nash, Acting Prime Minister, 15 August 1941, Archives NZ.
28 Nash Papers-2029-1041, 3 December 1941, Archives NZ.
29 Nash Papers-2029-0277 D.W. 26.2.42, Archives NZ.
30 MS-Papers-7783-3, p.367, ATL.
31 *New Zealand Herald*, 12 March 1942, p.7.
32 *New Zealand Herald*, 13 March 1942; *New Zealand Observer*, 18 March 1942.
33 'The Man in the Street Speaks', n.d., price 3d.
34 Nash Papers-2029-0043, D. Wilson, handwritten notes, 9 June 1942; and Nash Papers-2029-0045 J.T. Paul to D. Wilson, 22 June 1942, Archives NZ.
35 Nash Papers-2029-0195, Memo for Minister in Charge of Broadcasting – C.G. Scrimgeour, 6 May 1942, Archives NZ.
36 *NZPD*, Vol. 263, House, 10 August 1943, Supply, Fraser, p.643.
37 Nash Papers-2029-0452, D. Wilson to Hon Mr McLagan by phone 15.2.43, Archives NZ.
38 M.S. Bullivant and others, Appeal against military service in respect of Mr C.G. Scrimgeour, 12 February 1943, AAFL. 563, Box 46, 1/-/-, Broadcasting Corporation of New Zealand, Archives NZ; Hon D. Wilson to Mr M.S. Bullivant, 15 February 1043, AAFL, 563 43, Broadcasting Corporation of New Zealand, Archives NZ.
39 *Dominion*, 24 February 1943; *Evening Post*, 24 February 1943; *Standard*, 4 March 1943.

40 Nash Papers-2029-028, 24 February 1943, Archives NZ.
41 Lee, *NZPD*, Vol. 262, House, 4 March 1943, p.133.
42 Nash Papers-2029-0186, J.T. Paul to D. Wilson, 2 March 1943, Archives NZ.
43 Nash Papers-2029-093, proposed public statement, handwritten text written by Wilson but not distributed, Archives NZ.
44 Ian Keith Mackay Papers. MS 83-001/2-2/01, p.36. n.d. ATL.
45 Nash Papers-2029-0186, message to M. Bullivant, C.G. Scrimgeour, afternoon of 3 March 1943, Archives NZ.
46 Nash Papers-2029-0188, Greenberg to Minister, 4 March 1943, Archives NZ.
47 *Dominion*, 5 March 1943.
48 *Dominion*, 5 March 1943; Rt Hon P. Fraser, Supply Debate, 10 August 1943, *NZPD*, Vol. 263, p.640.
49 *Dominion*, 5 March 1943.
50 *Truth*, 3 March 1943; *Auckland Star*, 3 March 1943; *Press*, 8 March 1943; *New Zealand Observer*, 20 March 1943.
51 Minhinnick cartoon, 'Three Live Ghosts', *New Zealand Herald*, 4 March 1943, p.4. The Hon Frank Langstone is the 'ghost' in the centre of the ambush. He was an irascible left-wing member of the Labour government, and the only one to side in caucus with Lee and other left-wing opponents of Savage's proposals for paying the country's overseas loans. Fraser decided that he would rather have Langstone out of the country than in Parliament, and in May 1941 sent him to Washington with Coates to negotiate war supplies with the Americans and make arrangements for the setting up of a New Zealand legation. Langstone favoured himself as the man to head the legation. But when the United States entered the war, Fraser decided that Langstone would not be up to the job, and that Nash would head the legation. Langstone was angry at being passed over, and was not mollified by being appointed high commissioner to Ottawa. He had a blazing row with Fraser in Ottawa in September 1942, resigned his post, and gave a lengthy account of his grievances to the Canadian press, which was reported in New Zealand. Minhinnick's cartoon foresees further outbursts from Langstone during election year.
52 Nash Papers-2029-0286, message from Greenberg to Wilson, 3 March 1943, Archives NZ.
53 Nash Papers-2029-0290, Bullivant to Wilson, confidential, 14 April 1943, Archives NZ.
54 Nash Papers-2029-0246, cabinet submission, D.W. 23. 3. 43, Archives NZ.
55 C.G. Scrimgeour to Rt Hon P. Fraser, 31 May 1943, MS-Papers-2151-397, Bollinger Papers, ATL.
56 F.P.Walsh to Rt Hon the Prime Minister, 10 June 1943, MS-Papers-2151-397, Bollinger Papers, ATL.
57 Solicitor general to Rt Hon the Prime Minister, 15 June 1943, Nash Papers-2281-0145, Archives NZ.

58 *Evening Post*, 15 June 1943.
59 For the decision of the governor in council, 18 June 1943, Nash Papers-2281-0159, Archives NZ; Hon D. Wilson, Minister in Charge of Broadcasting, to C.G. Scrimgeour Esq, 18 June 1943, Nash Papers-2281-0156, Archives NZ.
60 *Dominion*, 20 September 1943.
61 *Evening Post*, 30 July 1943.
62 *New Zealand Observer*, 23 June 1943, p.6.
63 W.J. Polson, *NZPD*, Vol. 263, House, 10 August 1943, p.639.
64 Rt Hon P. Fraser, *NZPD*, Vol. 263, House, 10 August 1943, pp.639–40.
65 *NZPD*, Vol. 263, House, 10 August 1943, John A. Lee, pp.640–41; F. Doidge, p.641.
66 *New Zealand Observer*, 23 June 1943, p.5.
67 Ian Keith Mackay Papers, MS-Papers-83-001-2/01, p.39, ATL.
68 Mackay resigned from the NBS in 1953. He then worked in Australia, Nigeria, and Papua New Guinea. His *Broadcasting in New Zealand*, 1953, an informed history of New Zealand broadcasting from its inception, included his critical appraisal of the fortunes of the commercial branch after its incorporation in the NBS and his assessment of the shortcomings of the Service.
69 Ian Keith Mackay Papers, MS-Papers-83-001-1/02, pp.178–81, ATL.
70 Ian Keith Mackay Papers, MS-Papers-83-001-1/02, pp.178–81, ATL.
71 Ibid, p.181.

## Chapter 11

1 Scrim persistently wrote Frazer for Fraser.
2 L.M. Isitt, Air Commodore, Deputy Chief of the Air Force to Rt Hon Prime Minister, 24 June 1943, Nash Papers-102-0144, Archives NZ.
3 In fact, it was the 14th Reinforcements.
4 MS-Papers-4104-107, ATL; C.G. Scrimgeour interview with Michael King, n.d. [1978], MS-Papers-2096, ATL; C.G. Scrimgeour, Personal File, New Zealand Defence Force, Personnel Archive.
5 C.G. Scrimgeour, Personal File, New Zealand Defence Force, Personnel Archive. Sir James Elliott was Fraser's physician; See Bassett and King, *Tomorrow Comes the Song*, p.257.
6 *Evening Post*, 7 July 1943; MS-Papers-4104-49, ATL, for the Communist Party statement.
7 MS-Papers-4104-99, ATL.
8 Statement issued by C.G. Scrimgeour on the eve of his entry into the ranks of the RNZAF training camp at Linton, MS-Papers-4104-9, ATL.
9 C.G. Scrimgeour to Dr W.B. Sutch, 8 May 1974, MS-Papers-4104-3, ATL.
10 The *Dominion* published George Searle's cartoon on 1 September and Scrim's advertisements on 15, 16, 17 and 20 September 1943; *New Zealand Observer*, 29 September 1943, p.6.
11 *New Zealand Observer*, 8 September 1943, p.5.
12 Ian Keith Mackay Papers, MS-Papers-83-001-2/01, p.36, ATL; Scrimgeour

Papers MS-Papers-4104-81, n.d., ATL.

13 For the government's policies on these matters see Nancy Taylor, *The Home Front*, Vol. II, Wellington, Historical Publications Branch, 1986, pp.1291–2 for wages and prices; C.E.Beeby, *The Biography of an Idea*, Wellington, NZCER, 1992, chapter 8 for educational reforms; Bassett and King, *Tomorrow Comes the Song*, pp.248–9 for rehabilitation and pp.294–5 for relations with peoples living in New Zealand dependencies in the South Pacific; and Malcolm Templeton, *Top Hats Are Not Being Taken*, Wellington, NZIIA, 1991, for diplomatic relations with the USSR.

14 Allison Buchan, from 'William Appleton' biography, in Orange, ed., *DNZB*, Vol. 4, pp.18–19.

15 *Evening Post*, 23 September 1943.

16 *Evening Post*, 24 September 1943.

17 MS-Papers-4104, pp.81 and 97, ATL; *Dominion*, 20 September 1943.

18 Michael King in Margaret Clark, ed, *Peter Fraser: Master Politician*, Palmerston North, Dunmore Press, 1998, p.21; James Thorn, *Peter Fraser: New Zealand's Wartime Prime Minister*, London, Odhams Press, 1952, pp.33–5; Bassett and King, *Tomorrow Comes the Song*, pp.44–51 and 72–3.

19 Handwritten analysis of the Wellington Central vote in MS-Papers-4104-18, n.d., ATL; Bassett and King, *Tomorrow Comes the Song*, p.256.

20 Bassett and King, *Tomorrow Comes the Song*, p.256.

21 C.G. Scrimgeour, Personal File, New Zealand Defence Force, Personnel Archive.

22 MS-Papers-4104-14, n.d., ATL.

23 Autobiographical note in MS-Papers-4104-18, n.d, ATL.

24 H.F. James to air force member of personnel, Air Department, Wellington, 21 June 1944; Squadron Leader S.L. Gilkison to Air Commodore R.B. Bannerman, Air Department, Wellington, 14 April, 1944, in C.G. Scrimgeour, Personal File, New Zealand Defence Force, Personnel Archive.

25 H.J.V. James to Hon D. Wilson, 14 July 1943 (attached), Nash Papers-2029-0276, Archives NZ.

26 Hon D. Wilson to H.J.V. James, 15 July 1943, Nash Papers-2029-0276, Archives NZ.

27 B.C. Ashwin to Minister of Finance, 3 June 1943, AAFL 563 4B, Broadcasting Corporation of New Zealand, Archives NZ.

28 Hon D. Wilson to H.J.V. James, 19 January 1944; H.V.J. James to Hon D. Wilson, 19 January 1944, Nash Papers-2029-0274, Archives NZ.

29 C.G. Scrimgeour interview with Michael King, n.d. [1978], MS-Papers-2096, p.38ff, ATL.

## Chapter 12

1 Passport application, C.G. Scrimgeour to J.W. Heenan, secretary of internal affairs, 21 June 1946, MS-Papers-1132-209, ATL.

2 MS-Papers-4104 , ATL, unidentified newspaper clipping.

3 MS-Papers-4104, ATL.

4 This and the four paragraphs that follow are based on correspondence in MS-Papers-4104-38, ATL.
5 MS-Papers-4104-38, C.G. Scrimgeour, 'Television Today', n.d., ATL.
6 Ibid, passim.
7 Russell Campbell, in 'Cecil Holmes' biography, in Orange, ed., *DNZB,* Vol. 5, p.232.
8 MS-Papers-4104-96, n.d., ATL.
9 MS-Papers-4104-36, passim, ATL.
10 MS-Papers-4104-36, ATL.
11 Notes of a speech made by Mr C.G. Scrimgeour, president, Associated TV Pty at Metropole Sheraton, Rose Bay, 21 January 1953, MS-Papers-4104-87, ATL.
12 See *Sydney Morning Herald,* 16 January 1953; 6 February 1953; and 19 March 1953.
13 Associated Television Information Bulletin, No. 7, 23 July 1953, MS-Papers-4104-38, ATL.
14 Suggestions (of legal counsel) re answer to personal attacks on Mr Scrimgeour, n.d., MS-Papers-4104-38, n d, ATL.
15 C.G. Scrimgeour to Allan [Martin], 26 May 1971, MS-Papers-4104-104, ATL.
16 *Sydney Morning Herald,* 19 March 1954; and 30 September 1954.
17 See note 13 above.
18 Associated Television Information Bulletin, Special Edition, n.d., MS-Papers-4104-39, ATL.
19 C.G. Scrimgeour to Dear Norman [Collins], Associated Television Ltd, London, 15 March 1963, MS-Papers-4104-59, ATL.
20 Transcript of a discussion between Lena Scrimgeour and Gary Scrimgeour, n.d, fMS-Papers-7289, ATL.
21 Gary Scrimgeour to Scrim, 11 July 1977, fMS-Papers-7289-2, ATL.
22 C.G. Scrimgeour to Tony Simpson, 20 June 1974, MS-Papers-4104-29, ATL; C.G. Scrimgeour to the management, Radio Peking, Peking, 17 December 1957, MS-Papers-4104-61, ATL.
23 Letter of appointment, 1 January 1959, MS-Papers-4104-55, ATL.
24 Gary Scrimgeour to Scrim, 25 February 1959' fMS-Papers-7289-2, ATL.
25 C.G. Scrimgeour to Beau Sheil, 15 March 1959' MS-Papers-4104-56, ATL.
26 MS-Papers-4104, p.54, ATL.
27 C.G. Scrimgeour to H.G.R. Mason, 10 June 1959, MS-Papers-4104-56, ATL.
28 See, for example, William A. Gunn, chairman, Australian Wool Board Ltd, to C.G. Scrimgeour, 21 December 1964, MS-Papers-4104-59, ATL.
29 C.G. Scrimgeour to Dear Charlie, 22 July 1963, MS-Papers-4104-61, ATL.
30 C.G. Scrimgeour to Mai Yi, director, Radio Peking, 9 October 1964, MS-Papers-4104-61, ATL.
31 MS-Papers-4104-61, Cres Jenkinson to Scrim, 28 April 1959, ATL.
32 C.G. Scrimgeour to Sir Henry Kelliher, 4 January 1968, MS-Papers-4104-18, ATL.
33 *Auckland Star,* 11 October 1967.

## Chapter 13

1 *Sunday News*, 14 January 1968.
2 MS-Papers-4104-39, ATL, letters between Scrim and the NZBC, between the general manager of Watties and Scrim, solicitors' opinions, and between Sir James Wattie and Scrim.
3 Annual report, New Zealand Broadcasting Authority, *AJHR*, 1969.
4 C.G. Scrimgeour to Gary Scrimgeour, 12 February 1969, fMS-Papers-7289-1, ATL.
5 C.G. Scrimgeour to Gary Scrimgeour, 12 November 1970, ibid.
6 See, for example, memo from Gordon Dryden to 'the Group', 24 July 1970, MS-Papers-4104-42, ATL.
7 Scrim to Gary Scrimgeour, 12 November 1970, fMS-Papers-7289-2, ATL.
8 *AJHR*, 1974, F3, Annual Report of the New Zealand Broadcasting Authority, p.3.
9 *New Zealand Herald*, 31 May 1972, Section I.
10 MS-Papers-7783-3, 'Three Circuits and a City', p.333, ATL.
11 '"Scrim" is Still a Man With a Mission', a profile by Kevin Clements, *New Zealand Methodist Times*, 27 February 1969; Les Clements to Scrim, 8 March 1969, MS-Papers-4104-105, ATL.
12 Interview with Russell Marshall.
13 *Evening Post*, 24 March 1973.
14 Les Edwards to Gary Scrimgeour, 4 December 1971, fMS-Papers-7289-4, ATL.
15 Edwards, *Scrim*, p.9.
16 Ibid, p.87.
17 Ibid, p.93.
18 Ibid, p.100.
19 Ibid, p.105.
20 Ibid, pp.128, 138.
21 Ibid, p.120.
22 Ibid.
23 Ibid, p.120.
24 Ibid.
25 Ibid, pp.128, 138.
26 *New Zealand Herald*, 25 September 1971, Section 2:2.
27 *Christchurch Star*, 2 October 1971.
28 Scrim to Gary Scrimgeour, 6 February 1972, fMS-Papers-7289-1, ATL.
29 Gary Scrimgeour to C.G. Scrimgeour, 29 October 1971, fMS-Papers-7289-2, ATL.
30 G.C. Peterson, ed., *Who's Who in New Zealand*, 10th edition, Wellington, A.H. & A.W. Reed, 1971, p.299.
31 George Bryant to Scrim, 27 March 1972, MS-Papers-4104-104, ATL.
32 'Uncle Scrim is Coming', *CANTA*, No. 23 [1972].
33 *Christchurch Star*, 28 September 1972.
34 Brian Edwards, *Public Eye*, Wellington, A.H. & A.W. Reed, 1971, p.105. TV

Archives does not hold a copy of the interview.

35 Scrim to Brian Edwards, 17 October 1971, MS-Papers-4104-12, ATL.

36 John A. Lee to Scrim, 21 August 1974, MS-Papers-4104-019, ATL.

37 *NZ Listener*, 4 October 1975, p.9.

38 Sound Archives does not have a record of James McNeish's programme.

39 MS-Papers-4104-91, ATL, interview with Michael King, pp.23–4. In this interview Scrim also gave his account of how he smoothed the way for George Bernard Shaw to land in New Zealand.

40 MS-Papers-4104, n.d., ATL.

41 Interview with Patrick Downey, 12 June 2009.

42 TVNZ, 'Seven Days' programme, 24 August 1975, Television Archive.

43 Interview with Tony Simpson, 5 June 2009.

44 John A. Lee to Rob Muldoon, 12 October [1974], MS-Papers-4104-019, ATL.

45 John A. Lee's note, 23 December 1975, Lee Papers, Box 25/19, APL.

46 See Scrim to Bill Rowling, Prime Minister, n.d.; Scrim to Martyn Finlay, 7 March, 1973; Scrim to Minister Douglas, 3 August 1973; Scrim to Hon M. Rata, 6 September 1975; MS-Papers-4104-01, ATL.

47 Interview with Hugh Templeton, 28 May 2009.

48 John Smythe, *Downstage Upfront, The First 40 Years of New Zealand's Longest-Running Professional Theatre*, Wellington, Victoria University Press, 2004, p.175.

## Chapter 14

1 MS-Papers-7783, 'Three Circuits and a City', p.48, ATL.

2 The quotes in this paragraph are from 'Three Circuits and a City', MS-Papers-7783, ATL.

3 Ibid.

4 Ibid, p.210.

5 Ibid, p.254.

6 Ibid, p.372.

7 Ibid.

8 Michael Holyroyd, *Bernard Shaw, 1918–1950: The Lure of Fantasy*, Vol. 3, London, Chatto & Windus, 1991, p.319; *New Zealand Herald* Shipping movements, passim.

9 Scrim to Ray Richards, 19 May 1974, MS-Papers-4104-27, ATL.

10 Ray Richards to Scrim, 26 June 1974, MS-Papers-4104-27, ATL.

11 John A. Lee to Scrim, 10 May 1974, John A. Lee Papers, Box 13, April 10 and 10 May 1974, APL.

12 John A. Lee to Scrim, MS-Papers-4104-19, n.d, ATL.

13 Ibid.

14 Ibid.

15 John A.Lee to Stephen Barnett, 2 January [1976], Lee Papers, Box 25: 52, 55, APL.

16 Interview with Tony Simpson, 5 June 2009.

17 Tony Simpson, *The Slump: The Thirties Depression, Its Origins and Aftermath*, Auckland, Penguin Books, 1990.
18 Scrimgeour, Lee, and Simpson, *The Scrim-Lee Papers*, pp.2–3.
19 Ibid, pp.6–7.
20 Ibid, p.9.
21 Ibid, pp.9, 19, 39.
22 Ibid, p.35.
23 Ibid, pp.46–51.
24 Ibid, pp.55, 57, 66.
25 Scrimgeour, Lee, and Simpson, *The Scrim-Lee Papers*, pp.74, 77, 82.
26 Ibid, p.79.
27 Ibid, p.84.
28 Ibid, p.102.
29 Ibid, p.101.
30 Ibid, pp.108, 109.
31 Ibid, p.110.
32 Ibid.
33 Ibid, p.113.
34 Ibid, p.124.
35 *NZ Listener*, 26 March 1977, pp.60–61.
36 O.S. Hintz in *New Zealand Bookworld*, February 1977, MS-Papers-4104-105, ATL.
37 Gary Scrimgeour to Scrim, 24 October 1977, fMS-Papers-7289-2, ATL.
38 Scrim to Ray Richards, n.d., MS-Papers-4104-27, ATL; Ray Richards to Scrim, 3 October 1974, MS-Papers-4104-27, ATL.
39 Sound Recordings of C.G. Scrimgeour, LCD -0438-0453, Oral History Centre, ATL.
40 Ibid, disk 12.
41 Ibid.
42 Edmund Bohan, *The House of Reed 1907–1983: Great Days in New Zealand Publishing*, Christchurch, Canterbury University Press, 2005, chapters 15 & 16, passim.
43 An interview with Trevor James Constable, *Frontiers of Science*, Vol. III, No. 5, July–August 1981, pp.18–21, 29.
44 See Ray Richards' comments on page 251, above.
45 Trevor Constable to Gary Scrimgeour, fMS-Papers-7289-3, n.d. [1984], ATL.

## Chapter 15

1 Interview with C.G. Scrimgeour, 'Encounter', 18 July 1976, Television Archive.
2 Scrim and Pam, to Gary and Helen Scrimgeour, 22 April 1976, fMS-Papers-7289-2, ATL.
3 Pam to Helen and Gary Scrimgeour, 28 August 1978, fMS-Papers-7289-2, ATL.

4 Pam to Helen and Gary Scrimgeour, 28 May 1981, fMS-Papers-7289-2, ATL.
5 TVNZ 'Lookout' programme on John A. Lee, 15 April 1984, Television Archive.
6 Loc.cit, p.25.
7 C.G. Scrimgeour interviewed by Barry Gustafson, 15 April 1981, OHC-9149-50, Oral History Centre, ATL.
8 Ibid.
9 Scrim and Pam, to Gary and Helen Scrimgeour, fMS-Papers-7289, passim, ATL.
10 Gary Scrimgeour to Dad and Pam, 22 August 1976, fMS-Papers-7289-2, ATL.
11 Gary Scrimgeour to Scrim and Pam, 29 April 1977, fMS-Papers-7289-2, ATL.
12 MS-Papers-4104-73, n.d., ATL.
13 Pam Scrimgeour to Helen and Gary Scrimgeour, 24 October 1977, fMS-Papers-7289-2, ATL.
14 10 July 1980, District Public Trust Office, New Lynn, Archives NZ, Auckland BAZZ 1570 1791/ 1987.
15 Pam Scrimgeour, to Helen and Gary Scrimgeour, 25 February 1983, fMS-Papers-7289-3, ATL.
16 Pam Scrimgeour to Helen and Gary Scrimgeour, 25 January 1984, fMS-Papers-7289-3, ATL.
17 Pam Scrimgeour to Helen and Gary Scrimgeour, 11 May 1985, fMS-Papers-7289-3, ATL.
18 Gary Scrimgeour note, August 10 1985, fMS-Papers-7289-4, ATL.
19 Pam Scrimgeour to Helen and Gary Scrimgeour, 7 April 1986, 18 May 1986; 21 October 1986, fMS-Papers-7289-3, ATL.
20 Pam Scrimgeour to Gary Scrimgeour, 7 April 1986, fMS-Papers-7289-3, ATL.
21 *New Zealand Herald*, 17 January 1987, Section I.
22 'When Scrim Spoke', by Gary Scrimgeour, *NZ Listener*, 28 February 1987, pp.16–17.
23 Edwards, *Scrim*, pp.166–7.
24 Denzil Ward to editor, *NZ Listener*, 11 April 1987.
25 These comments are derived from Michael King's interview with Sir Alister McIntosh (MS-Papers-2096, folders 1 and 2), and from conversations the author had with Dr C.E. Beeby on several occasions during the 1970s and 1980s.
26 Allan K. Davidson in 'Colin Graham Scrimgeour' biography from Orange, *DNZB*, Vol. 4, 1921–40, Wellington, 1998, pp.465–6.

# Index